B

*f*P

CIVILIZATION AND ITS ENEMIES

THE NEXT STAGE OF HISTORY

LEE HARRIS

FREE PRESS

NEW YORK   LONDON   TORONTO   SYDNEY

*f*P

FREE PRESS
A Division of Simon & Schuster, Inc.
1230 Avenue of the Americas
New York, NY 10020

For information regarding special discounts for bulk purchases,
please contact Simon & Schuster Special Sales at 1-800-456-6798
or business@simonandschuster.com.

Book design by Ellen R. Sasahara

Manufactured in the United States of America

1   3   5   7   9   10   8   6   4   2

Library of Congress Cataloging-in-Publication Data
Harris, Lee.
Civilization and its enemies : the next stage of history / Lee Harris.
p. cm.
Includes bibliographical references throughout and index.
l. Civilization, Modern 1950– 2. World politics—21st century. I. Title.
CDB428.H375 2004
909.08—dc22
2003063136

ISBN 0-7432-5749-9

To Andy Fuson
and
Sundown Walker,
for asking me questions I could not answer.

. . . history is strewn with the wrecks of nations which have gained a little progressiveness at the cost of a great deal of hard manliness, and have thus prepared themselves for destruction as soon as the movements of the world gave a chance for it.

—WALTER BAGEHOT, *Physics and Politics*

CONTENTS

PREFACE

The peoples of the Western world have for some generations now been familiar with systems where armies and navies are rigidly subject to civil authorities, and they are wont to regard the military rebellion as something exceptional and monstrous. Actually the human beings who have lived on this earth in security from the brutal rule of the soldier are so few in number, on the background of the whole of human history, as hardly to count. The military tyranny in some form or other is in fact the common rule in human society; and even in the best-ordered societies . . . any serious disturbance of an established order of a nonmilitary type is likely to result in a reversion to the military dictatorship.

—ARTHUR LIVINGSTON, from the Introduction to Gaetano Mosca's *The Ruling Class*

T HE SUBJECT of this book is forgetfulness.
     By this I do not mean our tendency to misplace valuable objects, or our inability to recall the name of the boss's dog, but the collective and cultural amnesia that overcomes any group of human beings who have long benefited from the inestimable blessings of civilization—an amnesia first observed nearly eight hundred years ago by the Arab philosopher of history Ibn Khaldun, contemplating the rise and fall of those great human feats of organized life that we call by such terms as *societies, states,* and *empires.*
Forgetfulness occurs when those who have been long accustomed to

civilized order can no longer remember a time in which they had to wonder whether their crops would grow to maturity without being stolen or
whether their children would be sold into slavery by a victorious foe. Even
then it is necessary for the parents, and even grandparents, to have forgotten as well, so that there is no living link between the tranquility of the
present generation and those dismal periods in which the world behaved
very much in accordance with the rules governing Thomas Hobbes's state
of nature, where human life was "solitary, poore, nasty, brutish, and
short." When parents have forgotten what that world was like, they can
hardly be expected to teach their children how it was or what one had to
do in order to survive in it.

Civilized people forget that in order to produce a civilization there
must be what the German sociologist Norbert Elias has called "the civilizing process," and that this process, if it is to be successful, must begin
virtually at our birth, and hence many long years before the child can
have any say about the kind of training he would have preferred. They
forget that the civilizing process we undergo must duplicate that of our
neighbors, if we are to understand each other in our day-to-day inter-
course. If you are taught to spit at a man who offers to shake your hand,
and do when I offer you mine, we will not easily get along.

Civilized people forget how much work it is to not kill one's neighbors,
simply because this work was all done by our ancestors so that it could be
willed to us as an heirloom. They forget that in time of danger, in the face
of the enemy, they must trust and confide in each other, or perish. They
forget that to fight an enemy it is necessary to have a leader whom you
trust, and how, at such times, this trust is a civic duty and not evidence
of one's credulity. They forget, in short, that there has ever been a category of human experience called the enemy.

That, before 9/11, was what had happened to us. The very concept of
the enemy had been banished from our moral and political vocabulary.
An enemy was just a friend we hadn't done enough for yet. Or perhaps
there had been a misunderstanding, or an oversight on our part—something that we could correct.

Our first task therefore is to try to grasp what the concept of the enemy
really means. The enemy is someone who is willing to die in order to kill
you. And while it is true that the enemy always hates us for a reason, it is
his reason and not ours. He does not hate us for our faults any more than
for our virtues. He sees a different world from ours, and in the world he

sees, we are his enemy. This is hard for us to comprehend, but we must if we are to grasp what the concept of the enemy means.

For Himmler, the Jewish children whom he ordered the SS to murder were the enemy because they would grow up to avenge the deaths of their fathers, who had been the enemy before them. We have killed their parents; they will want to kill our children. Hence we have no choice but to kill them first. The fact that they had done nothing themselves, and were incapable of doing anything themselves, was irrelevant.

This is how mankind has always thought of the enemy—as the one who, if you do not kill him first, will sooner or later kill you. And those who see the world in this way see it very differently from those who do not.

This is the major fact of our time. We are caught in the midst of a conflict between those for whom the category of the enemy is essential to their way of organizing all human experience and those who have banished even the idea of the enemy from both public discourse and even their innermost thoughts.

But those who abhor thinking of the world *through* the category of the enemy must still be prepared to think *about* the category of the enemy. That is, even if you refuse to think of anyone else as an enemy, you must acknowledge that there are people who do in fact think this way.

Yet even this minimal step is a step that many of our leading intellectuals refuse to take, despite the revelation that occurred on 9/11. They want to see 9/11 as a means to an end and not an end in itself. But 9/11 was an end in itself, and that is where we must begin.

Why do they hate us? They hate us *because* we are their enemy.

THIS WAS THE REVELATION that came to Theodor Herzl when as a young newspaperman he had been sent to cover the Dreyfus trial in Paris during the 1890s.

Herzl had been born in Budapest, a part of that great polyglot cosmopolitan Austro-Hungarian Empire in which Jews had done so remarkably well. As a student, he had thought that the solution to "the Jewish question" lay in complete assimilation of Jews, or what his biographer Alex Bein called their "disappearance without a trace in the ocean of the surrounding world."

But the reaction of the French crowds to the condemnation of Colonel

Dreyfus shattered this illusion. The crowds had shouted: "Death to the Jews!" But why, Herzl asked himself, did they want death to *all* Jews, rather than death to the *one* Jew whom they believed guilty of treason?

Herzl realized that even in France, one of the most liberal and civilized countries in the world, assimilated Jews were still hated for being Jews; and this meant that Herzl too was still hated for being a Jew. Not for having grandparents who were Jews, but for being a Jew himself. This meant that being a Jew had nothing to do with how Herzl defined himself, but everything to do with how his enemy defined him. If his enemy wished to hate him because he was a Jew, he would, and Herzl's own self-definition mattered to him not all—a truth that was echoed by Karl Lueger, the virulently anti-Semitic demagogue who was elected mayor of Vienna in 1895, one year after Dreyfus's arrest, and who was reputed to have said, "I decide who is or is not a Jew."

This disillusionment spelled the end of Herzl's belief in the Enlightenment dream that all men could one day embrace in the spirit of universal cosmopolitanism and, ultimately, turned Herzl from the path of assimilation to Zionism.

It is the enemy who defines us as his enemy, and in making this definition he changes us, and changes us whether we like it or not. We cannot be the same after we have been defined as an enemy as we were before.

That is why those who uphold the values of the Enlightenment so often refuse to recognize that those who are trying to kill them are their enemy. They hope that by pretending that the enemy is simply misguided, or misunderstood, or politically immature, he will cease to be an enemy. This is an illusion. To see the enemy as someone who is merely an awkward negotiator or sadly lacking in savoir faire and diplomatic aplomb is perverse. It shows contempt for the depth and sincerity of his convictions, a terrible mistake to make when you are dealing with someone who wants you dead.

We are the enemy of those who murdered us on 9/11. And if you are the enemy, then you have an enemy. When you recognize it, this fact must change everything about the way you see the world.

Once someone else sees you as the enemy, then you must yourself deal with this category of human experience, which is why societies that have enemies are radically different from societies that do not. A society that lacks an enemy does not need to worry about how to defend itself against him. It does not need to teach any of its children how to fight and how not to run when they are being attacked by men who want to kill them. It does not need to appoint a single man to make instant decisions that affect the well-being of the entire community, and it does not need to train the community to respond to his commands with unthinking obedience.

But societies with enemies must do all of these things, and do them very well, or else they perish.

Yet there is a problem with each of these various things that must be done to protect a society against its enemy. They are illiberal and they are at odds with those values that express the highest that civilized life has to offer—tolerance, individual liberty, government by consensus rather than by fiat, and rational cooperation. Thus it is not unnatural for those who prize such values to be reluctant to acknowledge the existence of an enemy serious enough to require illiberal measures, and they are correct to feel this way.

Those who argue that war is not the answer are almost invariably right, and if civilization can be said to inhere in any one single characteristic more conspicuously than in any other, it must certainly be in the preference for peaceful over violent methods of resolving conflict. To be sure, civilization consists in more than this, but this more is always dependent on the prereflective certainty that the people you must deal with will not resort to force or threat or intimidation when they are dealing with you.

The first duty of all civilization is to create pockets of peaceableness in which violence is not used as a means of obtaining one's objective; the second duty is to defend these pockets against those who try to disrupt their peace, either from within or from without. Yet the values that bring peace are the opposite values from those that promote military prowess, and this poses a riddle that very few societies have been able to solve and then only fitfully. If you have managed to create your own pocket of peace—and its inseparable companion, prosperity—how will you keep those who envy you your prosperity from destroying your peace?

There is only one way: you must fight back; if your enemy insists on a war to the finish, then you have no choice but to fight such a war. It is your enemy, and not you, who decides what is a matter of life and death.

Once you have accepted this reality, however, you are faced with the problem of how to fight. If your enemy is composed of men who will stop at nothing, who are willing to die and to kill, then you must find men to fight on your side who are willing to do the same. Only those who have mastered ruthlessness can defend their society from the ruthlessness of others.

This was the plight faced by the peasants in Kurosawa's masterpiece *The Seven Samurai* and by the dirt farmers in the American remake, *The Magnificent Seven*. Men and women who knew nothing of battle, the impoverished peasants of a remote village found themselves at the mercy of a gang of ruthless bandits who each year came at harvest to steal what the peasant farmers had managed to eke from their soil. In their desperation the farmers turned to the seven samurai, all of whom had fallen on hard times. But then, once the samurai had defeated the bandits, the question immediately arose in the peasants' minds: "Now how do we rid ourselves of the samurai?"

Such has been the lot of most of mankind: a choice between the gangsters who come across the river to steal and the gangsters on this side of the river who do not need to steal because they have their own peasants to exploit. How else could it be? Given what we know of human nature, how could we expect there to be a government that wasn't, in the final analysis, simply a protection racket that could make laws?

Yet this is not how Kurosawa's movie ends. The samurai do not set themselves up as village warlords but instead move on, taking only the wages due them for their services. How was this possible? It was possible only because the samurai lived by a code of honor.

Codes of honor do not come cheap, and they cannot be created out of thin air upon demand. The fact that you need samurai and not gangsters is no guarantee that you will get them; indeed you will almost certainly not get them when you need them unless you had them with you all along.

A code of honor, to be effective when it is needed, requires a tradition that is blindly accepted by the men and women who are expected to live by this code. To work when it must, the code of honor must be the unspoken and unquestioned law governing a community: a law written not in law books but in the heart—something like an instinct.

A code of honor cannot be chosen by us; it can only be chosen for us. For if we look on it as one option among many, then we may opt out of it at will. In which case the community will never be quite sure of us when the chips are down.

All of which explains why those who subscribe to the values of the Enlightenment find the existence of the enemy so distressing.

The enemy challenges the Enlightenment's insistence on the supremacy of pure reason by forcing us to respect those codes of honor whose foundation is far more visceral than rational, a fact that explains the modern intellectual's hatred for such codes in whatever guise they lurk. The enemy requires the continued existence of large groups of men and women who refuse to question authority and who are happy to take on blind faith the traditions that have been passed down to them. The enemy necessitates the careful cultivation of such high-testosterone values as brute physical courage and unthinking personal loyalty to a leader. The enemy demands instinctual patriotism and what Ibn Khaldun called "group feeling," that is, the sense of intense identification with one's own people. The enemy propels into postitions of command men who are accustomed to taking risks and who are willing to gamble with the lives of others, and shunts aside those who prefer the leisure of contemplation to the urgency of action. Lastly, the enemy shatters the enlightenment's visions of utopia, of Kant's epoch of perpetual peace and of the end of history. And this is why so many American and European intellectuals refuse to acknowledge today even the possibility of the enemy's existence, concocting theories to explain the actions of Al-Qaeda as something other than what they were.

This is also why all utopian projects are set either on a distant island or in a hidden valley: they must exist in isolation from the rest of the world, to keep even the thought of the enemy at bay. Otherwise they would have to deal with the problem of how to survive without abandoning their lofty ideals.

This is the problem that confronts us today.

The ideals that our intellectuals have been instilling in us are utopian ideals, designed for men and women who know no enemy and who do not need to take precautions against him. They are values appropriate for a world in which everyone plays by the same rules, and accepts the same standards, of rational cooperation; they are fatally unrealistic in a world in which the enemy acknowledges no rule except that of ruthlessness. To insist on maintaining utopian values when your society is facing an enemy who wishes only to annihilate you is to invite annihilation. And that is unacceptable.

The only solution is for us to go back and to unforget some of what we have forgotten, for our very forgetfulness is an obstacle to understanding the lessons of the past, so long as we insist on interpreting this past in ways that give comfort to our pet illusions. We want to believe that civilization came about because men decided one fine morning to begin living sensible, peaceful, rational lives; we refuse to acknowledge what it cost to achieve even the first step in this direction. Unless we can understand this first step, none of the rest will make sense to us, and we will fail to see what is looming right in front of us.

The Greek way of expressing past and future differed from ours. We say that the past is behind us and the future is in front of us. To the Greeks, however, the past was before them, because they could plainly see its finished form standing in front of them: it was territory they had passed through and whose terrain they had charted. It was the future that was behind them, sneaking up like a thief in the night, full of dim imaginings and vast uncertainties. Nothing could penetrate the blackness of this unknown future except the rare flash of foresight that the Greeks called *sophos,* or wisdom. Yet even these flashes of wisdom depended entirely on the capacity to remember what is eternal and unchanging— which is precisely what we have almost completely forgotten.

The past tells us that there can be no end of history, no realm of perpetual peace, and that those who are convinced by this illusion are risking the survival of all that they hold dear. The past tells us that there will always be an enemy as long as men care enough about anything to stake a claim to it, and thus enmity is built into the very nature of things. The past tells us that the next stage of history will be a tragic conflict between two different ways of life, which both have much that is worthy of admiration in them but which cannot coexist in the same world. But the past does not, and cannot, tell us how it will end this time.

That is why it is impossible simply to stand by and not take sides. No outcome is assured by any deep logic of history or by any iron law of human development. Individual civilizations rise and fall; in each case the fall was not inevitable but due to the decisions—or lack of decision—of the human beings whose ancestors had created the civilization for them, but who had forgotten the secret of how to preserve it for their own children.

We are ourselves dangerously near this point, which is all the more remarkable considering how close we still are to 9/11. It is as if 9/11 has become simply an event in the past and not the opening up of a new epoch in human history, one that will be ruled by the possibility of catastrophic terror, just as previous historical epochs were ruled by other possible forms of historical catastrophe, from attack by migratory hordes to totalitarian takeover, from warrior gangs to the threat of nuclear annihilation.

Our journey of recollection, must therefore begin with 9/11, for this was the moment when one epoch closed, and another opened. With 9/11 commenced the next stage of history, one whose direction will be determined by how the world responds to the possibilities that it has opened up.

And yet, have we even begun to understand it?

CIVILIZATION AND
ITS ENEMIES

1

THE RIDDLE OF THE ENEMY

K NOW YOUR ENEMY" is an admirable maxim of prudence, but one that is difficult to observe in practice. Nor is the reason hard to fathom: if you are my enemy, it is unlikely that I will go very much out of my way to learn to see things from your point of view. And if this ignorance exists even where the conflict is between groups that share a common culture, how much more will it exist when there is a profound cultural and psychological chasm between the antagonists?

Yet, paradoxically, this failure to understand the enemy can arise not only from a lack of sympathy with his position but also from a kind of misplaced sympathy: when confronted by a culturally exotic enemy, our first instinct is to understand his conduct in terms that are familiar to us, terms that make sense to us in light of our own fund of experience. We assume that if our enemy is doing X, it must be for reasons that are comprehensible in terms of our universe.

Just how unfortunate—and indeed fatal—this approach can be was demonstrated during the Spanish conquest of Mexico. When Montezuma learned of Cortés's arrival, he was at a loss to know what to make of the event. Who were these white-skinned alien beings? What had they come for? What were their intentions?

These were clearly not questions that Montezuma was in a position to answer. Nothing in *his* world could possibly provide him with a key to deciphering correctly the motives of a man as cunning, resourceful, and determined as Cortés. Montezuma, who after all had to do *something*, was therefore forced to deploy categories drawn from the fund of experience that was readily available within the Aztec world.

By a fatal coincidence, this fund of experience chanced to contain a remarkable prefiguring of Cortés—the myth of the white-skinned god, Quetzalcoatl. Indeed, the parallels were uncanny. Of course, Cortés was not Quetzalcoatl, and he had not appeared on the coast of Mexico in order to bring blessings.

Yet we should not be too hard on Montezuma. He was, after all, acting exactly as we all act under similar circumstances. We all want to make sense of our world, and at no time more urgently than when our world is suddenly behaving strangely. In order to make sense of such strangeness, we must be able to reduce it to something that is not strange—something that is already known to us, something we know our way around.

Yet this entirely human response, as Montezuma quickly learned to his regret, can sometimes be very dangerous.

AN ACT OF WAR?

On September 11, 2001, Americans were confronted by an enigma similar to that presented to the Aztecs—an enigma so baffling that even elementary questions of nomenclature posed a problem: What words or phrase should we use merely to *refer* to the events of that day? Was it a disaster, like the sinking of the *Titanic*? Or perhaps a tragedy? Was it a criminal act, or was it an act of war? Indeed, one awkward TV anchorman, in groping for the proper handle, fecklessly called it an "accident." Eventually the collective and unconscious wisdom that governs such matters prevailed. Words failed, then fell away completely, and all that was left were the bleak but monumentally poignant set of numbers, 9/11.

This resolution did not solve the great question, What did it all *mean?*

In the early days there were many who were convinced that they knew the answer to this question, arguing that the explanation of 9/11 was to be sought in what was called, through an invariable horticultural metaphor, the "root cause" of terrorism. Eliminate poverty or economic imperialism, or pull our troops out of Saudi Arabia, or cease supporting Israel, and such acts of terrorism would cease.

Opposed to this kind of analysis were those who saw 9/11 as an unprovoked act of war, and the standard comparison here was with the Japanese attack on Pearl Harbor on December 7, 1941. To this school of thought, ably represented by, among others, the distinguished classicist Victor Davis Hanson, it is irrelevant what grievances our enemy may believe it has against us; what matters is that we have been viciously attacked and that, for the sake of our survival, we must fight back.

Those who hold this view are in the overwhelming majority among Americans. Yet there is one point on which this position does not differ from the position adopted by those, such as Noam Chomsky, who place the blame for the attack on American policy: both points of view agree in interpreting 9/11 as an act of war, while disagreeing only on the question of whether or not it was justifiable. This common identification of 9/11 as an act of war arises from a deeper unquestioned assumption—an assumption made both by Chomsky and his followers on the one hand and by Hanson and *The National Review* on the other, and indeed by almost everyone in between.

The assumption is this: An act of violence on the magnitude of 9/11 can only have been intended to further some kind of *political* objective. What this political objective might be, or whether it is worthwhile—these are all secondary considerations. Surely people do not commit such acts unless they are trying to achieve some kind of recognizably political purpose.

Behind this shared assumption stands the figure of Clausewitz and his famous definition of war as politics carried out by other means. The whole point of war, on this reading, is to get other people to do what we want them to do: it is an effort to make others adopt our policies and/or to further our interests. Clausewitzian war, in short, is rational and instrumental. It attempts to bring about a new state of affairs through the artful combination of violence *and* the promise to cease violence if certain political objectives are met.

Of course, wars may still backfire on those who undertake them, or a particular application of military force may prove to be counterproductive to one's particular political purpose. But such pitfalls do not change the fact that the final criterion of military success is always pragmatic: Does it work? Does it in fact bring us closer to realizing our political objectives?

Is this the right model for understanding 9/11? Or have we, like Montezuma, imposed our own inadequate categories on an event that simply does not fit them? If 9/11 was not an act of war, then what was it?

Oddly enough, the post 9/11 "celebrity comment" that came closest to capturing the true significance of the event was the much-quoted remark by the German composer Karlheinz Stockhausen, that 9/11 was "the greatest work of art of all time." Despite its repellent nihilism, Stockhausen's aesthetic judgment comes closer to a genuine assessment of 9/11 than the competing Clausewitzian interpretation. For Stockhausen did grasp one big truth: 9/11 was the enactment of a fantasy—not an artistic fantasy, to be sure, but a fantasy nonetheless.

A PERSONAL RECOLLECTION

My first encounter with this particular kind of fantasy occurred when I was in college in the late sixties. A friend and I got into a rather odd argument. Although we were both opposed to the Vietnam War, we discovered that we differed considerably on what counted as permissible forms of antiwar protest. To me the point of such protest was simple—to turn people against the war. Hence anything that was counterproductive to this purpose was politically irresponsible and should be severely censured. My friend thought otherwise; in fact, he was planning to join what by all accounts was to be a massively disruptive demonstration in Washington, and which in fact became one.

His attitude greatly puzzled me. For my friend did not disagree with me as to the likely counterproductive effects of such a demonstration. Instead, he argued that this result simply did not matter. What then was the point of the demonstration, if not to achieve our political objective, namely, an early conclusion of the Vietnam War?

His answer was that even if it was counterproductive, even if it turned people against war protesters, indeed even if it made them more likely to support the continuation of the war, he would still participate in the demonstration and he would do so for one simple reason—because it was, in his words, "good for his soul." What I saw as a political act was not, for my friend, any such thing. It was not aimed at altering the minds of other people or persuading them to act differently. Its whole point was what it did *for him*.

And what it did for him was to provide him with a fantasy—a fantasy, namely, of taking part in the revolutionary struggle of the oppressed against their oppressors. By participating in a violent antiwar demonstration he was in no sense aiming at coercing others to conform with his view, for that would still have been a political objective. Instead he took part in order to confirm his ideological fantasy of marching on the right side of history, of being among the elect few who stood with the angels of historical materialism. Thus, when he lay down in front of hapless commuters on the bridges over the Potomac, he had no interest in changing the minds of these commuters, no concern over whether they became angry at the protesters or not. They were there merely as props, as so many supernumeraries in his private political psychodrama. The protest for him was not politics, but theater; the significance of his role lay not in the political ends his actions might achieve but rather in their symbolic value as ritual. His was not your garden-variety fantasy: it did not, after all, make him into a sexual athlete, or a record-breaking race car driver, or a Nobel prize–winning chemist. And yet, in terms of the fantasy, he was nonetheless a hero; but a hero of the revolutionary struggle, for his fantasy—and that of many young intellectuals at that time—was compounded purely of ideological ingredients, smatterings of Marx and Mao, a little Fanon, and perhaps a dash of Jean-Paul Sartre. I have therefore elected to call the phenomenon in question, if only for lack of a better term, *fantasy ideology*—political and ideological symbols and tropes used not for political purposes but entirely for the benefit of furthering a specific personal fantasy. It is, to be frank, something like Dungeons and Dragons carried out not with the trappings of medieval romances—old castles and maidens in distress—but entirely in terms of ideological symbols and emblems. The only important difference between them is that one is an innocent pastime while the other has proven to be one of the most terrible scourges to afflict the human race.

But before tackling this subject outright, let us approach it through a few observations about the normal role of fantasy in human conduct.

THE NATURE OF FANTASY IDEOLOGY

It is a common human weakness to wish to make more of our contribution to the world than the world is prepared to acknowledge; it is our fantasy world that allows us to fill this gap. Normally, for most of us at least, this fantasy world of ours stays relatively hidden, and indeed a common criterion of our mental health is the extent to which we are able to keep our fantasies firmly under our watchful control.

Yet clearly there are individuals for whom this control is, at best, intermittent; its failure results in behavior that ranges from the merely obnox-ious to the clinically psychotic. The man who insists on being taken more seriously than his advantages warrant falls into the former category; the maniac who murders an utter stranger because God—or his neighbor's dog—commanded him to do so belongs to the latter.

What is common in such interactions is that the fantasist inevitably treats other people merely as props: there is absolutely no interest in, or even awareness of, others as having wills or minds of their own. The man who bores us with stories designed to impress us with his impor-tance or his intellect or his bank account cares nothing for us as individ-uals, for he has already cast us in the role that he wishes us to play: we are there to be impressed by him. Indeed, it is an error even to suggest that he is trying to impress us, for this would assume that he is willing to learn enough about us to discover how best we might be impressed. Nothing of the kind occurs. And why should it? After all, the fantasist has already projected onto us the role which we are to play in his fantasy. And no matter what we may be thinking of his recital, it never crosses his mind that we may be utterly failing to play the part expected of us; indeed, it is sometimes astonishing to see how much exertion is required of us in order to bring our own profound lack of interest to the fanta-sist's attention.

Tragically, the same problem occurs in the more significant aspects of life, and nowhere more insidiously than in our relationship with those we love. Jane falls in love with Bob, or so Bob thinks. But in point of fact Bob is nothing more than a prop around which Jane weaves her roman-tic and erotic fantasies. Often what Freud called the idealization of the love object is something far more sinister: it is a systematic canceling out of the real person of the beloved and its replacement by a fictional char-acter devised purely in order to fulfill the lover's fantasy of true love—a transformation, curiously enough, in which the beloved often takes an active and even aggressive role.

To an outside observer, the fantasist is clearly attempting to compen-sate by means of his fantasy for the shortcomings of his own present real-ity, and thus it is tempting to think of the fantasist as a kind of Don Quixote impotently tilting at windmills. But this is an illusion, for make no mistake about it, the fantasist often exercises great and terrible power precisely by virtue of his fantasy: the father who wishes his son to grow up to become a major league football player will clearly exercise much more control over his son's life than a father who is content to permit his child to pursue his own goals in life.

This power of the fantasist is entirely traceable to the fact that for him the other is always an object, never a subject. A subject, after all, has a will of his own, his own desires and its own agenda; he might rather play the flute instead of football. Anyone who is aware of this fact is automatically put at a disadvantage in comparison with the fantasist—the disadvantage of knowing that other people have minds of their own and are not merely props to be pushed around.

For the moment I stop thinking about you as a prop in my fantasy, you become problematic. If you aren't what I have cast you to be, then who are you, and what do you want? In order to answer these questions, I find that I must step out of the fantasy realm and enter the real world. If I am your father, I may still wish you to play football, but I can no longer blithely assume that this is obviously what you have always wanted; hence I will need to start paying attention to you as a genuine other and no longer merely as a ready-made prop. Your role will change from "born football player" to the mysterious stranger.

The very enormity of the required mental adjustment goes a long way toward explaining why it is so seldom made and why it is so often tragically impossible to wean a fantasist from even the most destructive fantasy. Fortunately, the fantasizing individual is normally surrounded by other individuals who are not fantasizing or, at the very least, who are not fantasizing in the same way, and this fact puts some limit on how far most of us can allow our fantasy world to intrude on the precinct of reality. But what happens when it is not an individual who is caught up in his fantasy world but an entire group—a sect, or a people, or even a nation?

That such a thing happens is obvious from a glance at history. The various end-time movements, such as those studied in Norman Cohn's *Pursuit of the Millennium,* are splendid examples of collective fantasy. Periodically, from the early Christian Era to the American "Great Disappointment" of 1843, hundreds or even thousands of people become convinced that the world will end on a certain date and begin to act accordingly.

For most of history, such large-scale collective fantasies appeared on the world stage under the guise of religion. But with the coming of the French Revolution, this changed. From that event onward, there have been eruptions of a new kind of collective fantasy, one in which political ideology has replaced religious mythology as the source of symbolism and in this way has provided a new, and quite dangerous, outlet for the fantasy needs of large groups of men and women. Hence the designation "fantasy ideology" to describe a fantasy that makes no sense outside of the ideological corpus in terms of which the fantasy has been constructed. From the ideology the roles, the setting, and the props are drawn, just as for the earlier adventists the relevant roles, setting, and props arose out of biblical symbolism.

The symbols by themselves, however, do not create the fantasy. There must first be a preexisting collective need for the fantasy.

In even the most casual survey of history, one is repeatedly struck by the fact that certain groups do not seem to have the knack for a realistic appraisal of themselves: they seem simply incapable of seeing themselves as others see them or of understanding why other groups react to them the way they do. A fantasy ideology is one that seizes the opportunity offered by such a lack of realism in a political group and makes the most of it. This it is able to do through symbols and rituals, all of which are designed to permit the members of the political group to indulge in a kind of fantasy role-playing. Classical examples of this are easy to find: the Jacobin fantasy of reviving the Roman Republic; Mussolini's fantasy of reviving the Roman Empire; Hitler's fantasy of reviving German paganism in the thousand-year Reich.

This theme of reviving ancient glory is an important key to understanding fantasy ideologies. It suggests that fantasy ideologies tend to be the domain of those groups that history has passed by or rejected—groups that feel that they are under attack from forces that, while more powerful perhaps than they are, are nonetheless inferior to them in terms of true virtue; they themselves stand for what is pure.

Such a fantasy ideology was current in the South before the Civil War and explains much of the conduct of the Confederacy. Instead of seeing themselves as an anachronism, attempting to prolong the existence of a doomed institution, Southerners chose to see themselves as the bearers of *true* civilization. Imperial Germany had similar fantasies before and during the Great War, fantasies well expressed in Thomas Mann's *Notes of an Unpolitical Man:* Germans possess true inwardness and culture, unlike the French and English—let alone those barbarous Americans. Indeed, Hitler's even more extravagant fantasy ideology is incomprehensible unless one puts it in the context of this preexisting fantasy ideology.

In reviewing fantasy ideologies, especially those associated with Nazism and Italian fascism, there is always the temptation for an outside observer to regard the promulgation of such fantasies as the cynical manipulation by a power-hungry leader of his gullible followers, but this would be a serious error, for the leader himself must be as steeped in the fantasy as his followers. He can only make others believe because he believes so intensely himself.

The concept of *belief,* as it is used in this context, must be carefully understood, in order to avoid ambiguity. For most of us, belief is a purely passive response to evidence presented to us: I form my beliefs about the world for the purpose of understanding the world as it is. This belief is radically different from what might be called *transformative belief*—the secret of fantasy ideology. Here the belief is not passive but intensely active, and its purpose is not to describe the world but to change it. It is, in a sense, a deliberate form of make-believe, in which the make-believe is not an end in itself but rather the means of making the make-believe become real. In this sense it is akin to such innocently jejune phenomena as "the power of positive thinking," or even the little train that thought it could. To say that Mussolini, for example, *believed* that fascist Italy would revive the Roman Empire does not mean that he made a careful examination of the evidence and then arrived at this conclusion. Rather it means that Mussolini had *the will to believe* that fascist Italy would revive the Roman Empire.

The allusion to William James's famous essay "The Will to Believe" is not an accident. James exercised a profound influence on the two thinkers essential to understanding both Italian fascism in particular and fantasy ideology in general—Vilfredo Pareto and Georges Sorel. All three men begin with the same assumption: if human beings were limited to acting only on those beliefs that can be logically and scientifically demonstrated, they could not survive, simply because this degree of certainty is restricted only to mathematics and the hard sciences, which, by themselves, are not remotely sufficient to guide us through the world as it exists. Hence human beings must have a large set of beliefs that cannot be demonstrated logically and scientifically—beliefs that are therefore irrational if judged by the hard sciences.

The fact that such beliefs cannot be justified by science does not mean that they may not be useful or beneficial to the individual or to the society that holds them. James was primarily concerned with the religious beliefs of individuals: did a man's religious beliefs improve the quality of his personal life? For Pareto the same question could be asked about all beliefs, religious, cultural, and political. Both James and Pareto viewed nonrational belief as outside observers: they took up the beliefs that they found already circulating in the societies in which they lived and examined them in light of whether they were beneficial or detrimental to the individuals and the societies that entertained them, exactly as a botanist examines the flora of a particular region; he is interested not in creating new flowers but simply in cataloguing those that already exist. So too James and Pareto were exclusively interested in already existing beliefs and certainly not in creating new ones.

Sorel went one step further. Combining Nietzsche with William James, he discovered the secret of Nietzsche's will to power in James's will to believe. James, like Pareto, had shown that certain spontaneously occurring beliefs enabled those who held these beliefs to thrive and to prosper, both as individuals and societies. But if this were true of spontaneously occurring beliefs, could it not also be true of beliefs that were deliberately and consciously manufactured?

Sorel's was a radical innovation. Just as naturally existing beliefs could be judged properly only in terms of the benefits they brought about in the lives of those who held them, the same standard was now applied to beliefs that were deliberately created in order to have a desired effect on those who came to believe in them. What would be important about such "artificially inseminated" beliefs (which Sorel calls myths) was not their truth value but the transformative effect they would have on those who placed their faith in them and the extent to which such ideological make-believe could alter the character and conduct of those who held these beliefs.

Sorel's candidate for such a myth—the general strike—never quite caught on, but his underlying insight was taken up by Mussolini and Italian fascism with vastly greater sensitivity to what is involved in creating such galvanizing and transformative myths in the minds of large numbers of men and women. After all, it is obvious that not just any belief will do and that, furthermore, each particular group of people will have a disposition, based on their history and their character, to entertain more readily one set of beliefs than another. Mussolini, for example, assembled his Sorelian myth out of elements clearly designed to catch the imagination of his time and place—a strange blend of imperial Roman themes and futurist images, but one that worked.

Yet even the most sensitively crafted myth requires something more in order to take root in the imagination of large populations, and this was where Mussolini made his great innovation. For the Sorelian myth to achieve its effect it had to be presented as *theater.* It had to grab the spectators and make them feel a part of the spectacle and not merely outside observers. The Sorelian myth, in short, had to be embodied in a fantasy— a fantasy with which the "audience" could easily and instantly identify. In addition, the willing suspension of disbelief, which Coleridge had observed in the psychology of the normal theatergoer, would be enlisted in the service of the Sorelian myth; in the process, it would permit the myth-induced fantasy to override the obvious objections based on mundane considerations of realism. Thus it came about that twentieth-century Italians became convinced that they were the successors of the Roman Empire.

Once again, it is a mistake to see the promotion of such fantasies as merely a ploy on the part of fascist leadership—a cynical device to delude the masses, in order to further the real interests of certain other groups— for in all fantasy ideologies, there is a point at which the make-believe becomes an end it itself. This fact is nowhere more clearly exhibited than in the Italian conquest of Ethiopia, an event that decisively proved that Mussolini's imperial fantasy was not a smoke screen for other interests but was instead the motivating factor even in such a critical area as the decision to invade a foreign country on a forbidding continent.

Any attempt to see this adventure in Clausewitzian terms is doomed to fail: there was no political or economic advantage whatsoever to be gained from the invasion of Ethiopia. Indeed, the diplomatic disadvantages to Italy in consequence of this action were tremendous, and they were in no way to be compensated for by anything that Italy could hope to gain from possessing Ethiopia as a colony.

Why then did Italy invade Ethiopia?

The answer is quite simple. Ethiopia was a prop—a prop in the fantasy pageant of the new Italian Empire—that and nothing else. The war waged in order to win Ethiopia as a colony was not a war in the Clausewitzian sense: that is to say, it was not an instrument of political policy designed to induce concessions from Ethiopia, or to get Ethiopia to alter its policies, or even to get Ethiopia to surrender. Ethiopia had to be conquered not because it was worth conquering, but *because the fascist fantasy ideology required Italy to conquer something,* and Ethiopia fit the bill. The conquest was not the means to an end, as in Clausewitzian war; it was an end in itself. Or, more correctly, its true purpose was to bolster the collective fantasy that insisted on casting the Italians as a conquering race, the heirs of imperial Rome.

AMERICA AS A PROP

To be a prop in someone else's fantasy is not a pleasant experience, especially when this someone else is trying to kill you, but that was the position Ethiopia was placed in by the fantasy ideology of Italian fascism. And it is the position Americans have been placed in by the quite different fantasy ideology of radical Islam. The terror attack of 9/11 was not designed to make us alter our policy but was crafted for its effect on the terrorists themselves and on those who share the same fantasy ideology: it was a spectacular piece of theater. The targets were chosen by Al-Qaeda not for their military value—in contrast, for example, to the Japanese attack on Pearl Harbor—but entirely because they stood as *symbols* of American power universally recognized by the Arab street. They were gigantic props in a grandiose spectacle in which the collective fantasy of radical Islam was brought vividly to life: a mere handful of Muslims, men whose will was absolutely pure, as was proven by their martyrdom, brought down the haughty towers erected by the Great Satan. What better proof could there possibly be that God was on the side of radical Islam and that the end of the reign of the Great Satan was near at hand?

Just as the purpose of the Italian invasion of Ethiopia was not to conquer Ethiopia but to prove to the Italians themselves that they were conquerors, so the purpose of 9/11 was not to create terror in the minds of the American people but to prove to the Arabs that Islamic purity, as interpreted by radical Islam, could triumph over the West. The terror, which to us seems the central fact, is, in the eyes of Al-Qaeda, merely an incidental by-product, an irrelevancy. In the same way, what Al-Qaeda and its followers see as central to the holy pageant of 9/11, namely the heroic martyrdom of the nineteen hijackers, is interpreted by us quite differently. For us the hijackings, like the Palestinian "suicide" bombings, are viewed merely as a modus operandi, a technique incidental to the larger strategic purpose. Consider the standard Arab apologist's "explanation" of such acts: They don't have jet fighters, so what other means do they have of fighting back? But even those who are most unsympathetic to the Arab fantasy ideology look upon the suicide of the hijackers, like that of the Palestinian terrorists, as merely a makeshift device, a low-tech stopgap, and nothing more. In our eyes, these attacks represent simply Clausewitzian war carried out by other means—in this case by suicide.

But in the fantasy ideology of radical Islam, suicide plays an absolutely indispensable role. It is not a means to an end but an end in itself. Seen through the distorting prism of radical Islam, the act of suicide is transformed into the act of martyrdom—martyrdom in all its transcendent glory and accompanied by the panoply of magical powers that religious tradition has always assigned to it.

In short, it is a mistake to try to fit such behavior into the mold created by our own categories and expectations. We must continually remind ourselves that one and the same physical act, such as 9/11, does not have the same significance for us as it does for those who follow radical Islam. And nowhere is this difference more telling than in the interpretation of the final collapse of the World Trade Center. Tapes of bin Laden have made it clear that this catastrophic event was not part of the original terrorist scheme, which apparently assumed that the twin towers would not lose their structural integrity. The unlooked-for collapse gave to the event—in the terms of Al-Qaeda's fantasy ideology—an even greater poignancy: precisely because it had not been part of the original calculations, it was immediately interpreted as a manifestation of divine intervention. The nineteen hijackers did not bring down the towers; God did.

9/11 AS SYMBOLIC DRAMA

Most of our misunderstandings of Al-Qaeda's goals have come about for one fundamental reason: in the first weeks after 9/11, no one knew what was going to happen next. That Al-Qaeda had not embarked on a systematic and calculated Clausewitzian strategy of terror simply could not be ascertained in the immediate aftermath because we did not know, and could not know, *what was coming next.*

In the days and weeks following 9/11 there was a universal sense that *it* would happen again at any moment—something shocking and terrifying, something that would again rivet us to our TV screen. But, in fact, it didn't happen. Nor does the possibility that it might still happen in the future change the fact that it didn't happen during this initial period, and this in itself is a remarkably telling fact.

Acts of terror can be used to pursue genuine Clausewitzian objectives in the same way that normal military operations are used, as was demonstrated during the Algerian War of Independence. But this use requires that the acts of terror be planned with the same kind of strategic logic that applies to normal military operations. If you attack your enemy with an act of terror—especially one on the scale of 9/11—you must be prepared to follow up on it immediately. The analogy here to time-honored military strategy is obvious: if you have vanquished your enemy on the field of battle, you must vigorously pursue him while he is in retreat (i.e., while he is still in a state of panic and confusion). You must not let him regroup psychologically but must continue to pummel him while he is still reeling from the first blow.

This Al-Qaeda has utterly failed to do. And the question is, Why?

Of course, given our limited state of knowledge, it is possible that Al-Qaeda did plan immediate followup acts of terror but was simply unable to carry them out, thanks to our own heightened state of awareness, as well as our own military efforts to cripple Al-Qaeda in its base of operations in Afghanistan. But it is hard to believe that these factors could have precluded smaller-scale acts of terror, of the kind employed during the Algerian War of Independence and, presently, by the Palestinian suicide bombers. What was to keep Al-Qaeda operatives from blowing themselves up at a Wal-Mart in Arkansas or a McDonald's in New Hampshire? Very little. And while it is true that such acts would lack the grandiose effect of 9/11, this would not in fact be a disadvantage from a strategic point of view. If the objective of Al-Qaeda were to instill psychological terror and panic among the American people, then such geographically dispersed small-scale attacks could be of great strategic advantage. In the highly charged aftermath of 9/11, the psychological impact of each attack would have been immensely amplified by the media's twenty-four-hour news cycle; most critically, a string of such attacks would have had the effect of making all people in the United States feel themselves under the direct threat of terrorism, not merely those who live and work in national landmarks and in the great symbols of national power. The strategy would have brought terrorism home to the average American in a way that even 9/11 had not done, and it would have multiplied exponentially the already enormous impact on the American psyche of Al-Qaeda's original act of terror.

This was the reason that I, like millions of Americans, spent the first few weeks after 9/11 either watching TV constantly or turning it on every fifteen minutes: we were prepared to be devastated again. Our nerves were in a state of such anxious expectation that a carefully concerted campaign of smaller-scale, guerrilla-style terror, undertaken in out-of-the-way locales, could have had a catastrophically destabilizing effect on the American economy and even on our political system.

Nothing of the sort happened, and the reason, I believe, is simple: 9/11 was not an act of Clausewitzian terror—that is to say, terror used as a strategic weapon for the sake of its psychologically debilitating effect on the American people. It was a symbolic drama, a great ritual demonstrating the power of Allah, a pageant designed to convey a message not to the American people but to the Arab world. Smaller-scale followup acts would have had no glamour, and it was glamour—and grandiosity—that Al-Qaeda was seeking in its targets. These targets, let it be said one last time, were selected not for any strategic value but simply because they were the most suitable props for the great symbolic fantasy drama that Al-Qaeda had devised—a drama, once again, designed to be decoded not in American living rooms but in the Arab street. The pure Islamic David required a Goliath. After all, if David had merely killed someone his own size, where would be the evidence of God's favor toward him?

IS WAR THE RIGHT METAPHOR?

If our enemy is motivated purely by a fantasy ideology, what sense can it make to look for the so-called "root" causes of terrorism in poverty, lack of education, lack of democracy, and so forth? However bad such conditions may be in themselves, they play absolutely no role in the creation of a fantasy ideology. On the contrary, fantasy ideologies have historically been produced by members of the intelligentsia, middle-class at the very least and vastly better educated than average. Furthermore, fantasy ideologies have historically arisen in a democratic context. As the student of European fascism Ernst Nolte has observed, parliamentary democracy was an essential precondition of the rise of both Mussolini and Hitler.

Equally absurd, in this interpretation, is the notion that we must review our own policies toward the Arab world—or the state of Israel— in order to find ways to make our enemies hate us less. That is like the Ethiopians trying to make themselves more likable to the Italians in the vain hope of persuading Mussolini to rethink his plans of conquest. In the eyes of the radical Islamic fantasy ideology, we are simply necessary props in the grandiose psychodrama that Al-Qaeda and its followers have devised for their own consumption. The reaction of the props themselves is unimportant: there is absolutely no political policy that we could adopt that would in any way change the attitude of our enemies.

We need therefore to reconsider the metaphor of war as it is currently used. As I have tried to show, *war* is a misleading term if by it we mean what I have called Clausewitzian war. In Clausewitzian war, the enemy has a set of political objectives which he tries to achieve through the use of organized force, including acts of terror. For example, the Japanese bombed Pearl Harbor because it was a large naval base and because the Japanese had the quite rational strategic goal of crippling the American Pacific fleet in the first hours of the war. The attack would not have taken place if the Japanese had believed themselves capable of securing their political goals, namely, American acceptance of Japanese hegemony in Asia and the Pacific. Lastly, the war would have immediately ceased if the United States, in the days following the attack, had promptly asked for a negotiated settlement of the conflict on terms acceptable to the Japanese.

In the case of 9/11, as we have seen, the terror attack was not the outcome of a preexisting conflict over differing political objectives, despite the various attempts to concoct such explanations. In the case of the attack on Pearl Harbor or, going further back, the sinking of the *Lusitania,* all the parties knew exactly what was at issue and there was no need of media experts to argue over the "real" objectives behind these attacks: they were obvious to everyone. The *Lusitania* was sunk because German strategy dictated that all vessels bound for England were appropriate military targets, since any one of them could be carrying war materials that could be used by Germany's enemies to attack it. Likewise, everyone knew that Pearl Harbor was the result of a strategic decision to go to war with America rather than accept the American ultimatum to evacuate Manchuria. In both of these cases, war was entered into by both sides, despite the fact that a political solution was available to the various contending parties. The decision to go to war, therefore, was made in a purely Clausewitzian manner: the employment of military force was selected in preference to what all sides saw as an unacceptable political settlement.

This was not remotely the case in the aftermath of 9/11. The issue facing the United States was not whether to accept or to reject Al-Qaeda's political demands, because it made none. Indeed, it did not even claim to have made the attack in the first place! And the United States was placed in the bizarre position of first having to prove who the enemy was—a difficulty which, by definition, does not occur in Clausewitzian war, where it is absolutely essential that the identity and goals of the conflicting parties be known to each other, since otherwise the conflict would be pointless.

The fact that we are involved with an enemy who is not engaged in Clausewitzian warfare has serious repercussions for our policy. We are fighting an enemy who has no strategic purpose in anything he does, whose actions have significance only in terms of his own fantasy ideology. It means, in a strange sense, that while we are at war with them, they are not at war with us; indeed, our position would be enormously improved if they were. If they were at war with us, they would be compelled to start thinking realistically, in terms of objective factors such as their overall strategy as well as their war aims. They would have to make a realistic and not a fantasy-induced assessment of the relative strength of us versus them. But because they are operating in terms of their fantasy ideology, such a realistic assessment is impossible for them. It matters not how much stronger or more powerful we are than they; what matters is that God will bring them victory.

This point must be emphasized, for if the fantasy ideology of Italian fascism was a form of political make-believe, that of radical Islam goes one step further: it is, in a sense, more akin to a form of magical thinking. While the Sorelian myth does aim, finally, at transforming the real world, in the fantasy ideology of radical Islam it is almost as if the "real" world no longer matters. Our "real" world, after all, is utterly secular, a concatenation of an endless series of cause and effect in which all events occur on a single ontological plane. The "real" world of radical Islam is different. Islam itself has traditionally tended to postulate a universe which, to use philosophical language, is thoroughly *occasionalist*. That is to say, event A does not happen because it is caused by a previous event B, with both events occurring on the same ontological plane. Instead, event B is simply the occasion for God to cause event A, so that the genuine cause of all events occurring on our ontological plane of existence is God— God and nothing else. If this is so, then the "real" world that we take for granted simply vanishes, and all becomes determined by the will of God. Thus the line between realist and magical thinking dissolves.

HOW DO WE FIGHT AN IDEOLOGICAL EPIDEMIC?

The fantasy ideologies of the twentieth century spread like a virus in susceptible populations. Their propagation was not that suggested by J. S. Mill's marketplace of ideas; fantasy ideologies were not debated and examined, weighed, and measured. The people who accepted them did not accept them as tentative or provisional. They were unalterable and absolute. They drove out all other competing ideas and ideologies. They literally turned their host organism into an instrument of their own poisonous and deadly will.

The same thing is happening today. The poison of the radical Islamic fantasy ideology is being spread through the Muslim world, through schools and through the media, through mosques and through the demagoguery of the Arab street. Does this mean that history is repeating itself? Are we again facing challenges like those we faced in our confrontations with Fascist Italy, Nazi Germany, and Soviet Russia?

The answer is an emphatic no. For while fantasy ideologies may have inspired Mussolini and Hitler, the threats that they posed could always be clearly apprehended in Clausewitzian terms. The threats we faced during World War II were precisely the kind of threat that one classical nation state poses to another, so confrontations between us and them could be expected to follow a certain set of rules. Diplomacy came first, even in Mussolini's attack on Ethiopia, and war followed after an elaborate procedural prelude, in which a medley of various feints and bluffs and threats were employed prior to the formal and official declaration of war. No possible doubt remained about who was fighting whom. Each position became transparent.

Such is no longer the case, as was made clear by 9/11. Against whom do we retaliate for such an act? Do we simply begin to bomb Arab countries at random, taking up the challenge as if it were a blood feud, thereby embracing the struggle in the same apocalyptic terms so beloved of radical Islam? Or do we treat the perpetrators as ordinary criminals, to be hauled before either the criminal courts of the United States or perhaps the World Court at The Hague? In which case, what do we do when the perpetrators are already dead, when indeed they have taken a martyr's delight in death?

How, in short, do we deter those who, driven by a fantasy ideology, are prepared to pointlessly sacrifice themselves to murder us?

This in turn raises the most important question: How do we defeat such ruthlessness? And can we defeat it without becoming ruthless ourselves?

These are the questions that we must keep in mind if we are to comprehend the nature of the world-historical gamble that the United States has embarked on, first with the invasion of Afghanistan, and then with that of Iraq—a gamble that will be world-historical, no matter what the outcome may be.

2

OUR WORLD-HISTORICAL GAMBLE

T HE TERM *world-historical gamble* takes its inspiration from the *Lectures on the Philosophy of History* by German philosopher Georg Wilhelm Friedrich Hegel.

World-historical gambles arise from—and offer the only possible response to—situations of historical impasse or deadlock for the human race. They emerge in situations where mankind cannot simply stay put, where the counsels of caution and conservatism are no longer of any value, and where to do nothing at all is to take an even greater risk than that contemplated by the world-historical gamble. Examples include the end of the Roman Republic, when Caesar literally crossed the Rubicon, violating the code of honor that had kept generals from bringing an army into a city for the purpose of intimidation; Martin Luther nailing his theses to the door of his local cathedral and thus launching the Protestant Reformation; the signing of the Declaration of Independence in Philadelphia by the members of the American Continental Congress, thereby precipitating the American Revolution.

In all of these cases, there was a conflict between two different systems of value: one old and one new. In all of these cases, both of the conflicting systems were backed by men who were willing to risk everything, including their own lives, in defense of what they felt to be the absolute claim of their own point of view. In all of these cases, once the new system had emerged into being, it was committed to a life-and-death struggle against the system that it was determined to replace. In all of these cases, the outcomes of these struggles were inherently unpredictable—each was, quite literally, a gamble. In all of these cases, an old world was swept away, and a new one emerged—and yet, in none of these cases was this new world quite what anyone had expected, including those who worked the most zealously toward its birth.

This is how Hegel expresses the nature of a world-historical crisis: "It is precisely at this point that we encounter those great collisions between established and acknowledged duties, laws, and right, on the one hand, and new possibilities which conflict with the existing system and violate it or even destroy its very foundations and continued existence, on the other." This fact explains why the old concepts and categories are of so little use in guiding us to an understanding of such transformative events: the essence of the world-historical moment is the disclosure of new and hitherto unsuspected historical possibilities. It is their absolute novelty, their quality as epiphanies, that accounts for their inevitable collision with, and transcendence of, the old categories of understanding.

Today we are in the midst of this collision. It is the central fact of our historical epoch; it is this we must grasp. Unless we are prepared to look seriously at the true stakes involved in America's world-historical gamble, we will grossly distort the significance of what is occurring by trying to make it fit into our own prefabricated—and grotesquely obsolete—set of concepts. We will be like children trying to understand the world of adults with our own childish ideas, and we will miss the point of everything we see. This means that we must take a hard look at even our most basic vocabulary—and think twice before we rush to apply words like "empire" or "national self-interest" or "multilateralism" or "sovereignty" to a world in which they are no longer relevant. The only rule of thumb that can be unfailingly applied to world-historical transformations is this: None of our currently existing ideas and principles, concepts and categories will fit the new historical state of affairs that will emerge out of the crisis. We can only be certain of our uncertainty.

THE DISSOLUTION OF THE LIBERAL WORLD ORDER

Since the events of 9/11, the policy debate in the United States has been primarily focused on a set of problems—radical Islam and the war on terrorism, the conflict between Israel and the Palestinians, and weapons of mass destruction in the hands of Saddam Hussein in Iraq. We feel that these are related problems, but we are not quite sure how. Superficially, of course, they are connected by Islam, and yet we are troubled to think that this could be the ultimate source of the problems.

What unites all these issues, from our point of view, is that we do not seem able to get a handle on them. They elude us. Did the war on Iraq promote our goals in the war on terror? And what about the Palestinians? If they are given a state of their own, will there be peace in the Middle East? Will the second Iraq war increase incidents of terror by Islamic radicals? How does it all connect?

The debate has taken many different forms and has been approached from a variety of perspectives. With few exceptions, each side in this debate is working with a set of ethical and political categories that have been derived from an earlier historical era. For example, those who opposed war with Iraq often justified their position by an appeal to the Iraqi people's right to self-determination. On the other hand, those who argued that America should try to contain Iraq or to deter it by sanctions, and even many of those who argued for a limited military intervention, justified their position on the principles of classical realpolitik. And there is a similar problem with the various recommendations about what should be done with the new Iraq. Do the neoconservatives who advocate democracy in the Middle East grasp the true nature of the fantasy ideology that is spreading through that region; and if they do, how can they possibly think that formal democracy would not be swept away before it?

All of these positions are fatally undercut by the fact that they appeal to the outmoded conceptual categories of an earlier epoch—an epoch in which all the relevant actors in an international conflict were playing by the same basic rules. They were all nation states, each deploying a foreign policy—in both war and peace—that was designed to advance their own interests, interests which could be realistically predicted by the other actors in the conflict. An illuminating metaphor here is a game of chess between two equally skilled players: no matter how bitter the conflict between them, each can understand the rationale and motivation behind the other player's moves. In fact, if the other player appears to make an irrational move, his opponent will be hesitant to conclude that the move was a mere mistake and will be far more likely to suspect that it is a trap and act accordingly.

But what happens when you play chess with someone who refuses to accept the rules of the game? How do you respond if your opponent begins to jump his knight in all sorts of bizarre zigzag patterns, so that you cannot predict where he will land or what piece he will seize? In a game of chess the answer is obvious: you stop playing with the madman and go your separate way. Unfortunately, withdrawal is not an option in dealing with genuine conflicts arising in the real world. That is why the supposed realism expressed by the concept of realpolitik can only be of value in a world made up exclusively of rational actors.

This incongruity is what gives so much of the American public discussion of the present crisis an almost surreal air. If we in fact lived in a world where concepts like self-determination and realpolitik could be applied, there would be no crisis, since there would have been no Saddam Hussein in Iraq, no terrorist organizations like Al-Qaeda, no conflicts like the Israeli-Palestinian conflicts. In such a world the players would all be limited to making rational calculations and pursuing predictable policies: their undesirable actions could be deterred through the traditional methods, and there would be no fear that a player might suddenly undertake risks that any realist would know to avoid. Everyone could be counted on to consult his self-interest in a way that was generally recognized, even by his most bitter opponents, as realistic. For a sense of the realistic, unlike one's taste in music or physical beauty, is not a culturally specific construct but transcends all such bounds. It embodies, so to speak, the fundamental rules of play between different cultures, even those cultures that, on other counts, may be bitterly opposed in any number of other ways.

That precisely is the nature of the crisis we are facing. The liberal world system has collapsed internally: there is no longer a set of rules that governs all the players. Here I do not mean ethical rules, for that cannot be expected, but what Kant called *maxims of prudence,* those regulatory principles that enforce a realistic code of conduct on all the participants in a well-ordered system, a code which allows us to know for a near certainty what the other players will not even conceive of doing. Such rules, once again, are transcultural, and must be transcultural if they are to permit all the players to participate in them. They constitute the precondition of any politically stable system, for without them there is the danger of *cognitive anarchy*—a situation in which no one can any longer predict with confidence what the others will do. Cognitive anarchy is the gateway to disaster, for when you do not know what to expect, it becomes prudent to expect the worst, but when all expect the worst, the worst is bound to happen.

This collapse of the well-ordered liberal system has come about exclusively from the side of the Islamic world. No other party has contributed to it. The cause of this disruption is the lack of a sense of the realistic on the part of certain elements in the Islamic world. This is not a cultural judgment, but a fact—at least as much a fact as any such judgment can ever be. This lack is the common thread that unites Iraq, Al-Qaeda, and Palestinian terrorism.

Yet it would be too facile to reduce this lack of a sense of the realistic to some inherent flaw in Islam, either as a culture or a religion, or in Arabs as a race or as an ethnos. It arises from an altogether different source, and in order to understand the source of the problem, we need to go back to the writings of Karl Marx.

THE LESSONS OF MARX

All previous threats in the history of mankind have had one element in common. They were posed by historical groups that had created by their own activity and with their own hands the weapons—both physical and cultural—that they used to threaten their enemies. In each case, the power that the historical group had at its disposal had been "earned" by them the hard way: they had invented and forged their instruments; they had disciplined and trained their own armies; they had created the social and economic structures that allowed the amassing of their armies and navies; they had paid their own way.

In each of these cases, to use Marx's language, the societies in question had achieved through their own labor and sacrifice the *objective* conditions of their military power. Their power to threaten others derived entirely from their own skill and genius. This, of course, is not to deny some amount of borrowing from earlier cultures, but in each case this borrowing was only the foundation upon which the affiliated culture proceeded to build its own unique structure, as evidenced, for example, by Japan's stunningly successful response to the Western challenge at the end of the nineteenth century—a vivid example of how a sense of the realistic can transcend cultural boundaries.

The threat that currently faces us is radically different. It comes from

groups who have utterly failed to create the material and objective conditions within their own societies sufficient to permit them to construct,
out of their own resources, the kind of military organization and
weaponry that has constituted every previous kind of threat. In the case of
Al-Qaeda, this failure is clearly evident, as V. S. Naipaul has observed: the
only technical mastery displayed by the terrorists of 9/11 was the ability
to hijack and to fly jumbo airliners into extremely large buildings, neither
of which they were capable of constructing themselves. The same is true
in the case of Saddam Hussein's Iraq: the money that funded both the creation of his conventional forces and his forays into devising weapons of
mass destruction came not from the efforts of the Iraqi people, but from
money paid by the West for the purchase of petroleum—a natural re-
source that Iraq had done absolutely nothing to create or even to produce
for sale.

Why does this matter? The answer, provided by Hegel, was subsequently taken up as a fundamental theme of Marx's own thinking.
When people are forced to create their own material world through
their own labor, they are certainly not setting out to achieve a greater
insight into the nature of reality; they are merely trying to feed themselves and to provide their children with clothing and a roof over their
heads. And yet, whether they will or not, they are also, at every step of
the way, acquiring a keener grasp of the objective nature of world. A
man who wishes to build his own home with his own hands must come
to grips with the recalcitrant properties of wood and gravity: he must
learn to discipline his own activities so that he is in fact able to achieve
his end. He will come to see that certain things work and that others
don't. He will realize that in order to have A, you must first make sure
of B. He will be forced to develop *a sense of the realistic,* and this, once
again, is a cultural constant, measured entirely by the ability of each
particular culture to cope successfully with the specific challenge posed
by the world it inhabits.

All of this grappling with reality is lost on the man who simply pays
another man to build his home for him. He is free to imagine his dream
house and to indulge in every kind of fantasy. The proper nature of the
material need not concern him; gravity doesn't interest him. He makes the
plans out of his head and expects them to be fulfilled at his whim.

If we look at the source of Arab wealth, we find nothing that the Arabs
created for themselves. Wealth has come to them by magic, much as in a

story from *The Arabian Nights,* and it allows them to live in a feudal fantasyland. What the Saudis and Saddam Hussein have in common is that they became rich because the West paid them for natural resources that the West could simply have taken from them at will and without so much as a thank-you, if the West had been inclined to do so. They were, by one of the bitter paradoxes of history, the preeminent beneficiaries of the Western liberalism that they despise and reject. Their power derives entirely from the fact that the West had committed itself, in the aftermath of World War II, to a policy of not robbing other societies of their natural resources simply because it possessed the military might to do so. Nor does it matter whether the West followed this policy out of charitable instinct, or out of prudence, or out of a cynical awareness that it was more cost-effective to do so. All that really matters is the quite unintended consequence of the West's conduct: the prodigious funding of fantasists who are thereby enabled to pursue their demented agendas unencumbered by any realistic calculation of the risks or costs of their actions.

Here we have one of the deepest contradictions of the liberal system of national self-determination. A world has been virtually achieved where each nation-state is an inviolable entity, its borders protected by an international consensus, and the benefits of such a system are so obvious that there is no need to enumerate them. And yet it is precisely here that the problem arises, through what Hegel called a *dialectical reversal.*

If the existence of a nation-state is guaranteed by some external authority—whether by the United Nations or the United States—then one of its chief incentives to a realistic policy, both domestic and foreign, has been removed from play. To see this problem, think back to the old chaotic world in which the rules of realpolitik operated: there, if a state pursued a domestic or a foreign policy that was too grossly unrealistic, it would inevitably pay the price for doing so. It would be invaded, or annexed, or partitioned, as the example of eighteenth-century Poland made clear. The price of any nation-state's survival was the cultivation of a heightened sense of realism.

This is no longer the case. Indeed, the current international arrangement might be compared to an economic system in which each business enterprise has been assured of not going broke by a guarantee of a government subsidy in the face of financial insolvency. Would such a system be inclined to produce hard-nosed realism among the operators of these business enterprises, or would it rather induce them to pay less attention to the complaints of their customers or to the innovations of their competitors?

The principle of self-determination in a world of perpetual peace may not in fact be the panacea for mankind's ills but rather a means for prolonging these ills unnecessarily, by sanctioning a status quo of despotism and tyranny, by virtually underwriting the brutal caprice of petty dictators, and by furthering the fantasies of ruthless fanatics. Self-determination at the level of the nation-state may entail complete loss of freedom and dignity at the level of the individual—and all in the name of liberalism.

Nor can this issue be addressed by any kind of multilateral organization such as the United Nations, for it is unlikely that a league of small nation-states will act in concert to liquidate a system of which they are the chief beneficiaries. It would be easier to imagine businessmen in our imaginary economic system voting to strip themselves of their subsidies. It will not happen, and it is utopian to think that it will.

Yet blind trust in the sacred principle of national self-determination seemingly cannot be shaken in certain quarters. In September 2002, Richard Butler, the chief arms inspector of the United Nations, berated the United States for its "double standard" in opposing the proliferation of nuclear weapons to any nation-state that wanted them. What blessing does he believe that the United States is trying to deny to smaller nations? Is he thinking about the citizens of those nations who will have to foot the bill for such fantasy projects? Or those who will likely die if the United States decides to abandon its "double standard"? Or the state of the world that would result from such an abandonment?

Can anything make clearer the fact that intelligent men of our time are stuck with grotesquely outmoded concepts and categories?

THE END OF CLASSICAL SOVEREIGNTY

We must first begin by realizing that both the "liberal" concept of national self-determination and the "conservative" one of realpolitik are no longer adequate to the historical actuality that is unfolding before our eyes. They are obsolete for the same reason: the epoch of history governed by the principle of classical sovereignty is in the process of dissolution.

Classical sovereignty is the basis of the classical nation-state. Its defining characteristic is the de facto achievement of a monopoly of physical force under the control of a single central authority. It is not enough merely to have a monopoly of legitimate force, for if there is enough outstanding illegitimate force, then the state dissolves back into the anarchic condition symbolized by the rule of warlords, in which case the so-called legitimate state is merely one of several contenders for the prize of genuine authority. It is not enough to declare your internal enemies illegal; you must in fact be able to vanquish and crush them. You must be able, in short, to rule alone, in fact as well as in theory.

With the achievement of the classical nation-state, one historical threat was put to rest and another emerged, for the classical nation-state was itself an instrument of enormous power—just how enormous would require centuries to discern. The classical nation-state brought with it an abrupt change in the rules of the game: if a society wished to compete against an efficiently centralized state, it too would have to become efficiently centralized. This was the lesson the Kingdom of Poland learned the hard way at the end of the eighteenth century. Unable to relinquish the near anarchy that constituted Poland's "golden freedom," the Polish parliament could not resist the pressure of the highly centralized autocratic states that surrounded it and was helpless to prevent the series of partitions that ended Poland's existence as an independent and sovereign state.

With the advent of the nation-state the rules governing conflict between societies took on the characteristic form of Clausewitzian war. Such war is carried out as the policy of a central organized command; it is rational in its design and instrumental in its purpose, this purpose being to change the behavior of other classical nation states in a desired direction. The basic terms of Clausewitzian warfare, in other words, are simply a logical consequence of the principle of classical sovereignty, for only a unified entity such as the classical state can be said to have a policy in the first place, since a policy is a conscious articulation of a coherent set of aims—something quite beyond the reach of a barbarian horde or a mere aggregate of contentious warlords.

During the last half of the twentieth century, however, the concept of the classical nation-state has been replaced, without anyone's seeming to notice the fact, by a radically different concept, though one that shares the same term: it is what might best be called the *honorific* concept of the state.

How has this change come about? Through the very success of the

liberal world order in the later part of the twentieth century. It is precisely through the triumph of the Pax Americana that the substantive
content of the term *state* has been imperceptibly subverted and transformed out of all recognition. The state, as this term is now used, is no
longer restricted to a political entity that can in fact defend itself against
all comers and that exists as a viable unit in defiance of those who would
absorb or annex it; the state is no longer locked in a continual struggle
for its independent survival in a world full of hostile forces, where a failure to face up to the imperatives of reality spells social death, as in the
case of the Kingdom of Poland or the American Confederacy. It is now,
instead, something very different: an entity called into being by the formal recognition of the international community. This purely honorific
sense of the term *state* is reflected in the assertion, for example, that the
Palestinian people "deserve" their own state. Such language makes completely clear that we are no longer even talking about the same thing.
Gladstone, for example, in his famous blunder during the Civil War
when he came close to formally recognizing the Confederacy as an independent nation, did not think that he was conferring an honorary status
on it but thought that he was simply acknowledging a brute and exis-
tential fact—that the Confederacy by its own struggle and sacrifice had
de facto become a genuine state.

There is, of course, nothing to keep one from applying the purely honorific title of "state" to the Palestinians, for example, just as the English are
perfectly entitled to dub a pop singer a knight, though it would be dangerous to rely on him to defend the realm. But merely to call the Palestinian
community a "state" does not and cannot transform it into a viable subsis-
tent entity if those who govern and decide its course are utterly lacking in a
sense of what is realistically available to them. Nothing highlights this
point more than the official explanation, on the part of Palestinian spokes-
men, for those acts of terrorism committed by the suicide bombers, the assertion that these are acts of war. The bitter truth is that if the Palestinian
people were indeed a genuine state fighting a genuine war, they would have
long since been annihilated root and branch—or else forced to make a realistic accommodation with the state of Israel, based on a just assessment of
the latter's immense superiority of resources, both military and political.
The reason for this superiority, by a paradox typical of history, is not American aid or funding but the fact that the state of Israel has been forced to
struggle for every moment of its existence from the very day of its birth. It

is this struggle that has made Israel into what no assembly of nations can ever call into being—a viable state. Unless the Palestinians as a people can set aside their fantasies of pushing a vastly superior enemy into the sea instead of seeking a realistic modus vivendi with him, they may demand a state and even be "recognized" as a state, but that state will exist as a viable entity only by virtue of the liberal conscience—and seemingly inexhaustible forbearance—of the Israeli people.

The Palestinians are not alone in their fantasy. It is a common feature of much of the Arab world to entertain the illusion of viability. In a world that had abandoned the liberal system, they would have long been extirpated, or else—a far happier and more probable outcome—they would have rapidly shed their delusions for a more realistic manner of proceeding.

There is a sense of Greek tragedy, with its dialectic of hubris and nemesis, to what has been unfolding in the Islamic world. If Muslim extremists continue to use terror against the West, their very success will destroy them. If they succeed in terrorizing the West, they will discover that they have in fact only ended by brutalizing it. And if subjected to enough stress, the liberal system will be set aside and the Hobbesian world will return, and with its return, the Islamic world will be crushed. Whom the gods would destroy they first make mad. The only way to avoid this horrendous end is to bring the Islamic world back to sanity sooner rather than later.

THE THREAT OF A ROGUE NUCLEAR STRIKE

The greatest threat facing us—and one of the greatest ever to threaten mankind—is the collision of this collective fantasy world of Islam with the horrendous reality of weapons of mass destruction, for weapons of mass destruction are unlike any other previous kind of military threat.

The capacity of one nation-state to threaten another, prior to the advent of nuclear weaponry, depended on its mastery of an enormous number of diverse circumstances. It had to be internally united; it had to have economic strength; it had to possess an abundant, and not easily threatened, supply of necessary natural resources; it had to have a military tradition that instilled a fighting spirit into its troops; it had to have an efficient system of transportation; it needed a clear-cut and reliable chain of command; it needed to have a substantial base of technological expertise; it required a settled tradition of authoritative command. In other words, a society's capacity to threaten depended on its successful coping with its own internal and external challenges.

But a stockpile of nuclear weapons will remain a threat even when those who originally put them together have long vanished. The example of the former Soviet Union is a clear case. Here a social order, no more viable than the Kingdom of Poland, has perished, and yet its weapons of mass destruction still exist.

We now live in a world in which a state so marginal that it would be utterly incapable of mounting any kind of credible conventional threat to its neighbors or to anyone else, a state unable to field a single battalion or man a single warship, a state whose level of technological sophistication may be generally so low that it would be incapable of providing for itself even the most elementary staples of modernity—such a state could still make a devastating use of a nuclear weapon that literally *chanced* to come into its hands.

The procedure would be simplicity itself. Such a state figures out a covert method by which it detonates a nuclear device, then simply fails to claim the act as its policy. Why, after all, may not a state act covertly, without declaring an attack to be official policy? After all, isn't this act covered by the right to self-determination? Who are we to tell another country what kind of covert policy it may employ?

Before 9/11 the first question that an intelligent person would think upon hearing of such a scenario was, Why on earth anyone would want to do such a thing? That is no longer our first question. Our first question has become, Who will do it to us first?

Like 9/11, this kind of attack would have no Clausewitzian justification; indeed, from a realistic point of view it can serve no purpose. But what if those who chose to use nuclear devices were merely acting out of a fantasy ideology? In this case, the act of violence need possess only a magical or fantasy significance to the perpetrator in order to motivate him to perform it. It need not bring him any other goal than the sense of achievement in having brought it off.

Beyond this scenario there is even a danger that rogue states, unable to maintain their domestic viability, will degenerate into being merely front organizations for the social force of radical Islam, as occurred in Afghanistan under the Taliban. In such a scenario the forces of radical Islam—having become the true focus of loyalty—could play a kind of shell game with the West, making use of the state's convenient façade of legality for its own purposes. It would accept the rules of the international liberal system, represented, for example, by the UN, in order to destroy the viability of this system. It would be doing, in effect, precisely what the Nazi Party did with the Weimar parliamentary system: force it into a deadlock in order to destroy it.

This is one of the dangers inherent in a fantasy ideology: it forms the primary group identity of its adherents, cutting across and annihilating other group loyalties, so that one is a Nazi before being a German and a true believer in radical Islam before being a Pakistani or a Saudi or an Egyptian. The fantasy ideology is the underlying reality, of which this or that state regime becomes merely an epiphenomenon, a formal and legal cover to conceal the machinations of the party—in this case, the party of radical Islam.

The motivation of those who want to murder us is not complicated: to watch an American city go up in a fireball is its own reward. This is the lesson that 9/11 should teach us in dealing with the fantasists of the Islamic world. A fantasy does not need to make any sense; that is the whole point of having one.

SO WHAT ARE the chances of another 9/11 happening? The problem here is that the very non-Clausewitzian nature of the radical Islamic terror cult, combined with the possibility of the rogue nuclear strike, makes it impossible to calculate the risk.

In dealing with previous enemies, such as the Japanese or the Soviet Union, we were never forced to wonder whether they might delegate their actions to such utterly informal and irresponsible entities as Al-Qaeda. The threat they posed they posed in their own right, and hence they were accountable for their actions and knew that we would hold them accountable. This is no longer the case. For example, even today, there is still debate about the possible connection between Iraq and the events of 9/11, a debate that may well never be resolved. This means that if a nuclear device were to be detonated in downtown Chicago tomorrow, from an unknown source, could we really count on being able to find its "return address"? We know that the answer is no, and we know that "they" know this as well, and they know we know—which only begins to suggest the surrealism of the crisis with which we are faced. If our enemies chose to delegate such a horrendous act to an entity like Al-Qaeda, they would force us into an impossible choice: either we accept such an attack without retaliating, or else we are forced to lash out blindly—and in the same spirit of blood feud and vendetta with which the attack was made. Either choice transcends our present categories of comprehension.

The *first* rogue nuclear strike—a strike from an unknown and even unknowable source—is a genie that once out of the bottle can never be put back in. It would cause an overnight catastrophic transformation of the world. In many ways we must be grateful that Al-Qaeda's fingerprints were all over 9/11. For what if we had no clue—even today—who had perpetrated the attacks?

In sum, the modern liberal world system has permitted the growth of power in the hands of those who have not had to cope with reality in order to acquire this power. Power has simply been given to them, out of the sense of fair play prevalent among Western liberal societies. Iraq was paid for its oil, which in turn paid for its weapons, and both were produced by us, to be used against us. Tragically, this genesis has had the unintended consequence of diminishing the value of the sense of realism in the eyes of those who have thus acquired their power and wealth—a fact just as much in evidence in the behavior of Saudi Arabia as in that of Iraq. It is the reenactment, on a world-historical scale, of what has been done by many well-meaning Americans in the case of their own children: by giving them so much, we have robbed them of that indispensable sense of realism that can only be earned by head-on collisions with the immovable object called the real world. We have nourished their fantasies instead of forcing them to face the facts of life. And in doing so, we have done no one any service—least of all, the hapless multitude of impoverished human beings who have themselves derived no benefit whatsoever from the West's fair play, and whose children's lives will continue to be wasted in the counterproductive pursuit of their leaders' delusional dreams.

The greatest danger, however, arises from the coalescing of these delusional dreams into the fantasy ideology of radical Islam, the essence of which is that the West must be destroyed. What this fantasy ideology seeks to accomplish is the abrogation of liberal modernity and its greatest symbol, the United States of America. Therefore its "war aims" cannot be reduced to Clausewitzian terms: the fantasy ideology of radical Islam requires the West not to do its will but to cease to exist. *To achieve this end, any historical catastrophe will do.*

*   *   *

THIS IS THE brave new world we are destined to live in for the foreseeable future. It is a world where bit players may well be in a position to bring down the house—literally.

Yet how we decide to live in this world, and what actions we need to take in order to survive in it, and to survive with our liberal civilization intact, are not predestined; they remain up to us. That is why it is so critical that our decisions be ones that are guided by the tenets of political realism—the insistence on seeing things precisely as they are and refusing to be misled by wishful thinking and utopian illusions. Nowhere is this more important than in how we conceive and define the category of the enemy. Not this or that particular enemy, but the enemy in general. To put it another away, we must learn what motivates men to be willing to kill each other, and to be willing to die in the process. What is it that drives men to fight to the death? Only after we have discovered what causes men to act this way can we even begin to see the answer to the question, Must there *always* be an enemy?

3

DEFINING THE ENEMY

P RIOR TO 9/11, all the experts and all their paradigms had assured us that the enemy had been defeated. All the bad ideologies of the twentieth century had been discredited; therefore, it was impossible for people to commit themselves to any more such nonsense. Capitalism or liberal democracy or both would make sure that the world would never need to resort to life-and-death struggles over anything of importance, since everything of importance would be forthcoming from the automatic expansion of Western values through the process of globalization.

True, there had been dissenting voices that warned of a clash of civilizations, but even these voices argued that the main concern was our own insistence on imposing our values on others.

The enemy was not supposed to exist according to any of the major geopolitical paradigms that were current prior to 9/11. The one point on which all of these paradigms agreed was this: there was no longer any underlying *necessity* for two different groups of humanity to be enemies to each other, since it was now possible, at least in principle, for men to work out their differences. In its own way, each of these paradigms offers an optimist view of mankind's future development, based on a theory of the enemy that glossed over what is most essential to his nature.

Remarkably enough, these theories of the enemy are still with us post

9/11, and they continue to influence our understanding of the present crisis. None of them is dead wrong; yet all of them are only half-truths, which is precisely why they are so dangerous.

THREE THEORIES OF THE ENEMY

We will begin with "the end of history" paradigm or, more precisely, with the *first* end of history paradigm, for as it turns out, there have been three quite distinct formulations of the end of history thesis, each of which is dependent on one of three distinct theories of the enemy.

In the first theory, the enemy is a rational actor seeking his economic advantage and prepared to use force to obtain certain economic goods. We will call this enemy the Greedy.

In the second theory, the enemy is someone struggling for the recognition of his equal state by those who refuse to grant this to him. We will call this enemy the Oppressed.

In the third theory, the enemy is someone who seeks to force us to recognize his superior status. We will call this enemy the Overbearing.

THE FIRST THEORY of the enemy was presented in a version of the end of history thesis that predated Francis Fukuyama's by nearly two centuries, appearing in this passage from *The Spirit of Conquest and Usurpation and Their Relation to European Civilization*, written by the French novelist and political thinker Benjamin Constant and published in 1814.

> We have finally reached the age of commerce, an age which must necessarily replace that of war, as the age of war was bound to precede it. War and commerce are only two different means to achieve the same end, that of possessing what is desired. Commerce is simply a tribute paid to the strength of the possessor by the aspirant to possession. It is an attempt to obtain by mutual agreement what one can no longer hope to obtain through violence. A man who was always the stronger would never conceive the idea of commerce. It is experience, by proving to him that war, that is, the use of his strength against the strength of others, is open to a variety of obstacles and defeats, that leads him to resort to commerce, that is, to milder and surer means of getting the in-

terests of others to agree with his own. (*The Spirit of Conquest,* in *Political Writings* [New York: Cambridge University Press, 1988])

This nineteenth-century end of history thesis was widely shared by those liberal proponents of capitalism and free trade, such as John Bright and Richard Cobden, who believed that war could and would be replaced by international arbitration. In this view, the enemy was simply the commercial rival; hence all that was necessary to deal with him was to make commerce and arbitration a more attractive proposition than war. The enemy, in short, was a rational player who could be counted upon to make rational choices; it was this fact that permitted a vision of a future world order in which those nations that were dedicated to commerce—the capitalist nations—could induce those nations still given over to the spirit of conquest to abandon that method of obtaining their objectives by making war a less attractive instrument of policy than commerce.

This theory of the enemy was, in fact, one side of the Clausewitzian legacy—its optimist side. If war is politics by other means, then by making these other means less appealing, people could envision a world in which war could be eliminated simply because there were better ways of getting what you wanted—namely, commerce. Capitalism, then, was the path to the realization of Kant's dream of perpetual peace. It would succeed because it would eventually educate all men into being rational calculators of their self-interest, in which case all would finally come to the conclusion that peace was a better way of getting what they wanted than war. From that point there emerged a clear-cut pattern of what the international order should be like. It should be a consortium of commercial nations that would cooperate for the purpose of preventing the spirit of conquest from paying off for any nation who resorted to it. The consortium would have a wide range of deterrence options, from economic sanctions to military intervention.

In this view, it is capitalism, and capitalism alone, that will usher in the end of history. And since capitalism can provide all the things that men want more efficiently and far more predictably than war, then war would soon be seen by all parties to be pointless.

This theory of the enemy can be called the rational actor theory: it assumes that the decision to be someone's enemy is a purely rational economic choice, much like any other economic decision. If I can get what

I want from you by commerce cheaper and more efficiently than by brute force, then I will chose commerce. If not, then force will do quite nicely.

Francis Fukuyama's end of history thesis, from an article that appeared in 1989, was slightly different from Constant's. Fukuyama's thesis was derived from a difficult philosophical text called *Introduction to the Reading of Hegel* by the Russian émigré Alexandre Kojève—a Marxist and an admirer of Stalin—written about an even more difficult philosophical text: Hegel's first great philosophical work, *The Phenomenology of Mind*. At the center of Kojève's text was his interpretation of Hegel's famous master/slave dialectic, and at the center of his interpretation was a new theory of the enemy.

According to the rational actor theory model just examined, if you have nothing that I could possibly want, in the way of material or commercial goods, then there could be no possible reason why I would choose to use violence against you. If you have nothing that I might be tempted to buy, you will also have nothing that I will be tempted to take by force. But the Kojèvean model asserts that the desire for pure prestige may still make me want to use force against you, even if you lack any material object that I could possibly desire, because what I desire from you is your recognition of me.

When I ask for your recognition of me, I am not asking for some economic good that you have; rather I am asking you to act and to conduct yourself in a certain way—a way that embodies your acknowledgment of the superiority that I am claiming, so that when I look at your behavior, I will see evidence to support my claim and nothing to refute it. For example, if I wish to claim the status of your superior, then whenever you are around me, you must treat me with the deference due a superior, and if you should fail to do so, I will use violence against you until your behavior is modified to conform to my desires. On the other hand, if I wish to claim the status of your equal, then you must put away any offensively superior airs, or I will compel you to put them away.

As a psychological insight, the Kojèvean model has its advantages, for clearly much human conflict arises precisely from the quest for pure prestige. In Castiglione's Renaissance classic *The Book of the Courtier*, for example, it is taken for granted that the reason a soldier fights is for the sheer glory he expects to gain from it and not for any vulgar economic motive. Much of the impetus for European imperialism at the end of the nineteenth century is best understood historically as an expression of the desire for pure prestige, to which the hypothetical prospect of economic or commercial gain was added as if a rationalizing afterthought. Men wanted an empire for the pure prestige of it but felt constrained to explain their motives in rational economic terms. Furthermore, the same principle can be seen at work when groups that have been marginalized or treated as inferior because of race or ethnic status or gender or sexual preference demand to be recognized simply as the equal of other human beings.

But there is an ambiguity here. For to say that the desire for recognition is the desire to have one's status acknowledged leaves open the critical question, Exactly what status is it that you wish to have recognized by others—your superiority to them and their inferiority to you, or your equality with them and their equality with you? Clearly these two quests are profoundly different. If our opponent simply wants us to treat him like an equal, then all we must do is to renounce our own claims to superiority. But if our opponent wants us to treat him like a superior, then we may have to renounce a great deal more.

This difference gives us two distinct conceptions of the enemy, beyond that offered by the rational actor theory: First, the enemy is someone whom we have mistreated and oppressed. Second, the enemy is someone who demands to be recognized for his superiority. These are two entirely different kinds of enemy, and the methods for handling one should not be expected to work on the other.

If the enemy is an oppressed group fighting to have equal recognition of its status vis-à-vis the other groups in the community, then the enemy may be eliminated by granting him the status he is seeking. By being treated as an equal, as a full-fledged citizen, his enmity will cease or at least abate over time. In Fukuyama's presentation of his end of history thesis, this equality seeker would appear to be the only enemy that mankind could have in the future. In that case the envisioned triumph of liberal democracy might be expected to gradually but eventually eradicate all such illiberal differences in status, thereby allowing the enemyless future required by the end of history thesis.

"Liberal democracy," Fukuyama writes, "replaces the irrational desire to be recognized as greater than others with a rational desire to be recognized as equal. A world made up of liberal democracies, then, should have much less incentive for war, since all nations would reciprocally recognize one another's legitimacy."

But this is puzzling, for Kojève's very interpretation of the struggle for recognition as it occurs in Hegel's master/slave dialectic makes it clear that, at least in its initial stage, the struggle for recognition was simply a struggle for pure prestige—for superiority, in other words, and not mere equality. So how is it possible that the mere introduction of liberal democracy could make people bent on having their superiority recognized decide not to insist on it? After all, the whole point of desiring the recognition of your superiority is that recognition of your mere equality is not enough.

Indeed it was precisely this thirst for superiority that made Kojève's original theory intuitively appealing. It permits us to grasp the narcissistic ego drive behind those world-historical figures such as Caesar, Napoleon, Hitler, and Stalin. Indeed, such figures are the reason why Kojève devised his theory in the first place: to try to find an answer to the embarrassing questions that the history of the twentieth century posed to Marx's theory.

MARX'S THEORY OF THE ENEMY

The truth is that Marx totally accepted the Benjamin Constant version of the end of history. He too believed that the Age of Commerce would replace the Age of War. Only in his version, there would be a third stage in which commerce would take place no longer on the capitalist basis of economic organization but on one that was entirely socialistic. The transition to socialism would in fact end the only remaining possible reason for the existence of the enemy—namely, the struggle between the capitalists and the proletariat. At this point the epoch of perpetual peace, prepared by commerce, would finally be achieved by socialism.

It was prepared by commerce because, according to Marx, capitalism had shown men how to eliminate scarcity as a source of conflict. More precisely, the technology that capitalism had introduced had so multiplied mankind's productive capacity that there would no longer be any economic motive for men to wish to seize the property of others; there would be enough to go around.

That, after all, was the whole point of Marx's economic determinism. Wars were always fought for material and monetary gain; therefore the enemy was just someone who had something you wanted. Fights for pure prestige were between persons and were no more significant than a common duel. Thus for Marx there were two kinds of war that could have genuine historical significance: war between economic rivals and class war, both of which could be entirely explained by rational choice theory.

If there was to be war in the twentieth century, it would have to be what the "Internationale" called the "final conflict"—the war between the capitalist and the laboring classes. Yet this is not at all what happened. Mussolini did not fit into this picture, nor did Hitler. How did Marxist theory explain them?

To answer this question, Kojève returned to what he regarded as the original source of Marx's theory, the philosophy of Hegel, and thought he discovered the answer in the master/slave dialectic: the fight for pure prestige. Men like Mussolini and Hitler were narcissists driven to assert their superiority over other men, and they were able to enlist support by appealing to their followers' own narcissistic promptings.

But there was a problem here. While the desire for pure prestige can explain a Hitler and a Mussolini, it poses an enormous difficulty for Marxism. For if the desire for pure prestige is in fact part of human nature, then how can we ever expect to escape its baleful influence on historical events—an influence epitomized by the cost of Hitler? If Hitlers could crop up at any moment, how could there ever be an end of history? If the desire for pure prestige was an inescapable part of the human condition, then man seemed doomed to face future ravaged centuries like the one just endured.

Was doom in fact inescapable? No, because by classifying narcissistic desire as a psychological pathology, Kojève could envision a future stage of history in which such character disorders could be therapeutically eliminated from the human race. Men, in short, could be cured of their unhealthy and purely narcissistic desires, and the realm of perpetual peace would be close at hand. This reading assumes, as Fukuyama puts it, that "the . . . desire to be recognized as greater than others" is irrational in and of itself; hence it is a legitimate target of anyone who wishes to make the world a more rational place, which in practice leads to a two-step solution.

First, you create societies that are liberal enough that all human beings will find all their needs satisfied, so that they will not be driven to seek compensatory fulfillment through the pursuit of a superior status. The assumption, simplified immensely, is that only those with inferiority complexes need to make others feel inferior. Hence, rid the world of reasons to feel inferior, and you rid the world of the Hitlers and Mussolinis.

Second, you stamp out all claims to superiority wherever they manifest themselves. You systematically rob everyone of any possible reason to claim superiority—based on their religion, or their class status, or their ethnic history, or their religious affiliation. No one is special, and you are condemned for thinking that you are.

At the end of these two steps you have arrived at Kojève's celebrated "homogenous and universal state" that will usher in the end of history. The world will thus be safe from the emergence of new Hitlers and Mussolinis because everyone will have been so thoroughly homogenized and universalized that they will not even be able to entertain the fantasy of superiority.

The homogenous and universal state is a world in which everyone has become a *rational cosmopolitan*—the German philosopher Immanuel Kant's term for that human being who lives and breathes pure reason and who no longer thinks of himself as belonging to any tribe or group or religion or class. Everyone is fungible with everyone else. It is therefore inconceivable that any one group of men might entertain the thought of advancing their own particular group interests, for there will be no groups.

Indeed, there will be no primordial loyalty to any body of men or ideas or customs or traditions; all will have been eradicated except the allegiance to the homogenous and universal state, that community of all the men and women on the planet that has been rendered entirely indifferent to any accident of birth that might distinguish them from each other. There will be no one group of people that you will trust more than others and none you will trust less.

The question is, Will you trust any at all?

THE CLASH OF CIVILIZATIONS?

The end of history paradigm is normally contrasted with the clash of civilizations thesis of Samuel Huntington, but, as it turns out, Huntington's paradigm offers nothing new; and in fact, when probed, it reveals itself to rest primarily on the third and last theory of the enemy—the enemy as the overbearing and irrational person who insists on having his superior status recognized by others. Only, according to Huntington, this enemy does not take the form of a person or even a society but of a whole civilization. Ours.

Before proceeding, let us first notice what Huntington is *not* saying. Nowhere does Huntington argue that civilizations are somehow doomed to clash; he is perfectly aware that different cultures can get along, as in fact they have done for millennia. Nor is he unaware that some of the bloodiest conflicts in history have been waged between members of the same culture. Thus, he is not proposing to identify the enemy as someone who simply belongs to a different culture or who possesses different cultural values.

Nor is he denying that war and conflict may in the future be brought about for reasons having nothing to do with culture. The invasion of Kuwait by Iraq in 1991, for example, was occasioned not by a clash of civilizations but by what looked suspiciously like old-fashioned greed. Constant's Spirit of Conquest carried out the invasion for a purely economic purpose, namely, to gain the extra revenue of the Kuwaiti oil fields. Certainly it is also easy to envision future struggles in which an oppressed minority fights to achieve recognition of its equal status.

But such actual and potential conflicts are not what concerns Huntington when he thinks about the future of our world. His anxiety arises from what he perceives as the West's insistence on its universal mission.

> Cultural and civilizational diversity challenges the Western and particularly American belief in the universal relevance of Western culture. This belief is expressed both descriptively and normatively. Descriptively it holds that peoples in all societies want to adopt Western values, institutions, and practices. If they seem not to have that desire and to be committed to their own traditional cultures, they are victims of a "false consciousness" comparable to that which Marxists found among proletarians who supported capitalism. Normatively, the Western universalist belief posits that people throughout the world should embrace Western values, institutions, and culture because they embody the highest, most enlightened, most liberal, most rational, most modest, and most civilized thinking of mankind.
>
> In the emerging world of ethnic conflict and civilizational clash, Western belief in the universality of Western culture suffers three problems: it is false; it is immoral; and it is dangerous. . . . Imperialism is the necessary logical consequence of universalism. (*The Clash of Civilizations and the Remaking of the World Order* [New York: Simon & Schuster, 1996], p. 310)

From this argument Huntington draws the unsurprising conclusion that "Western universalism is dangerous to the world because it could lead to a major intercivilizational war between core states and it is dangerous to the West because it could lead to a defeat of the West." (p. 311) This conclusion in turn leads to the stark maxim that "Western intervention in the affairs of other civilizations is probably the single most disastrous source of instability and potential global conflict in a multicivilizational world." (p. 312)

In short, the biggest problem facing the world today stems from the West's determination to have its own standards of civilization recognized as universally valid by the rest of the world; in which case, it is the West that presently looms as the Kojèvean enemy seeking to force others to acknowledge his superior status.

Yet at the same time Huntington notes that "as Asian and Muslim civilizations begin more and more to assert the universal relevance of their cultures, Westerners will come to appreciate more and more the connection between universalism and imperialism." This casual remark deserves some attention. If both Asian and Muslim civilization are asserting their own universal relevance, doesn't it follow that they must be suffering from the same hubristic condition as the West? If so, we have to ask the question, Why? Is the drive to assert the universal relevance of one's own civilization somehow inherent in any civilization, or is it just a pathology that overtakes certain ones but not others?

If it is inherent to any civilization, then the clash of civilizations, instead of being avoidable, becomes the necessary and inevitable result of having more than one civilization. But if this is the case, then there can never be an end to history so long as we live in a multicivilizational world, for each civilization will be struggling to impose its own standards on all the rest. It follows that the only possible solution would be for one of the civilizations to triumph and crush all the others.

On the other hand, if the need to supplant others is a pathology that develops only in certain civilizations—like Bernard Lewis's triumphalism—then in order for mankind to reach the state of perpetual peace, it would be necessary to either destroy these "diseased" civilizations or else transform them.

Both of these responses point in a radically different direction from the counsel that Huntington himself offers to America and to the West. "The principal responsibility of Western leaders . . . is not to attempt to reshape other civilizations in the image of the West, which is beyond their declining powers, but to preserve, protect, and renew the unique qualities of Western civilization. Because it is the most powerful Western country, that responsibility falls overwhelming on the United States."

What sense does this make if there will soon be other cultures that wish to impose their values on us? For even if the West and the United States could be brought to follow this advice, is that any reason to think that the Asian and Muslim civilizations might be less inclined to assert their own universal relevance? What happens if these other civilizations continue to assert their own style of universalism more and more insistently, just as the West was deciding to conserve its own dwindling strength?

These are questions that we will take up later; for the moment what is important is to ask ourselves if the three different theories of the enemy that we have examined exhaust all the possible ways in which human beings may turn into each other's enemy, willing to kill and to risk being killed. If so, then it is quite conceivable that the end of history thesis is right. On the other hand, if there still remains a fourth way of being an enemy, then we must come to a different conclusion.

In fact, the three theories of the enemy described here are serious distortions of the way the world works. This fact has been long apparent to anyone who was prepared to look at the history of the previous century without being seduced by the mirage of liberal internationalism.

It is to this mirage that we will now turn.

4

THE GRAND ILLUSION

The whole of history of civilization is strewn with creeds and
institutions which were invaluable at first, and deadly afterwards.

—WALTER BAGEHOT, *Physics and Politics*

IN THE MONTHS leading up to the Second Gulf War, liberal internationalism was the position taken by those who were opposed to what
they regarded, quite correctly, as a unilateral act on the part of one
nation and its allies to usurp the prerogative of the UN—the body that
they saw as the only possible source by which such an act could be legiti-
mately authorized. From their perspective, the only way that the United
States could assert legal authority to act would be if this authority had
been granted it by the explicit permission of the UN.

To hold this position it was not necessary to love Saddam Hussein and
to hate America. Indeed, a person could affirm this point of view and still
be deeply convinced that the regime of Saddam Hussein was an unmiti-
gated horror, nor is there anything logically inconsistent about this position. Consider the following analogy. Suppose that there is a man in our
town whom we know to be a murderer. Clearly we will want to see him
stopped. But will we want to see him stopped so badly that it will make
no difference to us *how* he is stopped? Will we be content to see him
lynched by an angry mob, for example, or assassinated in the dark of
night by an unknown assailant?

In a civilized community, it normally does make a difference to us how
such a man is stopped; that is why we insist upon a distinction between

acts of violence that are legitimate when carried out by persons authorized to commit them, such as the police, and those that are carried out by persons not so authorized, such as a crowd of vigilantes. In the same way, opposition to unilateral action by the United States and its small contingent of allies, *even in the pursuit of a good cause,* can be justified by a commitment to preserving an analogous distinction between legitimate and illegitimate authority on an international scale.

Indeed, liberal internationalism insists on this distinction, for what sense can there possibly be in setting up an authoritative international body, such as the UN, if its authority is not recognized by the nations whose conduct it is trying to control? It would be like setting up a judicial system that was entirely optional: if you failed to appear in court, well, that was your business. But a judicial system that functions like this is no longer a judicial system. This analogy between the legal and judicial system of a sovereign nation, on the one hand, and that of an international body like the UN, on the other, is the foundation of liberal internationalism, but as we shall see, it is also the source of its ultimate incoherence.

THE PROBLEM OF SELF-DEFENSE

The heart of the problem may be put this way: If you have a legal system that governs individual men and women, it will be based on the premise that all physical restraint and force must be either administered or authorized by the state. Therefore if I use violence to force you to hand over your collection of rare stamps, I have violated the system's ground rules and will be punished for doing so. But what if, while I was holding a gun to your head and demanding your stamps, you had kicked me in the groin, and in the ensuing struggle you had shot me dead—all in self-defense? It was not the state or the legal system that shot me dead, but you. So the question at once arises. Was your act of self-defense authorized by the state?

This same question may be put to the liberal internationalist. If he permits force to be used by nations in their self defense, then the question arises, Who is to judge whether this or that particular war is in fact a war of self-defense? Hitler justified the invasion of Poland in September 1939 as self-defense, as did all the parties to the conflict that opened World War I, with the exception of the English, who justified their entrance into war by their treaty with Belgium. But if *any* act of war can be alleged as self-defense, then the liberal internationalist has gained nothing by permitting only wars that are justified in this way. On the other hand, if the liberal internationalist insists that all claims of self-defense must be reviewed and approved by an international body in order to be deemed legitimate, he advocates a serious infringement of the most essential of all principles of national sovereignty—namely, the right of a nation to decide when there is a threat to its survival.

This poses a problem for the liberal internationalist. What distinguishes him from the proponent of a single world government is that the liberal internationalist both accepts and insists on the right of national self-determination on the part of individual nation states, whereas the advocate of a single united world federation rejects this right completely. For the latter, no nation can be allowed to decide on its own when to defend itself through the use of military force, in precisely the same way that Alabama and Oregon cannot decide on their own when to go to war against another country, even if they believe that such a war is justifiable self-defense.

Going back to the analogy between the individual and the state, and the state and the international community, consider the following argument: In any society individuals may be granted the right of self-defense, subject to review by the legal system of that society. An adult may not shoot an eight-year-old child who is flourishing a rubber knife at him. Nor may he kill the little old ladies who live in the apartment above him because he suspects that they are extraterrestrials who are tampering with his vital organs while he sleeps. This is something that we all grant. So what is wrong with establishing the same kind of review system for the international community?

Nothing, but to review a decision is not to deter that decision; no society has ever insisted that it alone could decide when its members could act in their individual self-defense *prior to* the act itself. Indeed, such deterrence would require a form of totalitarianism far beyond even Orwell's vision in *1984*—one in which Big Brother is not only watching but deciding for you at every step of your life. But if the liberal internationalist is merely asserting the right of an international body to review the self-defense claims made by nations that have already gone to war, then what is the practical value of this review? There is, of course, nothing wrong with condemning a war as illegal if you believe it to be such, but if the condemnation has no effect on the aggressor, then what?

This is the perennial quandary of the liberal internationalist. On the one hand, he accepts the system of national sovereignty for all the various countries of the world, and their right of national self-determination, including the right to decide when and if to fight in one's national self-defense; on the other hand, he wants a system of international law that will outlaw wars of aggression. However, the only way to effectively outlaw wars of aggression is to supply international law with a mechanism by which its verdict can be enforced, so that individual nations undertaking aggressive wars, like individual citizens undertaking criminal acts, can be compelled to cease and desist.

To deter a nation from aggression, more is required than a slap on the wrist, which is all that can be achieved by the moral censure of the international community. This fact was proven in the 1930s and again in the invasion of Kuwait by Iraq in the early 1990s. In neither case did the outrage of the world make the aggressor reverse his policy of aggression. Nor should he be expected to, so long as the liberal internationalist is not prepared to be consistent in making an analogy between the state and a criminal individual, on the one hand, and the international community and an aggressor nation, on the other.

The only reason that the state can compel the criminal individual is that the state maintains the virtual monopoly of force, so that even if the individual is capable of mounting a violent defense against the state's attempt to compel him, the state—if it is a genuine and not merely honorific state—will always have the means to apply overawing power to the recalcitrant individual. It must be able to literally overpower him, which can only happen if it possesses vastly superior physical might.

This means that, in order to structure the international system on the analogy of the legal system of a state, there would have to be an international body which had the same virtual monopoly on violence that the state had vis-à-vis the individual; otherwise the system would be forced to permit states stronger than the international body, like China, for example, to exercise unlimited sovereignty, simply because it could not overpower them, whereas weaker states, like Thailand, would not be permitted to exercise such unlimited sovereignty, simply because the international body *could* overpower them. Such an international system would have the perverse effect of outlawing war for precisely those nations *least* likely to disrupt the international system by engaging in it, but permitting it for those nations that were the *most* likely to disrupt the system by engaging in it. Such a system might possibly be beneficial, but its benefits would be inversely proportionate to the gap that separated the weakest nation from the strongest one. In a world in which all countries were equally weak, such a system might work quite effectively.

This was, in fact, the rationale behind the disarmament movements of the nineteenth century and the 1920s. If all nations could agree to keep their military might to the bare minimum required for their own national defense, it was conceivable that an international body could then collect a force that was *in fact* capable of deterring acts of aggression between one relatively weak nation and another. Such deterrence would be, in effect, merely a kind of policing, and hence it would not require colossal commitments on the part of those nations that agreed to undertake such a role.

Thus, if we push the analogy with the state and the individual to its logical conclusion, what we are looking for is a world in which the international body is provided with just enough power to police a world made up of nations that have all disarmed themselves, except for what is deemed, by the agreement of the international community itself, to be just sufficient for their self-defense.

THE GREAT WAR AND THE LEAGUE OF NATIONS

These two features—an international organization designed to outlaw war and an international agreement that aimed at universal disarmament—became the pillars of the first great effort to achieve the end of history, namely, the League of Nations.

The vision of an international body whose function would be to eliminate war is familiar to most of us as the brainchild of Woodrow Wilson, but the idea had been around for many generations prior to the Great War, and indeed, it is simply a working out of what is implicit in Benjamin Constant's vision of the coming Age of Commerce. Its enthusiastic revival at the conclusion of the War to End All Wars seemed not only fitting but long overdue.

Nevertheless, the League of Nations came into existence at the very moment when it should have been obvious to all that the idea upon which it was predicated had proven bankrupt. If the Great War could be said to have demonstrated anything, it was the woeful inadequacy of the theory of the enemy articulated by Benjamin Constant in *The Spirit of*

Conquest—the idea that the enemy was a rational player who was using war as an instrument of policy only because he could get away with it, but who, with the proper incentives, could be persuaded to abandon this instrument of policy and to replace it with peaceful commerce. No one could possibly argue that the Great War lasted five years because the antagonists were pursuing their rational economic self-interest, even if you accepted the idea that this is what got them started.

Here was another classic example of a world-historical transformation that, like the one we are living through in the post-9/11 epoch, went unobserved by the liberal internationalists. The Great War had destroyed any reason for looking at the enemy as a rational player attempting to maximize his economic well-being, and this fact by itself should have forced men to rethink the fundamental assumption behind a league of nations. Instead they simply reached back to a panacea from the historically superseded epoch and tried to apply it in a world where it simply didn't fit and couldn't possibly work.

What had changed after the Great War? Well, the whole nature of war, and with it the whole nature of the risks involved in going to war, and with the alteration of the risks involved in going to war came the alteration in the kind of deterrence that would be needed to effectively prevent future wars.

No one, of course, had meant the Great War to be the Great War. As is well known, almost all the belligerents in World War I expected the time frame of this war to be similar to that of the Franco-Prussian War—measurable in weeks and months, not years. Indeed, this schedule had been built into the German war plan. No one, in his worst nightmares, expected World War I to develop into the ghastly system of trench warfare, in which battles, like Verdun and the Somme, could last months and consume casualties reckoned in the millions. The horror of the war had been, prior to the event, simply unthinkable—which in the hindsight of the early 1920s, seemed like the best possible argument for why everything should be done to prevent such a terrible carnage from ever recurring.

Yet it was this same catastrophic carnage that made it impossible for the League of Nations to be the agent by which another such war could be avoided in the future. The problem confronting mankind after the Great War was that everyone now knew something they did not know before, namely, that such a war was *possible*. It could happen again, and this ever-present awareness radically changed the way in which men were forced to think of deterrence.

Similarly today, in the post-9/11 world, we know now that catastrophic terror is a possibility, and this knowledge can never be eluded. It changes the way in which we imagine our future, just as it changed the way those who had lived through the Great War were condemned to imagine theirs.

TO SEE WHAT this means, let us go back to the kind of deterrence that men like Benjamin Constant felt would be adequate to dissuade a nation from engaging in a war. If nation A wanted to go to war with nation B in order to gain an economic benefit Z, all that was required to keep nation A from going to war was for the international community to make a credible threat that it would force nation A to lose economic benefits equal to or greater than Z. In short, nation A would be deterred from going to war with nation B because it would perform a cost-benefit analysis in which it would weigh what it had to gain from the war against what it had to lose. All the international community had to do was make its sanctions, economic or military, greater than what nation A hoped to gain from war.

Now, since what any nation had to gain from going to war could be measured in finite economic terms, it was clear that any deterrence could also be measured in the same way. If nation A wants to seize the gold mines or the oil fields of nation B, the world community must first determine the economic and commercial value of these coveted targets, then announce that if nation A does in fact seize the gold mines or the oil fields, it will face some kind of economic loss greater than what it has gained. The enemy, in this model, always acts as a Benthamite calculator, weighing and measuring precisely quantifiable economic gains and losses; hence all that is required to make certain that he will not go to war is to make war simply too expensive for him—to make it unprofitable or, more precisely, less profitable than commerce.

This model was an essential component of any workable scheme for a league of nations, and if we reflect a moment, we can see why this is so. Suppose that you and I are two nations making up such a league, and we are trying to deter nation A from its contemplated act of aggression—say the invasion of a smaller country. We have made an accurate calculation of the economic advantages that would accrue to nation A from his seizure of the smaller country—a calculation with which nation A agrees—and jointly we have pledged to do whatever is necessary to inflict an economic cost on him greater than his anticipated economic gain.

Because we have accurately determined A's economic gain from the attack, we can accurately determine the cost we must impose on him to deter this attack, and this figure in turn permits us to calculate how much it will cost you and me to impose these economic costs on A. Suppose, for example, that our individual contributions, in money, matériel, and manpower, are arrived at by some kind of predetermined rule that all the members of the league have previously signed off on. In this case, you and I can both know, virtually to the penny or to the last man, what our own losses and costs will be if a joint decision is made to punish A. It follows that when we threaten action against A, we are perfectly aware of how much this act of deterrence will cost us if we are obliged to carry it out.

This state of affairs would greatly facilitate the operations of a league of nations, since all parties to such a league would know in advance how much it would cost, both collectively and individually, to deter acts of aggression undertaken for economic gain. Uncertainty and risk, on this model, would be minimized to the point where they would impose no obstacles to collective actions, since all the parties to the decision would know the costs of making any particular decision beforehand.

The unspoken assumption behind the actual League of Nations was the idea that war was an economic decision made by a rational actor, whose behavior you could change by finding the right combination of incentives to commerce and disincentives to war, a combination that could be worked out in advance for any possible act of aggression, so that deterring such an act involved no unforeseen or even unforeseeable risks. After all, if the enemy was a rational calculator, he would never go to war when it was not in his economic interest to do so, and this condition was something well within the power of the League of Nations to accomplish.

But what of the Great War itself? How was it possible for anyone to fail to see that this interminable conflict had made no sense economically for any of the belligerents? That, in fact, it was a startling refutation of the entire theory of war and of the enemy upon which the League of Nations was premised?

Here we have a classic example of the power of wishful thinking to distort the perception of reality of otherwise intelligent men and women. The Great War, according to the liberal internationalists, had been no one's fault—a point of view that was given its classical formulation in

John Maynard Keynes's enormously influential *Economic Consequence of the Peace*. Why seek to blame the Germans for what had in fact been a breakdown in the inherently anarchic system that had governed international relations prior to the League of Nations?

This exoneration of the Germans from any unique blame for the historical catastrophe that was the Great War was a common phenomenon in Europe during the 1920s. All Germans accepted it as an article of faith, the Left just as much as the Right. Look for it as hard as you wish, you will find not a single utterance of war guilt on the part of any German in the postwar environment. Among "enlightened" English, French, and American opinion, acceptance of the Keynes thesis became a badge of intellectual sophistication. Indeed it still passes for such in many circles, despite its complete refutation, implicitly in works such as Fritz Fischer's *Germany's Aims in World War One* and Barbara Tuchman's *The Guns of August*, and explicitly in Niall Ferguson's masterly debunking of both Keynes and his thesis in *The Pity of War*.

For our purposes the important question is not whether the Germans were responsible for causing the Great War but rather, Why were so many people who were not Germans so insistent on absolving their former enemy from any hint of responsibility for bringing about the greatest historical catastrophe since the collapse of the Roman Empire? Why, in other words, did Keynes's exoneration seem so convincing?

Because so many people had a need to be convinced. There had to be a plausible way of denying German responsibility for the war because if you accepted the idea that German conduct had caused the war, then you would have to rethink the fundamental premises of liberal internationalism—and at the very moment when the world most desperately wanted to accept liberal internationalism as the panacea for all mankind's ills. If, in short, liberal internationalism could not have prevented the first Great War, how could it be trusted to prevent the next one? Those who could not bear to envision the prospect of another, similar war had to believe that the Great War had been a malfunction in a system and not the result of deliberate strategy on the part of one of the belligerents.

That was why it was called the Great War in the first place; even the name was a sign of hopefulness, just we call the economic downturn that occurred in the 1930s the Great Depression, to underscore its uniqueness and the unlikelihood of its ever happening again. Our own insistence on the name World War I distorts our understanding of the postwar atmosphere in both America and Europe during the twenties and thirties. How, we ask, can men who have lived through World War I possibly fail to be aware that they were living in the shadow of an imminent and pre-destined *Second* World War? The answer is that the experience they had just lived through was not the experience of World War I but that of a unique and "never again" historical catastrophe, the Great War; unless we are able to share in this different way of imagining the experience of this event, we will fail to comprehend the entire postwar experience.

The Great War was shorthand for the War That Has Ended All Wars, the war that had made future war *unthinkable.* Yet there are two quite different ways in which something can be unthinkable. Either it cannot be thought, or we cannot bring ourselves to think it.

The idea of another Great War became almost an oxymoron for a whole generation because so many of that generation could not bring themselves even to think it possible. The idea that such an event could never again happen became the Grand Illusion—the title of Jean Renoir's masterpiece about the Great War. It was an illusion shared by all liberal internationalists.

Is it fair to call it an illusion, as opposed to misplaced optimism? Misplaced optimism occurs whenever you encounter someone who makes a good impression on you and whom you decide to trust on this quite reasonable basis, but who then disappoints your hopes by his subsequent behavior. It is a principle that can be applied equally well in the conduct of nations and communities. An illusion, on the other hand, requires a false interpretation of facts that are already right in front of your eyes. A mother whose son repeatedly takes advantage of her generosity and good nature, but who insists that he is really a devoted son, is an example of someone acting subject to an illusion. She has seen the same evidence as everyone else, but she interprets it in accordance with her own wishful thinking. She wants her son to be a good son and thus sees his behavior in a far more sympathetic light than is warranted by the facts.

Defined like this, the liberal internationalism that followed on the heels of the Great War was not misplaced optimism but an illusion. It required the systematic suppression of all memory of what had been the most obvious feature of German war policy during the conflict itself. The German word for it was *Schrecklichkeit,* which, thanks to the Teutonic flair for onomatopoeia, sounds precisely as bad as the idea being conveyed by it; according to my battered *Brockhaus Illustrated Ger-*

man/English Dictionary, the English synonyms for it include "dreadfulness, frightfulness, horror, horribleness, terror, terribleness, atrociousness, atrocity."

The word that I will use to translate the German is *ruthlessness*, and it is one of the most imortant categories for the rest of this book. Indeed, ruthlessness is the great driving motor of human history, and nowhere is this truth more readily apparent than in the course of World War I, where ruthlessness was deliberately and systematically employed by the Germans in their violation of Belgian neutrality, in their use of terror against the civilian population of Belgium, and in their policy of targeting ocean liners like the *Lusitania*—all actions that brought about the transformation of what had been originally planned as a short and swift Clausewitzian war into the inconceivable nightmare of a European holocaust.

To neglect the role that ruthlessness played in making the Great War what it was, the liberal internationalists not only willed themselves to believe an illusion, they also doomed the system that they hoped would make such a war an impossibility in the future. By refusing to take seriously the significance of the German policy of ruthlessness, liberal internationalism overlooked the possibility that such ruthlessness could be used again in the postwar period, but now with a new and utterly devastating force.

What the founders of the League of Nations refused to see was that the very horribleness of the Great War had created an entirely new kind of risk, one that could not even have been contemplated prior to the strewing of millions of corpses across a continent-long system of trenches and barbwire. For while the League of Nations might have been equipped to prevent the accidental eruption of another great war, how could it be expected to handle a nation that *deliberately* used the threat of yet another great war as a way of obtaining its political desires?

No one had intended the Great War. The German military staff had been initially willing to use *Schrecklichkeit* in order to assure a quick and decisive victory. The von Schlieffen plan called for the Germany Army to move through Belgium, in violation of its neutrality and, more generally, in violation of the rules of play that had governed European conduct for the previous century. The action was justified because it was seen as guaranteeing a short war.

What had originally come about as an accident, as the result of the law of unintended consequences, could subsequently be used as a deliberate strategy. Before the Great War, it was not possible for an opponent to use the threat of a great war, because such a threat did not exist in anyone's imagination: it was not thinkable. But after the Great War, all threats of war inevitably became the threat of a second great war, and it became impossible *not* to think it.

This is a pattern that, according to Hegel, holds the key to understanding human development. What first appears completely by accident is subsequently taken up as a deliberate method. The accident opens up a new possibility, one that was previously thought unimaginable or, more precisely, that was not thought of at all because it was unimaginable. Mankind's control of fire, for example, did not come about because men first thought, *How helpful it would be to have a source of energy and heat. Let's look about for one.* It occurred instead because certain natural phenomena—lightning and lava flows—produce fire. It is not only natural accidents that open up new possibilities for the human imagination, however; human action is capable of doing the same thing. The law of unintended consequences, normally thought of in a purely negative manner, also has its positive side, for it is equally productive of serendipity. The discovery of America by Columbus opened a new epoch in human history, yet it was notoriously the unintended consequence of Columbus's plans.

This pattern of accidents and/or unintended consequences that are subsequently taken up and turned into a deliberate strategy is the driving engine of human history. New possibilities are opened up to us entirely by accident, but once they are grasped as possibilities, then this new understanding alters the way in which human beings subsequently imagine and think about the world that they live in. Once known, it is impossible to "unknow" something. The same law applies both to good and bad innovations.

We know, for example, that diseases can be cured by the application of scientific methods because we have cured them this way—not all of them, but some of them; this possibility leads us to look for other cures. But we also know, after 9/11, that terrorists are capable of using catastrophic terror, and this is also a possibility that changes the realm of what is thinkable and what is imaginable in our time. That is the ultimate significance of 9/11: we can no longer imagine a future in which this possibility does not loom for us.

The same was true for those who had survived the Great War. There arose a new level of ruthlessness, one that involved not merely the willingness to violate neutral territory, to shoot civilians and sink ocean liners, but a willingness to risk another great war. It was not possible to deal with this threat in terms of the model of the enemy upon which the League of Nations had been founded. Any large industrialized nation that credibly threatened the willingness to precipitate another war of the same magnitude—*total war*—would expose the weakness of an international system set up to deal with the kind of small-scale wars that the liberal internationalist wanted so desperately to believe posed the only real threat to world peace.

The source of the League's weakness is not hard for us to see: to counter an armed force of several million men, well trained and well equipped, requires an equally serious commitment on the part of other nations with similar resources: where this is lacking, the one nation that has steeled itself to risk total war will be able to effect its will, whatever its will may be. In the aftermath of the most total war of all time, the Great War, it was widely assumed that no power capable of fighting a total war would risk waging one if it could possibly be avoided. But the problem with such a widespread assumption is that its very pervasiveness provides an enormous opportunity for any party who does not share the assumption.

We can see this problem clearly in the case of a small community in which everyone is so trusting of everyone else that no one locks his doors. Behind this trust is the implicit assumption that everyone else will obey the same rules that we obey, in which case no one will ever think of taking advantage of the community's habits of trustfulness in order to further his own ends. Yet, for someone who does not obey these rules—or merely pretends to—this very trustfulness provides a wonderful opening, literally and figuratively, by which he may enrich himself.

The same thing happened to Europe in the 1930s. Hitler grasped the enormous opportunity that the aftermath of the Great War gave to any power that could plausibly threaten to bring about another great war. For as long as he could even *imply* such a threat, those who were not prepared to commit themselves to such a conflict, from a lack either of popular support or of allies or of military might, would be forced to compromise over issues that they would otherwise have been willing to fight for, if only they could have been certain that the fight would not immediately escalate into total war.

This was the logic that underlay the French *military*'s refusal to respond to Hitler's invasion of the demilitarized Rhineland in 1936, something that the French *civilian* government demanded that they do. In hindsight we all know that this was a terrible mistake. We now know from German archives that had the French countered Hitler's move, he had planned to immediately withdraw his force, with the likelihood of his own removal from power.

At the time, however, the French military staff did not know this, and their failure to act was based on their belief that Hitler would not take such an enormous gamble unless he was prepared to escalate to total war. No one could possibly take such an action merely as a bluff, because, as they saw it, such a bluff involved the risk of total war, and no one would possibly risk total war who was not prepared to fight it. It was like playing poker with a man who is willing to stake the farm. It is unnerving to those who are playing against him. Yes, he may just be bluffing—but what a bluff!

This was why the French generals rejected the idea of pushing the Germans out with a police action; it was, for them, too much of a risk. Their rejection had nothing to do with faintheartedness. It resulted from their belief that the only prudent response to Hitler's provocation was a preparation for total war.

This is how William Shirer recounts the event in *The Collapse of the Third Republic.* "It quickly dawned on the astounded civilian ministers that what the . . . generals wanted was a *general mobilization,* starting with the *couverture,* which itself would take eight days to put a million men on war footing. What was called for on that crucial Saturday of May 7, 1936, was a police action by the French to chase out a few German troops who were parading into the Rhineland. . . . But the French High Command demanded a sledgehammer to kill a fly." (Italics in original text)

Shirer's lack of sympathy for the French High Command is understandable in retrospect, just as it is always clear to us what an idiot we have been whenever we allow someone to bluff us. But this attitude overlooks the fundamental problem faced in the aftermath of the Great War: from that point on, any move by a great power involved the risk of the Great War occurring all over again—as in fact ultimately happened. It was impossible to judge in advance when a sledgehammer might be needed and when a flyswatter would do.

THE PROBLEM OF RISK

The same problem faces the United States today in the aftermath of 9/11. When is a sledgehammer needed, and when a flyswatter? If we may be attacked at any time by enemies who are prepared to use catastrophic terror, how is it possible to calibrate in advance the magnitude of any threat or any risk?

There is, in fact, no answer to this problem. The color-coded Terror Index, while certainly harmless and well intended, only underscores the inherent difficulty—one for which it is absurd to blame the United States government. When an agency is put in charge of the defense of an entire people, and when it cannot possibly know in advance the magnitude of the danger it is defending against, what else can it do?

This is the problem with the very concept of risk. It requires measurement and rational calculation. If we are forced to choose between two courses of action, where these courses are capable of being measured on the same scale, then we can assess the risks involved. We are able, in advance, to see the very worst thing that could happen to us if we make the wrong choice.

Life abounds with such examples of measurable risk and simple calculation. In the once-popular game show *Let's Make a Deal,* if you chose the unknown envelope (full of an unspecified amount of cash), you knew you would not be taking home the brand-new refrigerator and dinette suite. When you invest your money in a stock, you can quantify exactly how much money you could lose under the most adverse conditions.

But where the risk is total war—and for the French High Command, the possibility of total defeat—the human tendency is not to quantify and to make a rational calculation. The tendency is to do anything to avoid the risk. This is the reason most of us are not willing to play Russian roulette even if we are promised large sums of money each time we successfully pull the trigger without blowing our brains out. When a risk involves life and death, for an individual or for a nation, there is a very natural tendency to accept any consequence less grave than death. And for a good reason. It allows us to live to fight another day.

Yet this very fact is precisely what gives an enormous advantage to any party who *is* willing to risk death or, in Hitler's case, total war. Because in those situations where it is irrational to voluntarily take a risk that involves life and death, those who are willing to act irrationally and to take this risk will be able to force any rational player into acceding to his will.

In a world where others are willing to risk death to get their way, you must be willing to risk death to keep them from getting their way.

Equally, if you live in a world where nations are willing to risk total war over minor issues, then you too must be willing to risk total war over minor issues—such as parading into the Rhineland. On the other hand, in a world where everyone else is accustomed to making rational economic choices, the man who is prepared to fight to the death will normally be appeased. The same logic applies to whole societies.

The result is an unsettling paradox: the more the spirit of commerce triumphs, the closer mankind comes to dispensing with war, the nearer we approach the end of history, the greater are the rewards to those who decide to return to the path of war, and the easier it will be for them to conquer. There is nothing that can be done to change this fact; it is built into the structure of our world.

This does not of course mean that some party *must* emerge that will behave in this way, yet the plain fact is that they always have emerged. Given what we know of human nature, there is simply no way of guaranteeing that they will not emerge in the future, and at precisely those points at which rational men and women are celebrating the end of history. All that is necessary is the will.

Forgetfulness overcomes every successful civilization. Its transformation of men into peaceful, commercially minded, liberal cosmopolitans is a large-scale version of the trustful community that leaves its doors unlocked. As it becomes harder and harder to imagine people playing by different rules from us, the advantage to those who are prepared to break the rules altogether increases.

That is why so many intellectuals have utterly failed to comprehend the role of fantasy ideology in the great totalitarian movements of the twentieth century. They have analyzed them as belief systems and looked to see if they were true or false, but their value lay elsewhere: they were purely transformative. What Nazism, fascism, and Communism had in common was their refusal to play by the same rules as their middle-class and liberal opponents or even to acknowledge these rules. In each case, the leaders of these movements were prepared to push their own societies into civil war in order to get their way, and since their opponents could think of nothing worse, they were allowed to do so. In the same way that any historical catastrophe will do for our current enemy, the totalitarian movements of the past were also prepared to take advantage of social, economic, or political catastrophe, in order to turn it to their own purpose. What their opponents could never think of was their first thought.

To see these movements as driven by their ideology is a tremendous error. Rather, they were driven by men who had been transformed by the fantasy contained in the ideology: the whole purpose of the fantasy ideology was to permit the true believer to overcome the middle-class and bourgeois inhibitions on violence that had been built into the character structure of the nineteenth-century European personality. It was a way of psyching themselves up to commit acts that they knew to be violations of the civilized norm, in order to achieve the degree of ruthlessness necessary to intimidate their opponents into acceding to their demands.

The ideologies that came to dominate Europe after the Great War were precisely the ones that preached the doctrine of ruthlessness most effectively, in each case justifying the doctrine by an appeal to a different myth. Each myth justified the use of ruthlessness by a certain select group of human beings. In Italian fascism, it was those who were naturally heroic and daring. In Nazism, it was the master race. In Communism, it was the Vanguard of the Proletariat. Each of these groups was entitled to behave ruthlessly and to scoff and make fun of the hypocrisy and cant of middle-class values, of the corruption and lack of direction of parliamentary democracy, of the selfishness and money grubbing of the self-satisfied bourgeoisie. And who could blame them?

This is a problem that those who wish to defend the spirit of commerce will always have—its complete lack of glamour and heroism, its poverty of incentives to the nobler and more adventurous side of our nature. There is nothing there to excite the imagination, even of those who most benefit from it. And yet this lack of glamour was not the worst disadvantage of those who wanted after the Great War to defend the values of civilization against the forces of ruthlessness. The worst disadvantage arose from the very nature of these values—their civility.

THE CIVILITY TRAP

"He was so generally civil that no one ever thanked him for it," Samuel Johnson once shrewdly remarked of a friend. The same can be said for societies that embody civility in their everyday practices: we are so accustomed to people behaving civilly with us that we never think to thank them or, more important, to thank the society that made them that way. Yet that is not the only problem with civility. Part of the beauty of civility is also its nemesis, and that is its refusal to acknowledge the incivility of others.

Everyone knows the story, true or not, of the Russian ambassador who, at a formal dinner with Queen Victoria, lifted up the finger bowl provided for him at the end of a course, stared at it with momentary bafflement, then gulped it down. Whereupon Queen Victoria, hesitating not a second, lifted hers up and did the same, followed by all the other guests. This story is usually retold at the beginning of every etiquette book as containing the soul of good manners, the refusal to offend others at all costs. What can be more offensive than to tell another person that he is not acting civilly?

The fundamental rule of civility is that you must behave with others as if you expected them to behave civilly themselves. But what if they are not behaving civilly? Then what? You can always pretend that they are, as Queen Victoria did. Or you can bring it to the other party's attention that he is not behaving by the rules of civility. To do this, however, requires that you step outside the condition of civility and into quite another zone—one in which it is no longer possible to assume that everyone will follow the rules of the game. If I tell a stranger that he is not behaving like a gentleman, will he thank me for it, or will he challenge me to a duel?

This is something that every practitioner of ruthlessness knows. People who have been trained in the practice of civility, and who find it second nature, will be reluctant to challenge the conduct of another on the ground that he is lacking in civility. The ruthless party therefore knows that he will be able to push very far before a break point is openly acknowledged. Because once the break point is acknowledged, all bets are off and you no longer can be sure of the next step.

Before the break point, the civil party thinks that the ruthless party can be accommodated to civilized standards by means of patience and forbearance, much in the same way that we might try to domesticate a feral animal. We are convinced that we will bring him around. We attribute his ruthlessness to some defect in his psychology. Perhaps he has an inferiority complex and is acting out with us. Perhaps we are an authority figure, and he is rebelling against us. (Who knows, he may have had a wicked stepfather somewhere in his childhood.) We may blame ruthlessness on someone's religion or culture or economic status. We never dream of identifying it for what it is—a strategy that works.

Every society, every culture, every civilization has produced exponents of ruthlessness; none has a monopoly on it. None will ever find a way of eliminating those who are prepared to resort to ruthlessness, as long as it continues to work, and it will continue to work so long as men civilize themselves, and to work all the more effectively whenever a civilization has succeeded so well in its civilizing task that it believes itself within sight of the end of history, because at no time is ruthlessness more effective. It works in some cases because its victims are easy to cow, in some cases because they genuinely can't fathom ruthlessness, and in some cases because their idealism refuses to countenance such an illiberal truth.

THERE CAN NEVER be an end to history. In a world in which everyone has accepted liberal values, the practice of ruthlessness will amply reward those who still practice it—so amply that it is sheer utopianism to expect no one to seize the opportunity when it offers itself. Ruthlessness, in short, is the fourth enemy of civilization. Unlike the other enemies that we have considered, it is not one that humankind can ever evade, for it is an essential component of civilization itself. It arose with civilization and can only cease to exist if mankind returns to the state of absolute savagery.

5

RUTHLESSNESS AND THE ORIGIN
OF CIVILIZATION

The great difficulty which history records is not that of the first step, but that of the second step. What is most evident is not the difficulty of getting a fixed law, but getting out of a fixed law; not of cementing . . . a cake of custom, but of breaking the cake of custom.

—WALTER BAGEHOT, *Physics and Politics*

TO FIND the origin of ruthlessness, we must first go back to the state once called savagery, but only in order for us to see the difference between these two conditions.

The savage state, as the twentieth-century English philosopher R. G. Collingwood explained it in *The New Leviathan,* is "a negative idea. It means not being civilized, and that is all." But ruthlessness does not arise from a lack of knowledge of civility, or civilization, on the part of its practitioners, but rather from that "hostility to civilization" that Collingwood dubs "barbarian."

Collingwood's choice of the term *barbarism* was no doubt influenced by the historical circumstances in which he wrote his book—namely, the period of the Nazi threat to European civilization, a time when the popular associations of the word *barbarian* would not have appeared to be too misleading. For our purposes I think it is best to replace the term *barbarism* with one that can avoid the potentially misleading association

69

of this term. For this purpose I propose the word *de-civilization*, defined as Collingwood defined *barbarism*: "the effort, conscious or unconscious, to become less civilized than you are, either in general or in some special way, and, so far as in you lies, to promote a similar change in others."

In terms of fantasy ideology, the function of de-civilization is not merely to promote ideas opposed to civilization, but to make men and women into human beings with a totally different set of visceral and emotional responses to atrociousness.

The example that first comes to mind is the SS officer who is devoted to Schumann's piano music and yet who oversees the operation of an extermination camp. We are puzzled by this, and we ask ourselves, *How could a man with such artistic sensitivity commit such acts?* The answer is that he has worked very hard to make himself into someone who can commit such acts. He has steeled himself to behave atrociously.

Thus while savagery and de-civilization can both produce atrocities, they do so in entirely different ways. To understand the atrociousness of the ordinary savage, consider this reaction of a sixteenth-century explorer to the ritual cannibalism of a Brazilian tribe. "Although they all confess that this human flesh is marvelously good and delicate, nevertheless they feast on it more out of vengeance than taste. . . . Their main purpose in . . . gnawing the dead down to the bones . . . is to fill the living with fear and horror. . . . Everything that can be found in the bodies of these prisoners is completely eaten by them."

An interesting question arises from the explorer's own interpretation of the purpose of such cannibalism. Is it really plausible that such a ritual could have been consciously created to engender fear and horror? Are we to suppose that a peace-loving and root-and-berry-eating tribe of vegetarians might have hit on this particular custom as a way of making others fear them? Or is it more natural to suppose that the cannibalism came about from some other motive entirely and that it merely occurred, quite by accident, and just so happened to have the effect of making those who practiced it both respected and feared by those civilized persons like the explorer who happened to observe it?

This question is important because it demonstrates that what you or I will count as an example of the atrocious and the horrible will depend very much on our imagination. If, for example, a person works in a slaughterhouse and spends his days killing animals, he is less likely to be shocked by the sight of a dead animal on the side of the road than someone who is accustomed to seeing only animals who are alive, such as his own pets. Yet both people are equally aware of the fact that animals die. The shock can only be measured by visceral impact—by the stab of sympathetic pain that is analogous to an electric shock when it hits us.

The explorer, when he watched the tribe gnawing the flesh down to the bone of a man who had been living just hours before, felt precisely the same kind of visceral shock; nothing in his own experience could have prepared him for seeing such a sight. He could think of such a thing, but he could not imagine it. And so when it was right there before him, he assumed that the same sight would have to arouse the same gut-level emotions that he felt—the emotions of fear and horror—in anyone else who witnessed the same scene, even if it was a scene that they had been familiar with from childhood. (According to his account, the adults "let the children eat whatever they especially enjoyed.")

But did the Indians in fact feel the same emotions as the explorer? By his own account, after the feast "for a space of three days they do nothing but dance and drinke day and night," which is not suggestive of remorse. Nor is there any evidence that the rites were done for the benefit of anyone other than those who enjoyed it—like the children feasting on their favorite tidbits.

The point here is not to illustrate the savagery of those who could perform such a ritual but rather the civilized imagination of the European who witnessed it. Keep in mind here that the eyewitness was the product not of our own time but of a much rougher period in history. The concept of civilization is notoriously subject to controversy; what is normally forgotten in these controversies is the fact that a civilization is first and foremost a product of the human imagination. A civilization comes into being whenever a large number of people begin to feel visceral shock whenever they are confronted with the state of savagery.

The foundation of civilized life is wired into our nervous system and into our sweat glands; its basis is in the pit of our stomach and in the queasiness and vertigo that come over us whenever we are face to face with something that is "beyond our imagination."

Consider this thought experiment: How well would you have to know a man for it not to disturb you if he happened to remark, "I often imagine violently raping your daughter, but of course it's only in my imagination." Would you want him to stay your friend or give your daughter a ride to her job?

In a civilization, we do not like to imagine that people have imaginations that are too different from ours, because it would radically subvert our trust in them. That is why we are startled, and indeed appalled, even to hear someone avow an act of the imagination suggestive of a violation of civilized conduct—cannibalism, or incest, or the rape of a child.

A civilization is protected by a twin barrier of shame, one external and one internal. The first defends against actions by punishing transgressions, while the second defends against acts of the imagination by not allowing most people even to think the unthinkable.

Those who argue, like Plato, that the state has a justifiable interest in what people imagine, and not merely in what they do, have a point, and it is one that all the blessings of free speech and artistic license cannot take away. When there is a shift within a society that makes it easier merely to imagine certain acts, then there has been a genuine change in the fabric of that society.

Changes in what is collectively permissible to our imagination cannot be dismissed as irrelevant to the quality of life in any society composed of real human beings. If the members of a society are permitted to begin the process of de-civilizing their imaginations, this change will ultimately have an impact on the day-to-day conduct of that society. When the unthinkable becomes increasingly thought, it begins to numb those visceral emotions that govern the shame system, and thus the very structure of civilization that it supports.

DEFINING CIVILIZATION

Throughout this book the word *civilization* is used to mean not this or that culture but rather a quality of all cultures that have obtained to a standard of civilization.

A standard of civilization is like any other standard of measurement. Meters and yards are different, yet they measure the same thing, and so too do the different standards of civilization. In one culture human beings might show they are civilized by bowing when they depart from each other's company, in another by shaking hands. Both embody the same civilized value, namely, the need to give a physical expression of respect for the other party. Naive and unsophisticated multiculturalists think that meters and yards measure different things, which explains how they accept the sophistical nonsense of cultural relativism. But does the recognition that the French measure in meters while we measure in yards mean that I am a different height when I am in Paris than when I am in New York?

The fact that cultures differ does not mean that you cannot measure perfectly objective differences between them, and without any degree of controversy. For example, my parents were raised eating the very nonspicy food of the American South. This experience did not keep them from being able to tell that Indian food was much spicier. You might like spiciness, or you might hate it, but presumably your preference does not keep you from being able to tell whether the food of one culture exemplifies this feature more than another.

Nor do we have an inescapable preference for the culture we were born into. Some of us even seem to have an inescapable aversion for it. This fact implies that we may have many quite objective standards available for measuring the inferiority or superiority of one culture to another. And of course we do.

By civilization what I mean is a standard like this: one that can be applied across cultures and across history. This concept of civilization goes back to one of the first great inquiries into the rise and fall of societies, that undertaken by the French novelist turned philosopher of history, Arthur de Gobineau, in his *Essay on the Inequality of the Races*.

This is how Gobineau characterized the four hallmarks of civilization: "By the side of stability, and the co-operation of individual interests, which touch each other without being destroyed, we must put a third and fourth characteristic of civilization, sociability [i.e., tolerance], and the hatred of violence—in other words the demand that the head, and not the fists, shall be used for self-defense."

Less analytic, but in the same spirit, is the definition by Gobineau's fellow countryman Guizot: "Civilization . . . in its most general idea, is an improved condition of man resulting from the establishment of social order in place of the individual independence and lawlessness of the savage or barbarous life. It may exist in various degree."

R. G. Collingwood expresses the same point in his own way: "Civilization is a mental process . . . whereby the members of [a] community become less addicted to force in their dealings with one another." (*The New Leviathan* [New York: Crowell, 1971], p. 299)

Thus the culture of New York City when Rudolph Giuliani became mayor was more addicted to violence than the culture that evolved during his administration, and this becoming less addicted was a phenomenon that could actually be measured in purely objective terms—by the number of murders and other crimes of violence. According to these definitions, New York City became a more civilized place to live during this period. Does this mean that the performances of *Der Rosenkavalier* at the Met were superior to what they had been under earlier administrations or that New York poets wrote finer poetry than they had ever written before? Of course not. The limited definition of civilization being used here has nothing to do with high or low culture but only to do with the way people get along with one another. By this standard, a lowbrow WASP town in North Georgia might be said to be a more civilized place to live than the turbulent, but artistically vibrant, Florence of the Medici.

This definition of civilization offers a completely objective way of determining which of two cultures is more civilized, a way that can be applied equally well by people who actually might prefer living in a nation that was less civilized.

It was one of the great masters of the French language, Jean-Jacques Rousseau, who voiced one of the most eloquent of all pleas for living a less civilized life—though hardly the life of either the noble or the ignoble savage, contrary to popular caricature. He argued in his famous "Discourse on the Progress of the Arts and Science" that civilization, defined much as above, inevitably produced a loss of vigor in any society that had pushed civilized values too far; if you look back to our definition, you can see why this must be so.

Getting people to practice sociability and to abstain from violence, while beneficial to the cause of civilization, if too successful, may weaken other important elements of character. A narrow-minded suspiciousness of others, accompanied by nasty outbursts of temper, may in certain contexts be exactly the right response to exhibit and, in fact, may prove to be of great value to the society in which such uncouth behavior is still acceptable. Ask yourself who would have the best chance of surviving an encounter with Ted Bundy or with a high-powered car salesman: the low-down redneck or the cultured gentleman?

Civilization may be grasped by an analogy to the concept of politeness. What is polite in Eskimo society may be considered quite rude in Tibetan society. Yet if these two protocols achieve the same end in their respective societies—namely, to avoid interpersonal conflict and hence deter violence—then they are both equally forms of politeness, just as a haiku and an English sonnet are both forms of poetry.

GOBINEAU'S PARADOX

What makes Gobineau's approach so interesting is the reason he hit upon to explain why so many human groups have been unable to go much past the stage of the cannabalistic Brazilian Indians: their inability to tolerate or socialize with their neighbor, if this neighbor was from another family or tribe.

We will call this the *biological barrier*. It puts an obstacle between neighboring tribes that do not recognize any blood kinship between them. The very sensible question that Gobineau asked is, Why was this barrier so hard for most human groups to cross? Why, in short, is tolerance in such short supply among savage peoples?

Looking over the whole of history, Gobineau was struck by the fact that mankind fell into two sharply divided patterns of collective conduct. In one, there was tolerance of people who were different; in the other, there was not. Intolerance predominated in both the world and in history, not just among cannibals. It thrived among people at all sorts of higher stages of tribal life, who still thought of the world as divided between us and them, where this division is grasped entirely in terms of blood kinship.

Such tribes had two completely different sets of rules—one for their members when interacting with each other, and one for their members when interacting with strangers. Within one's own tribe, you might be expected to be tolerant, to abide by the rules of fair play, to avoid violence, and to be honest and forthright in your dealings, but outside the tribe, in your dealings with strangers, you could practice trickery, deceit, and deception, at the upper end of the scale, or you could eat them, at the lower.

Set apart from these us-versus-them tribes were those strange and remarkable things that so fascinated Gobineau, groups of people that had miraculously been able to cross the primordial barrier between the biological Us and Them. As Gobineau writes:

> The human species seems to have a very great difficulty in raising itself above a rudimentary type of organization . . . the stronger

massacre the weaker, the weaker try to move as far away as possible from the stronger. This sums up the political ideas of these embryo societies, which have lived on in their imperfect state, without possibility of improvement, as long as the human race itself.

If then we are driven to admit that for a very large number of human beings it has been, and always will be, impossible to take even the first step towards civilization . . . we must assume that a part of mankind is in its own nature stricken with paralysis, which makes it for ever unable to take even the first step towards civilization, since it cannot overcome the natural repugnance, felt by men and animals alike, to a crossing of blood. (*Gobineau: Selected Political Writings* [London: Jonathan Cape, 1970])

Gobineau's empirical observation here is correct. Few and far between have been those societies that have been able to transcend the tribal us-versus-them stage; those societies that have been able to make this enormous leap have clearly been the big winners of history, for reasons that are quite obvious. If my society is able to get a million people to imagine themselves as an Us, and your society can only get eighteen people to imagine themselves like this, which will win in a conflict between them?

This advantage of numbers is yet another factor in the puzzle. The rule embodied in the motto, There is safety in numbers, is hardwired into the human condition: all things being equal, larger numbers triumph over smaller ones. Hence there is an obvious incentive for any society to enlarge to the maximum the number of people who collectively *and* mutually imagine themselves as being members of it.

If tolerance pays off so well, why did so many peoples fail to come even close to achieving it? Why did so many of the savages encountered in the New World continue to kill their neighbors without a qualm, even if they didn't eat them? And why do so many groups of people resort to the same behavior today—as was evidenced in the last decade in the Balkans?

This was the question that drove Gobineau to take up a position that his good friend and admirer Alexis de Tocqueville would repeatedly try to get him to abandon, but in vain. After exhibiting the unique value, and rarity, of tolerance, Gobineau goes on to explain it as the special inheritance of certain races. Some races were doomed to remain incapable of producing people who could mix sociably with others, while the superior race did produce such people. Gobineau thought this fact explained the rise and fall of civilizations. They are created by superior races that were born tolerant.

REASON AND RACISM

Why race?

Gobineau thought that this was the only way to explain why European cultures had produced the kinds of societies they had—ones in which the four qualities of civilization were in fact exemplified to a very high degree, though by no means perfectly. Of course it is easy to point out those aspects of European societies that were unenlightened, but it is idle to try to pretend that the audience that enjoyed the plays of Marivaux was not more civilized than the savages who feasted on their neighbors. I often suspect that the reason many Westerners who should know better produce so much cant in defense of savages is because they are sincerely, but quite falsely, convinced that any acknowledgment of Western superiority vis-à-vis the rest of the world must be predicated on some form of racism. If we are better than they, it can only be due to something in our genes or in our blood.

Their faulty logic goes like this: If European nations, circa 1500 or 1700, were more civilized than South American natives, it must be because the inhabitants of the former were racially superior to the latter. Therefore, to deny the conclusion, deny the premise.

But the premise is correct. The citizens of sixteenth-century Nürnberg *were* more civilized than the Brazilian tribe of cannibals. The truth of the premise, however, by no means implies the truth of the conclusion, as we can see the moment we go back and look at Gobineau's reasoning, for there we will discover an astonishingly naive and unsophisticated argument that is, in fact, the linchpin of his entire argument for racism—and indeed for much racist thinking ever since.

His reasoning goes like this: What if all men were equal? What kind of world would it be? Gobineau responds:

> If the human races were equal, the course of history would form
> an affecting, glorious and magnificent picture. The races would all
> have been equally intelligent, with a keen eye for their true inter-

ests and the same aptitude for conquest and domination. Early in the world's history, they would have gladdened the face of the earth with a crowd of civilizations, all flourishing at the same time, and all exactly alike . . . Mankind, at one with itself, would have nobly walked the earth, rich in understanding, and founding everywhere societies resembling each other.

Can Gobineau be serious? If men were equal, would this really imply that all their societies would be exactly alike? If four people all have IQs of 120, will they all want to live in societies that are "all exactly alike"? Would the case be different if they were all 140s or 87s?

The key to Gobineau's argument is that some people overcome the biological barrier imposed by kinship thanks to the fact that they are inherently more reasonable and tolerant than others. Once you buy into this proposition, logic inevitably leads you to conclude that civilization was the achievement of some specially endowed race of men. Kidnap a Westerner's newborn baby and leave him alone on a desert island, and he will invariably grow up to be a gentleman.

At one time it was actually believed that a newborn baby, if left to his own devices and without any adult companionship, would grow up to speak a language, though there was debate about what this language might be: some argued Hebrew, since this was clearly the language of Adam and Eve, others ancient Greek, since it was clearly the most logical language.

And yet the claim that a child would spontaneously begin to speak Greek is a modest one compared to the claim that the children of a certain race, if left to themselves, would not only begin by re-creating a previously unknown language but would create an entire civilization, with its elaborate codes and slowly evolved customs. Yet this absurdity is what the myth of certain "naturally" civilized races asks us to believe.

None of this follows if we adopt a much more realistic scenario, one in which civilization—along with reason and tolerance—does not emerge by spontaneous generation but rather comes into the world in the same way that human beings do, screaming and kicking. In the view I am proposing, no one was born civilized, and no one becomes civilized as the result of the decision to be civilized. Rather civilization occurred—in those few cases when it did occur—as the result of an utterly improbable chain of events, so improbable that we are forced to ask not why it did not happen more often but, Why did it happen at all?

THE AMBIGUOUS LEGACY OF SPARTA

In the memoirs that she composed while awaiting her execution during the Jacobin Reign of Terror, the Girondist leader Madame Roland tells us that as a girl she used to weep because she had not been born a Spartan. Nor was this sentiment at all unusual for the time: it was shared, for example, by the very men who were shortly to lead her to the guillotine, all of whom, like Madame Roland herself, had derived this passionate enthusiasm from the reading of Plutarch.

Nearly a half century earlier, Jean-Jacques Rousseau had commenced his brilliant career with his first discourse, "On the Progress of Arts and Science," in which he had written the following tribute: "Can it be forgotten that, in the very heart of Greece, there arose a city as famous for the happy ignorance of its inhabitants, as for the wisdom of its laws: a republic of demigods rather than of men, so greatly superior their virtues seemed to those of mere humanity? Sparta, eternal proof of the vanity of science."

Such sentiments are no longer with us. Sparta, for us, is apt to be seen as the precursor of totalitarianism. The contrast between these two images of Sparta presents a puzzle that can only be solved if we are prepared to recognize that both of these views contain an element of truth.

In discussing Sparta I will limit myself entirely to what we absolutely know for sure, and this is largely what the Spartans thought about themselves and what other people thought about them at the time.

To begin with, the Spartans claimed that their institutions were the conscious and deliberate creation of a single man, the lawgiver named Lycurgus. Whether or not such a person actually existed matters less than the fact that he was believed to have existed, for this meant that the Spartans, unlike the bulk of the human race, believed that their community was the product of human reflection and deliberation and not the result of the eternal cycle of nature.

This belief had a profound effect on how the Spartans imagined themselves. For most other peoples, their own folkways were self-evident. How else could human beings behave? Hence whatever they did was the natural way to do it—so much so that such an idea could not even have been expressed by them, since it would have required a consciousness of the possibility that other ways of ordering their community might exist. But the Spartans never had any illusions on this count. They knew that their ways were not the ways of other people. Nor did they ever claim that their ways were natural, because they knew they weren't. Other people might go the way of nature, but the Spartans did as their law, or *nomos,* commanded them to do, and what it commanded was often radically opposed to everyone else's natural order.

This difference began at birth. As soon as he was born, the Spartan child was taken immediately to be inspected by the Elders, who would determine whether the baby would live or die. The parents had no say in the matter. At the age of seven, Plutarch tells us in his life of Lycurgus, the Spartan boys "were to be enrolled in certain companies and classes, where they all lived under the same order and discipline, doing their exercises and taking their play together." At the very commencement of the Spartan educational system, known as the *agôge,* the Spartan boy was no longer under the supervision or protection of his own biological family, but became identified with one of a number of small units of age cohorts, and this unit replaced family. The Spartans themselves called these units by the Greek word for a herd of oxen, and the term was appropriate, for the brutality of what the Spartan boy had to endure was legendary, though it was a matter of boast to the Spartans themselves. But not a boast in too many words, because, according to Plutarch, Spartan boys were flogged for each unnecessary word they used to express their meaning.

There were penalties for men who did not marry and who therefore failed to produce children for the state, but the Spartan idea of marriage was quite unlike our own or indeed that of any other society of the ancient world. This is Plutarch's account of a Spartan wedding night:

> In their marriages, the husband carried off his bride by a sort of force [i.e., a make-believe rape]; nor were their brides ever small and of tender years, but in their full bloom and ripeness. After this, she who superintended the wedding comes and clips the hair of the bride close around her head, dresses her up in man's clothes, and leaves her upon a mattress in the dark; afterwards the bridegroom, in his everyday clothes, sober and composed, as having supped at the common table, and, entering privately into the room where his bride lies, unties her virgin zone, and takes her to himself; and after staying some time together, he returns composedly to his own apartment, to sleep as usual with the other young men. And so he

continues to do, spending his days, and, indeed, his nights, with them, visiting his bride in fear and shame. . . . In this manner they lived a long time, insomuch that they sometimes had children by their wives before ever they saw their faces by daylight. (*The Lives of the Noble Grecians and Romans*, trans. by John Dryden and rev. by Arthur Hough Clough [New York: Modern Library, 1932])

Yet the Spartans insisted that they did not engage in homosexual conduct. Everyone else in Greece scoffed at their claim, including Plato, who in his last work, *The Laws,* makes it clear that he believes that the Spartans practiced pederasty, not individually but collectively—a practice that he condemns in the strongest terms. Since Plato intensely admired the Spartan system in general, it is difficult to believe that he would have made this accusation without good reason.

Finally, the Spartans did something that no other Greek city-state had done: they enslaved their neighbors. Indeed, part of a Spartan boy's training was the chance to participate in sneak attacks on innocent and unsuspecting helots, usually those who had shown promise of leadership ability, killing them in the middle of the night.

Plutarch, in summarizing Lycurgus's achievement, writes: "To conclude, he bred up his citizens in such a way that they neither would nor could live by themselves; they were to make themselves one with the public good, and, clustering like bees around their commander, be by their zeal and public spirit carried all but out of themselves, and devoted wholly to their country."

To our ears this has the authentic ring of totalitarianism—the complete suppression of the individual; it forces us to wonder what on earth anyone could have ever found to admire in such a system.

But the above account has left out three facts about Sparta that, in the eyes of its many admirers, justified even the most bizarre of its many bizarre institutions. For a period lasting roughly from the eighth century B.C. to the third century B.C., Sparta was never conquered by an enemy, was never embroiled in a civil war, and was never ruled by a tyrant—three feats that no other society has been able to claim for so long a period, including our own.

It is strange, and almost paradoxical to assert it, but Sparta was the place where men first cured themselves of their addiction to lethal violence *within* their own community. The Spartans may have been hell on earth for their neighbors, but they did not kill each other. Their sense of loyalty to their own city-state transcended and trumped all other types of affiliation—kinship, class, party. No one else in the ancient world managed to pull off this trick. The Athenians, with whom we prefer to affiliate ourselves, did not, nor did any of the other societies whose cultural and artistic achievements were infinitely greater than the Spartans'.

But where, we ask, is the individual in all of this? For this is our overwhelming objection to the Spartan system—that it provides no place for our own concept of the individual.

Obviously there is a point to this objection: no one, for example, could possibly wish to revive such a system in the modern world. But what this objection overlooks is the fact that in the world of which Sparta was a part, there simply was no concept of the individual as we know it. It had not been discovered as a possibility yet.

This sounds strange to us, because we tend to confuse the fact that people are born as unique and separate biological entities with the fact that some people also happen to *imagine* themselves as unique and separate metaphysical entities—entities that we call the individual. We often overlook the fact that in order to imagine ourselves as unique and separate beings—with unique and separate interests, passions, hobbies, agendas, destinies—we must have been brought up imagining ourselves this way.

But this is not the way that anyone has ever brought up their children outside the West, and the modern West at that. All the rest of mankind insists that their children be brought up to imagine themselves as part of a family, whether in the small kinship circle of Brazilian Indians or the more elaborate kinship structure of more complex societies. They are trained to see themselves fitting into a particular slot, the most extreme example of which is the Hindu caste system, where this slot is fixed and permanent, part of the eternal order of things.

We in the West do not think this way. Why?

THE ANSWER TO this question has great importance for our world today, because much of the rest of the human race is still governed almost exclusively by the ethos of the family, whereas the West has long since transcended it. Yet it is not at all clear how the West did this.

For us it seems natural to judge individuals as individuals, without inquiring into the identity of their family, so much so that if asked to name the tribe with which our closest friends are affiliated, we would draw a complete blank. We could, of course, easily name all sorts of other affiliations that they might have—for example, the softball team they played on, their bowling league, the corporation they worked for, the church they attended, the civic clubs they belonged to, the political parties they volunteered for.

In the West, and nowhere more than in America, the individual is caught not in a web of kinship affiliations but in a web of team affiliations. The chasm between these two systems of affiliation is profound.

What seems perverse to us are those societies in which the ties of kinship trump all other forms of group loyalty, often to the point that it is virtually impossible for there to be any other kind of group loyalty than loyalty to the family. We insist that all men are born individuals, free to join whatever associations they wish to join, or equally free not to. Indeed, we often feel that this is just the way things are and that human beings if left to themselves would naturally produce the kind of individualistic society that we have produced.

This is why, in the West, we instinctively feel that it is tribalism that needs an explanation. We ask ourselves in puzzlement, What makes people behave like that? But the real question we must ask ourselves is: What makes us the way we are? For the tribal way is the way that comes naturally to the human race; it is simply our own penchant for forgetfulness that keeps us from realizing this fact.

This is why the case of Sparta is so critical, for it was here, for the first time, that the family was defeated. Spartan men grew up thinking of themselves not as members of a biological family but as citizens of Sparta, and this achievement changed the world. We can, of course, choose to look at this breakthrough negatively, as the failure to discover the individual as we know him. But such an approach would be like criticizing the inventor of the wheel for not having invented the vulcanized tire; the wheel had to come first. Before the individual could make his appearance, he first had to be liberated from the family.

The individual can only begin to emerge when he has the possibility of deciding with whom he wishes to affiliate himself. If all of his affiliations have been predetermined for him by the accident of his birth, then he will have no choice but to live and to die a prisoner of his system.

To put this in a way that makes it easier for us to understand, consider the perplexities facing the United States in its attempt to bring liberal democracy to Iraq. Here the very first problem is to somehow get the people of these societies to look upon themselves as bound by a common loyalty that is superior to their traditional loyalty to their tribe or sect. Yet our problem is a piece of cake compared to that faced by the first people who tried to transcend the biological barrier of tribal loyalties, since obviously the Iraqis already have a working model of what a society looks like that has in fact transcended this boundary—ours, and indeed the West, for centuries. The early Spartans had no such model to appeal to. No society before them had managed to overcome this seemingly insuperable obstacle; a glance at those parts of the world that did not derive their patterns of political culture from the Greeks shows that no other society ever came close to making this quantum leap.

If we are struggling to embody the values of liberal civilization in Iraq—by which is simply meant making Iraqis less addicted to the use of violence within their own national community—then we can only dimly imagine what a struggle must have faced the first people who set out to perform this miracle.

How do you divert men from feeling their primordial loyalty toward their own family to feeling primordial loyalty to the team?

The team is what Plutarch's translator John Dryden called "the commonwealth," the Greeks called the *polis*, the Roman *res publica*, and what we call the common good or general welfare. It is a target of loyalty that has nothing whatsoever to do with the traditional loyalty to one's family, tribe, and kin, and indeed, to be genuine, it must in fact trump all such loyalties.

But where does it come from?

6

THE BIRTH OF PATRIOTISM AND THE
HISTORIC ROLE OF THE UNITED STATES

T HE TEAM PRINCIPLE must not be understood as an abstract
ideal or an ideology but as a way of life, as an ethos, a kind of
doing rather than a style of thinking.

Intellectuals tend to forget that ethical ideals do not pop out of the human head but first manifest themselves in practice. Capitalism, for example,
did not come into being because one day everyone woke up and said, "Why
don't we switch from feudalism to capitalism," simply because the word *capitalism* could not possibly have any meaning before the practices that we
now think of as capitalism had already begun to emerge as a distinct social
phenomenon. Thus, when Adam Smith begins *The Wealth of Nations* with
his discussion of the division of labor and how much more efficiently men
can make pins by this method, he is not elaborating a vision that has come
to him in a dream; he is delineating the essential component of an actual
process that had evolved as a way of making more pins in the same amount
of time. The exigencies of modern education tend to make us overlook this
fact, and we imperceptibly fall into the strange way of thinking that sees
Adam Smith "inventing" capitalism, when in fact he simply noticed it. Noticed it very well, and profoundly, but it was already there to be noticed.

In this process of noticing and delineating, a new and almost magical effect occurred. By isolating the essential pattern, Smith was able to take what was originally only a factory for making pins and turn it into a conceptual model that could be employed to make not just pins but china or chairs or sailboats—in fact, virtually anything. Yet this abstract model—though amazingly useful—must never be confused with the original concrete behavior from which it has been abstracted. For in abstraction something important will always be left out.

For example, in analyzing the division of labor, Smith did not need to ask himself, "Why are these pin makers able to cooperate?" He was living in a world in which you could take it for granted that people, if you were willing to pay them money, would gladly do one small mindlessly repetitive task hour after hour. But would this idea have occurred to him if he had been living among cannibalistic tribes?

When the Spanish discoverers settled in the Caribbean lands in the early sixteenth century, their first thought was to put the native Indians to work. But the problem was they wouldn't work: even if you threatened them, they preferred either to run away or to die. Were they lazy? No, such a concept implies an acceptance of a standard that the Indians didn't have, because there was no earthly reason why they should have it. They had everything they needed—or could imagine—before the Spanish arrived. The Indians, in short, had a mode of existence that simply could not tolerate the kind of economic system that Smith saw functioning all around him; this meant that, as far as the tropical New World was concerned, capitalism was not an option.

In a world in which all human organization was a mode of the family, the principle of the team would have been in the same position as the principle of capitalism was in the New World: it would have been a form of daydreaming, assuming anyone had even been able to dream such a far-fetched fantasy. This is why any attempt to explain the fundamental institutions of Sparta by the military value that they may have proved to have *after* they came into existence is misguided. Men did not first see the value of the teamwork—even military teamwork—and then decide to make themselves into a team; rather the team needed already to be there in embryonic form, as an already existing behavior.

THERE ARE, as it turns out, only two different modes of loyalty that arise spontaneously. The first, of course, is the family. The second is the boys' gang.

The significance of the latter is normally overlooked, for the sound reason that, typically, the boys' gang is merely a passing phase, a brief and turbulent passage from the family of one's parents to the family in which one becomes a parent, so that the ethos of the gang is never permitted to play any fundamental role in determining the structure of the society in question: the family overwhelms the gang.

Furthermore, even if the gang can free itself from the family, for example, by the use of violence to impose its will, this too will be just a phase, for the family will always have the biological edge on the gang, for the simple reason that the boys' gang has no way of reproducing itself outside the biological family. Insofar as the gang member must marry and produce his own family, the overwhelming temptation to look after one's own kin will get the upper hand over loyalty to one's gang. Boys proverbially vow never to separate, and yet they almost invariably do, and always segregating themselves off into their own family.

This means that the eventual triumph of the family over the gang is unavoidable, unless the gang consciously decides to fight the family as an institution and to create powerful institutions that will deliberately act to restrict and subvert the family's enormous power. But how could this have come about? How could the gang continue to fight off the family not just for one generation but for centuries? Biology alone would seem to condemn such a project to the realm of make-believe.

Yet this is precisely what Sparta did. The male adolescent gang is the unifying principle behind all the otherwise bizarre aspects of Sparta's institutions and laws. Each of them was designed to institutionalize and domesticate the ethos of the boys' gang, to make it a permanent and self-reproducing social organism, one capable of existing not only for the first group of boys but for succeeding groups of boys generation after generation.

In fact, what was produced in Sparta was a community in which the anarchic testosterone energy of the adolescent gang was harnessed for the purposes of civilization, somewhat in the same way that an atomic reactor is able to harness the potentially catastrophic energy of a nuclear chain reaction. The system of Sparta was designed to keep the ruthlessness of the gang available to be used against its enemies, while controlling it in such a way that it would pose no danger to the society itself. The mechanism by which this was done was the invention of the team.

THE SPIRIT OF THE TEAM

It was Jacob Burckhardt who in his study of Greek culture stressed the centrality of the theme of agonistics—that is, of competitive struggle between males—and examined its ramifications through all areas of Greek life; like Hegel before him, Burckhardt traced the prominence of this cultural ideal back to the Greek glorification of male adolescence. Boys glory in competitive games, and team sports have been found in other cultures around the world, for example, among the Aztecs and the Seminoles.

The often lethal quality of such competition underscores how useful such training can be in preparation for the field of battle, and the Duke of Wellington's shrewd remark that the Battle of Waterloo was won on the playing fields of Eton is an aphorism concealing an entire philosophy of history.

In addition to being useful in the development of a community's military resources, adolescent agonistics provided something else of equal and, in the long run, even greater value: it was the prototype of a radically different way of achieving social cooperation or, more correctly, a way of achieving a radically different kind of cooperation—coordination rather than subordination.

Coordination is an utterly different, and far more challenging, process than subordination. In a hierarchical organization, a command is issued from the person at the top, and it is followed mechanically by the person underneath him, and so on down the chain of command. But in a team organization, each player can, and must, initiate his actions in response to an external challenge from the other team, and he can, and must, do this entirely on his own, without first obtaining permission from his superior, much less waiting for his command.

Compare two different armies, the first in which each soldier, facing a new threat, is unable to decide what action he should take and must therefore wait until he has received orders, and the second in which each soldier is able to decide what his action should be, whereupon his fellows will adjust their behavior in response to the action that their comrade has undertaken. Which one of these two systems of cooperation is easier to master?

In order to answer this question, you might wish to spend the afternoon watching a basketball game played by boys between the ages, say, of nine and ten. In the stands you will find very few people who are there to watch the games for their exciting sportsmanship. Almost all of them will be the parents or siblings of the boys, or friends who have accompanied them, and there is a profound reason for this. The boys, even at their best, play absolutely terrible basketball—so bad, indeed, that the thought must pass through the mind of anyone not related by blood to the participants, *Why on earth go through the pretense?*

Indeed, it is only after sitting through many hours of such "games" that it finally occurs to you that this is what human beings must go through if they are ever to master any activity that is characterized by that peculiar form of cooperation known as teamwork. We see this clearly when a child is learning to play the piano: no one expects a six-year-old to play Beethoven's *Hammerklavier Sonata,* and we understand that long before such a prospect comes into sight, the child must have spent untold hours of tedium mastering scales and all the other neighbor-annoying techniques indispensable for the production of anything eventually worth listening to. The child, we are well aware, must acquire all the manual skills requisite in accurately and effectively hitting the keys in the order and at the tempo demanded by the music.

Now, a child learning to play basketball must also acquire a repertoire of individual skills, but in addition to these he must also acquire an entirely different repertoire, the mutually collective or cooperative skills that are necessary for a set of boys to play together as a genuine team. He must learn when he is not to try to grab the ball because someone else on the team is in a better position; he must learn when to take initiative, and how to signal to his teammates that he wishes to do so; and while he is doing all of this, his teammates must also be mastering the same set of mutually collective skills, because in order to master the skills of the team, everyone on the team must have mastered them. Even one boy who is unable to coordinate his play with others can be fatal to the success of the team.

This is why the principle of blackballing—first used in Sparta—is found whenever the ethos of the team has emerged. Any member of the team has the right to reject any prospective candidate for membership on it. The soundness of this principle is self-evident. If two boys dislike each other that much, this rift creates the possibility of a breakdown in the mutual collectivity of the team and thus constitutes a threat to its wellbeing.

Though the principle of blackballing arose from the necessity of making teamwork work, its very logic resulted in a radically new form of social interaction: egalitarian self-government. When members of a team set about to resolve an issue or to come to a decision, each opinion or counsel offered by an individual member, or even by a faction, is subject to being scrutinized for any possible selfish motive that has influenced the individual member or faction to put it forward as a plan of action for the whole team. If such a motive is suspected, then the opinion or counsel is immediately seen as having been tainted.

For example, if you and I are members of a team, and we hear that another member is suggesting that we buy up a certain piece of land in order to build a temple to Artemis for the glory of our team, we will want to discover whether this member is suggesting this particular piece of land because he owns it and wants to profit from it. If he does, we will look upon his counsel with understandable suspicion. But since all the members know that this is the case, then it follows that they will themselves hesitate to put forward such an obviously self-interested idea, knowing full well that their deception is apt to be discovered by the other members of the team. The end result is that all the members of the team learn to judge both their own counsel and that offered by others by a new standard: Is it good for the team?

Here we find the origins of the concept of the common good, or public welfare, or *res publica* of the Romans. The common good could not be this or that particular person's idea of good but could only arise from consensus.

Rule by consensus was radically different from the kind of rule that mankind had previously experienced, that is to say, rule by the dominant member of a hierarchy. Rule by consensus was rule without hierarchy or oppression, but only if the members of the team had been able, to a high degree, to internalize the rules of fair play.

Indeed, the entire concept of fairness—as opposed to justice—arises out of the context of boys who are attempting to play together in a way that deliberately minimizes the potential for conflict. Taking turns, for example, is a universal principle of play, and it is natural that it is also the prototype of all notions of fair play. This is because taking turns is a solution that can be accepted by all the members of a team.

Take, for example, the famous Boy Scout rule for dividing up a candy bar fairly. The first boy cuts the candy bar, and the second one chooses which piece he prefers. This is an algorithm that can be applied in all sorts of ingenious forms, but the underlying principle that it embodies is the idea that fair is what all parties regard as fair: consensual fairness, as opposed to justice.

Justice is what occurs when two boys go to a third party and ask this party to decide for them. Fairness is what happens whenever the two boys are able to resolve their differences on their own, by compromise or by a device like the candy bar rule.

It is clearly the practice of fairness that provided the key to Sparta's greatest achievement: the Spartans were the first people to achieve autonomy. Not individual autonomy, as we understand it, but community autonomy, which meant a community guided by its own law—*autos nomos.*

This is what gives such great poignancy to Simonides' famous epitaph to the three hundred Spartans who died at the Battle of Thermopylae:

Go tell the Spartans, oh passer-by.
That here, obeying their laws, we lie.

By dying in obedience to the laws of Sparta, they were dying in obedience to their own laws. Thus the overwhelming impact of their boast: they have accepted their fate as the joint will of both themselves and of their community. They had not, in other words, fought as the Persian slaves had fought, in obedience to the lust for glory of a single man, but for an *ideal.*

The team is an ideal in two senses. It does not have a real existence that you can point to. That is, you can point to a ruling tyrant, and you can point to the members of an oligarchy, but what you cannot point to is the team, for the membership of the team will change over time and often in the course of a single day's battle. The Spartan team had a corporate permanence, and this is one of the first of the great gifts that Sparta left the world: the idea that institutions did not depend on the particular individuals that happened to make them up at any particular time, but that their composition could change—and change completely—without the essential nature of the team changing in the least.

In hoplite tactics, an individual may come to replace a soldier who has died in the previous battle, and yet the team is the same. Even if all the original soldiers are dead, so long as the new ones have gone through the same training, they too will constitute the very same team—a fact that is clear from the intensity with which military units zealously guard and pass on their own proud traditions, whose original creators have often died centuries before.

Spartans deliberately worked to make themselves individually fungible—interchangeable—and this is why they died not for personal glory or honor but from a sense of duty.

THE EMERGENCE OF A NEW KIND OF FREEDOM

Paradoxically enough, the Spartans, by being slaves to duty, achieved a radically new form of freedom, and one that was copied by the other Greek city-states, with varying degrees of success. This is, in fact, precisely the point that Hegel made in his famous division of human history into three distinct periods, each of which represents a stage in the evolution of human freedom.

Between the first stage, represented by the Oriental World in which only *one* was free, the despot, and all the others were his slaves, and the third stage, Protestant Europe, in which all were free, fell the second stage—the stage that the Greeks and the Greeks alone managed to achieve and which Hegel characterized as a world in which *some* were free, while others continued to be their slaves.

There is, in Hegel's philosophy, a special term for what transforms a collection of isolated individuals into teammates; it is *Sittlichkeit*. We will discard the German and keep the sense; we will call it *team spirit*. Those who do not like this term because it reminds them of pep rallies in high school are in fact responding to the underlying concept precisely as they should, for team spirit always requires a high degree of mindless and mechanical conformity, a going along just for the sake of going along, a willingness to cooperate for the sake of cooperation.

The sense in which *some* were free, at the Greek stage of history, is the sense in which a team of men, not just a group of individuals, is free. Their freedom was in fact a product of their status as a team, and it consisted of the freedom of the team to set its own course and to decide its own fate and not to be subject to the will of just a single individual. Hence, for us, Hegel's schema needs to be rewritten in order to underscore this distinction: in the Greek world, *the team was free*.

* * *

WHEN WE THINK we are free, we think of ourselves as free to do what we individually want; this is not at all how the members of the Greek team thought of their freedom, which was their freedom to act collectively, to get their own way as a team, a freedom that often required them to renounce and deny their own personal impulses—the very locus of our notion of personal freedom.

The team is a different way of imagining human relationships, and one that cannot be reduced to either the isolated individual or the hierarchical structure built into the very biology of kinship and tribal ordering. No family can be a team, because no family can be made up of equals. Age, if not gender, imposes a rank that cannot be altered, a position of superior and inferior that is hardwired into every form of family relationship— even that of identical twins, ever mindful of who came into the world first.

The very possibility of equality had to wait until the team came into the world; before its arrival, they were no pictures by which social equality could even be imagined. Everyone who entered the world fell into his own slot in a human taxonomic system, so that everyone's respective rank could be precisely determined in advance of their birth.

The coming of the first team changed all of this. Men could now look at a large number of their fellow human beings and think, "We are all equal. None takes precedence over the other." And they could live and eat and defend their community in the same spirit, which explains why Hegel considered the emergence of such an ideal into human consciousness as the pivotal event in the history of human freedom. The hardest step of all is the step from one to some. From some to all is, comparatively, a piece of cake.

HOW DID THE Spartans succeed in taking this step? Their secret, once seen, is simplicity itself: Model your entire society on a boys' gang. In Sparta, through some unknown set of circumstances, an entire community was organized as if it were one huge, immortal boys' gang. Every aspect of human biology worked against them—just as in the rest of the world it worked for the family. But the Spartan system, like the hedgehog in the famous poem by Archilochus of Paros, knew one great trick in comparison with which the multitude of tricks mastered by other societies counted for little.

Sparta was unsurpassed, and unsurpassable, as a military power. And those who wished to go toe to toe with it simply had to adopt the methods of the Spartans if they hoped to have a fighting chance against them.

Think of the brutality and conformity of the Spartan *agôge* as if it had been a secret weapon, equivalent to something like the nuclear bomb, and you can get some sense of the radical innovation that it had brought about in the world. In a world where all military might was directly proportionate to the number of physically strong and agile young men you could put on a field of battle, the ability to take the same number of these young men and make them work as a team created a multiplier effect whose full impact would be demonstrated in Sparta's unsurpassed military record.

After the Spartans had shown that the team was possible, they next proved that it was necessary, for if you could not achieve the same degree of coordination, you ran the risk of becoming helots, if not to the Spartans, then to those who had succeeded in imitating the Spartans.

This was a genie that, once released, changed everything that it came into contact with. If it can be called a meme, it was a supermeme that changed, sometimes radically, sometimes subtly, every other meme that it knocked up against. The maxim of this meme, if memes have maxims, was: To build up the team, you must break down the family. To break down the family, you had to encourage males to think of themselves as separate and apart from the family, as capable of managing completely by themselves—the fantasy of every boys' gang.

Precisely because this world was so unreal, and so artificial, it had to be governed by new rules and regulations—like the rules of the boys' clubhouse. Hence the emphasis of the team ethos on the concept of law, or *nomos,* understood as rules that we have made by ourselves for ourselves, not immemorial customs whose reasons have long since been forgotten. This explains the great outpouring of Greek creativity: they had no choice. Having thrown away the biologically determined model of the family, they were compelled to improvise, to invent, and to experiment.

Athens, for example, had a founding legend that said its first citizens had sprung out of the earth. This fantasy permitted the Athenians to imagine themselves as their own creations: to see themselves starting a new world from scratch, without either the help or hindrance of tribal traditions.

But was it a fantasy? Did the Greeks really start off as regular families, with the mother and father living together and having children; did one day the husband decide to evict his wife, in order to put his adolescent son in her place?

No. It is generally assumed that the cult of pederasty was brought by the Dorians—the group from whom Spartans claimed descent. But what made the Dorians depart so radically from the norm? A common way of answering this question is to argue that their homosexuality was situational: it was part of the cult of the warrior. This makes some sense, since we know that pederasty has been practiced by warrior groups in various historical settings. Yet this still doesn't solve the mystery of Sparta. For, once again, even if its peculiar institutions started this way, why didn't they disappear the moment the warrior gang settled down in one spot? Why didn't Spartan men want to go back to raising families and living with their wives, once they had shed their migratory habits? And what on earth would persuade them to go on living in the military barracks not just for a generation but for six or seven centuries?

Nothing like this ever happened outside of Sparta. Shaka Zulu employed the barracks system, as did others, but no one managed to make it the fundamental institution of an entire society for well over half a millennium.

But it is not only what Sparta managed to do for itself that is so striking. Thucydides, in *The Peloponnesian War,* says that in addition to freeing Athens from tyranny, "the Spartans put down tyranny in the rest of Greece, most of which had been governed by tyrants for much longer than Athens." The Spartans must therefore get the credit for the entire Greek breakthrough from the family to the team, because the rule of the tyrant always ends in the eventual return of the family. Thucydides tells us that "in the Hellenic states that were governed by tyrants, the tyrant's first thought was always for himself, for his own personal safety, and for the greatness of his own family. Consequently security was the chief political principle in these governments, and no great action ever came out of them—nothing, in fact, that went beyond their immediate local interests."

If this is true, then the entire Greek miracle—and with it all the unique characteristics of the West—can be traced back to the Spartan decision to go to war against the family and to drive it out by whatever means were necessary. Sparta, in short, domesticated the gang and turned it into the team. And the odds against this happening even once are astounding—a fact that we must always remember whenever we think about the uniqueness not only of the Greeks but of the West.

Ever since the Spartans, the West has refused to permit the family to rule the roost. Everywhere, and in every way, the West has succeeded in putting the team above the family—and often by quite violent revolutions.

The Romans were taught that *patria* came before family. Each generation of their young learned how Brutus the Elder had unhesitatingly ordered the execution of his two sons when it was discovered that they were prepared to turn the Roman team into a tyranny.

The Christian Church came into the world teaching that the family was about to be rendered extinct due to the immediate coming of the Kingdom of God—a Kingdom that, Saint Paul takes pains to remind us, does not recognize the bonds of the family, including marriage. Even after the initial period of the Church, this same antifamily impetus would reappear in the ideals of chastity and celibacy—ideals every bit as difficult for us to comprehend sympathetically as Spartan pederasty.

Finally, the modern corporation would create entirely new objects of loyalty in which the family came to play less and less of a role. Indeed, the gradual elimination of the family business in favor of the corporate team had the same world-historical impact that the elimination of the family army in favor of the team army had, for it permitted a vastly larger scale of organization and thus underlaid the possibility of the globalization of capitalism.

This, in fact, was one of the points of disagreement between Marx and defenders of classical capitalism like the nineteenth-century English economist Alfred Marshall. *Contra* Marx, who believed that capitalism would collapse because of its inevitable tendency to form monopolies, Marshall argued that the business corporation had an inherent life cycle that was organically rooted in the logic of the family.

For Marshall, the life cycle of a company followed this pattern: First, the company is founded by a risk-taking adventurer and entrepreneur; second, it is passed on to his son, who does not need to take risks but merely needs to uphold the position obtained by his father; and third, it finally descends to the original founder's grandson, who, having been raised without a worry about money, pays no attention to it and slowly permits the company to flounder thanks to his own extravagance and mismanagement.

What is intriguing about the dispute between Marshall and Marx is that it parallels the dispute between those who view history as an organic and thus inescapable cycle—such as Giambattista Vico, Oswald Spengler, Arnold Toynbee, and Samuel Huntington—and those who see the possibility of an onward and upward march of progress, such as Hegel and Marx.

It was the early twentieth-century Italian thinker Gaetano Mosca who observed, *contra* Spengler, that there was absolutely no reason to suppose that human *societies* had to follow the organic cycle of the human *individual,* and indeed, it is hard to imagine a better refutation of this analogy than the immortality of the modern business corporation, with its capacity to draw on fresh new blood in order to revitalize itself.

The ability to tap into new human resources will prove to be one of the preeminent reasons for the triumph of the team over the family, for the team, as long as it remains a team, will be able to coopt and absorb into it those who were previously outsiders. Nowhere is this clearer than in the prospective fate of a hardworking and ambitious employee in a family business and the fate of the same man in a modern corporation. In the family business, if he is unrelated to the boss, his only real chance of success is to marry the boss's daughter; in the team corporation, he may obtain the same end by dedication and hard work.

The team principle permits a way of breaking the inescapable organic life cycle of rise and decline, and thus it provides a realistic basis for envisioning a progressive future for mankind. Yet this possibility by no means should be taken as a refutation of the organic cycle view of history, because from our perspective, we can clearly see that this view contains a large measure of truth. We can even go so far as to say that this pessimistic view of history *should* be true, considering the odds against any society's breaking through what Walter Bagehot called "the cake of custom" imposed by the family principle.

The cycle, family despot–gang–tyrant–family despot, is in fact the normal cycle of human history, and it is this observation that provides the irrefutable foundation of all the pessimistic theories of man's fate. But in addition to this cycle, there is another one, one that goes family–gang–team. It is this pattern that may properly be said to commence history, since it is the only one that permits human beings to escape from the inevitable cycle that begins with the family and returns to it.

Yet the very thing that permits mankind to escape from this cycle condemns him to an ever escalating competition to see who can apply the team principle to master larger and larger masses of human populations. For it is the team principle alone that permits human beings to feel objects of loyalty ample enough to be embraced by literally millions of men and women, far beyond the scope of anything that could be achieved by the family.

Perhaps the best way to think of the impact that the team form of organization had on the world is to think in terms of a secret weapon that, once it had been discovered by one society, had to be copied at all costs by those who did not want to fall prey to it.

THE ORGANIZATIONAL ARMS RACE

This is what Rousseau is talking about when he says in *The Origin of Inequality,* "It is easy to see how the establishment of one [united and organized] community made that of all the rest necessary, and, how in order to make headway against united forces, the rest of mankind had to unite in turn." In other words, the first community that made the breakthrough that permitted it to organize its manpower on the model of the team left other communities no choice but to follow suit, if they wished to survive—a process that we saw happening in ancient Greece in response to the threat of Sparta.

When we think of "the arms race," we are apt to think exclusively in terms of technological innovations: the crossbow, the catapult, Lord Fisher's *Dreadnought,* the tank, the German V-1 and V-2 missiles, jet aircraft, the atomic bomb, the hydrogen bomb, Star Wars. But what we miss in this picture is the other race—the one that involves breakthroughs and competition not in the construction of new things but in the construction of new ways to organize human beings.

As we have seen, the Spartans did not gain power by inventing some new piece of military hardware; instead they innovated a new way of making men cooperate. This paid off not only in superior military prowess but also in the social cohesion that was obtained through the innovation of the team model. This kind of innovation, however, is radically different from the invention of a new piece of equipment, for it is obviously going to require sweeping and quite drastic changes in any social system that adopts it. A new design for a sword or a battleship or a bomb may be copied from your enemy without a major overhaul of your own social system, but this will not be the case when your enemy's innovation consists in a totally different form of social organization.

THREE CASES

During the seventeenth and eighteenth centuries, the Kingdom of Poland maintained a peculiar system of political organization, one in which no effort was spared to keep a single man from gathering to himself too much power. It was the period of the *liberum veto,* the notorious device by which any single member of the Polish parliament, the Sejm, was allowed to annul any piece of proposed legislation by simply crying *Nie pozwalam!* I will not allow it. This, indeed, was libertarianism with a vengeance—provided of course that you were one of Poland's enormous class of nobles and not a peasant or serf.

What is astonishing about this peculiar institution is that, as Norman Davis points out in *God's Playground,* it worked for so long. Indeed, for a period of over two centuries the Kingdom of Poland actually succeeded in ruling itself by methods that, by our standard, would appear to guarantee political suicide. Yet, in its own curious way, it provided the right political solution to the multitude of problems posed by the unique combination of factors that constituted Polish society—factors psychological, cultural, and historical.

Had Poland been an island in the middle of the vast Pacific, this political solution might well have persisted indefinitely. The problem was that all around Poland, during the course of the seventeenth and eighteenth centuries, its neighboring societies were moving, at immense human costs, from feudal aristocracies—like Poland's—to highly centralized autocratic nation-states, in which the entire design of the political system was founded on the principle of ruthlessly efficient executive action.

This was the kind of organizational analogue to the arms race that I am referring to, and it was this challenge that the Polish Sejm faced and to which it failed abysmally to respond. Its failure led to the series of partitions at the end of the eighteenth century by which Poland was literally dismantled by its hostile neighbors until nothing whatsoever was left of the original kingdom except the bitter memory of a glorious past. To put it in terms of our arms race metaphor, Poland was not able to alter its internal social and political structure enough to permit it to compete against those absolute states that had achieved the organizational break-through that gave them the power to act decisively.

A similar fate would await the American Confederacy in the next century. Born out of the belief that each state had the right to decide for itself what was in its own best interest, the central government of the Confederacy lacked the power to enforce coordinated action on the individual states that composed it. Its constitution, like the early Articles of Confederation that had preceded the United States Constitution, and like the constitution of Poland, was too wary of giving power into the hands of a single man. Hence, when challenged by the far more cohesively organized North, the Confederacy succumbed, like Poland, to the judgment of history.

The German poet Johann Wolfgang von Goethe was an eyewitness at the commencement of yet another organizational arms race. He was traveling, merely as an observer, with a number of German officers near the start of what became known as the French Revolutionary Wars. The night following an indecisive day of the battle—in which the French soldiers merely succeeded in holding their ground—Goethe was sitting around the campfire with his friends, the German officers, all of whom were in a blue funk. To break up the awkward silence, Goethe suddenly declared to the officers around him, "Today is a day that will go down in world history; and you will be able to say, 'You were there.'" This verdict would be confirmed by Sir Edward Shepherd Creasy in his classic book *Fifteen Decisive Battles of the World,* where he decided to include in his list the unimpressive skirmish that occurred that day in the northeast corner of France and that is now known to us as the Battle of Valmy.

What would make a mere skirmish an event of world-historical importance? And why were the officers sitting around the campfire in stunned silence, if their enemy had done nothing more than hold its ground against them?

The answer to these questions lies in the composition of the two armies that had clashed that day. The Germans and their allies were a professional army, made up entirely of career officers and career soldiers—men whose entire life was dedicated to mastering the craft of warfare. The French army was profoundly different. It was, as Creasy tells us, composed of merchants, cooks, lawyers, artisans, apprentices, all dressed in the clothes that they wore in their civilian life. Hence the shock that such a rabble had held its ground at all—an army of an odd lot of amateurs holding at bay an army of professionals. What was it about the nature of this encounter that made Goethe think of it as a decisive event in world history?

The answer to this question lies in the psychological motivation of those who were fighting for France. They were average people, untrained in military matters, who were nevertheless willing to risk their own lives in defense of their country, even against professional soldiers. They were not fighting because they were paid to do so, or for the honor of their professional caste, or because they had bayonets pointed at their own backs. They were fighting because they had volunteered to fight.

What Goethe saw was that, from now on, a society that was able to generate this kind of spontaneous enthusiasm would have the military edge over a society that was not. The French principle of civilians' flocking to defend their country in its hour of need, the *levée en masse,* could put staggeringly huge numbers of men onto the field of battle—men all of whom were prepared to kill and to be killed. This fact would have to be taken into account by any society that could not pull off this same trick.

Seen in terms of our arms race analogy, the *levée en masse* was a technological breakthrough far exceeding in significance the invention of a new piece of military hardware, but the technology in question was the technique of *political* organization. For only societies that were prepared to adopt the same form of political organization as Revolutionary France would be able to count on the *levée en masse* in times of war; states that could not, or would not, adopt this form would be forced to suffer the consequences, just as Poland was forced to suffer the consequences of its refusal to adopt the principle of the absolute state.

All the legitimate crowned heads in Europe were horrified. To fight against such men, you would need such men. But to get them, you would have to turn your own society upside down. The dynastic principle, so recently established, would have to be retired, and something new would need to take its place.

The Frenchmen at Valmy *imagined* themselves not as fighting for someone else but for themselves. They saw themselves as risking death for their republic, and this made all the difference. They called themselves "citizens" and they imagined themselves as citizens, and this had precisely the kind of transformative effect on their conduct that any fantasy ideology will have on those who are caught up in it. These men saw themselves as Roman citizens fighting in the defense of their *patria.* Their war cry was *"La patrie en danger!"* and in rallying to it each saw himself, in his mind's eye, as a new Cincinnatus abandoning his humble life to save his country.

This is what the poet in Goethe saw. He saw the world through the imagination of this ragtag crew of Frenchmen, and he grasped the way they saw themselves. His own uncanny capacity for empathetic identification allowed him to penetrate to a truth hidden from the German officers who had seen their enemy only externally and thus superficially.

Seen from within, these men *were* new Romans, men once again willing to die for the team, the team being identified not as their own particular caste or class, but as the entire social order. The motto of the French Revolution, Liberty, Fraternity, Equality, is the purest expression of the principle of the team, just as the overturned Bourbon dynasty had become the purest expression of the principle of family and hierarchy.

But once again, as we saw in the aftermath of World War I, the French Revolutionary Wars released a genie from its bottle that refused to be coaxed back inside. Just as the Great War would demonstrate the possibility of catastrophic warfare, so too the armies of the French Revolution and the armies of Napoleon demonstrated the immense power that was waiting for anyone who had the will and the genius to call it forth—the power of turning whole populations into armies. The power, in short, of fighting a total war.

THE ADVENT OF THE ERA OF TOTAL WAR

What was the secret by which you could make your ordinary civilian population willing to fight in a total war? This had always been one of the most serious problems facing any community; most people simply do not like the idea of dying, even for a good cause. In fact, it is this fear of death upon which Thomas Hobbes constructed his shockingly fragile Leviathan, fragile because not all men fear death, and when the enemy produces lots of men who no longer fear death, the Leviathan is doomed.

Making even a small team fearless in this way required the breakthrough made by Sparta. But a whole country—how could that be possible? The reason it didn't seem possible before is that it wasn't possible before—that is, until the French Revolution, whose ultimate significance is that it showed that this could be done and how to do it.

The technique involves three stages:

First, you must convince the population of your country that those who claim legitimate power are not justified in doing so. It makes no difference, of course, what principle this legitimacy may be founded on. Both the divine right of kings and parliamentary democracy could be, and were, equally dismissed as ideological camouflage by those who employed this technique.

Second, you must provide a new dispensation of enthusiasm. You have to find a source of psychological motivation that generates the exact same kind of loyalty and dedication that was displayed by the French soldiers at Valmy.

Third, you have to organize a team around you that is passionately devoted to the pursuit of its own power. All for one, and one for all, and the only requirement for admission onto the team is the willingness to sacrifice everything else to its interests. This, after all, was the hallmark of the Fascist, the Nazi, and the Communist parties: loyalty to them canceled out loyalties to anyone or anything else. The party member will betray his own family if required to do so, and in that, he is the genuine descendent of Sparta.

IN THE AFTERMATH of World War I, the first step of this process was rendered easy in those countries where the legitimate order had already crumbled—Imperial Russia, Imperial Germany, the Austro-Hungarian Empire, and the Ottoman Empire. Here the battle against legitimacy had already been accomplished. By "legitimacy" in this context, I mean simply the belief on the part of a population that those who presently have power are the people who should have power; again, it is of no importance by what political ideology this psychological attachment is justified. Legitimacy in this sense was destroyed by the Great War, and the only way that this kind of legitimacy can be reproduced is the slow organic process by which all habits and customs become entrenched in our nervous system.

Thus, in the period after World War I, those societies that had lost their moorings in the old legitimacy and had not had time to develop a new sense of legitimacy were prime targets for the seizure of power by dedicated gangs who had divined a way of eliciting mass enthusiasm for their project.

In every case, as seen earlier, the groups that gained power during this period did so by the deliberate exploitation of a strategy of ruthlessness. They behaved ruthlessly, in other words, not just to get their way, but in order to become supermen, to whom the conventions of middle-class and ordinary people meant nothing. Ruthlessness was not merely instrumental but an end in itself, and those who had the will to be ruthless were the natural masters of those who didn't—the point of connection between Hitler's admiration for Nietzsche and the latter's admiration for the ancient Greeks. These new forms of ruthlessness, however, differed radically from the ancient ones, because the new ones had at their disposal the weapon of total war.

This returns us to the point at which liberal internationalism broke down. It did not have the resources to cope with an enemy, such as Hitler, who was prepared to threaten total war and whose reputation for ruthlessness made such a threat all too real. Once such an enemy came on the scene, then the whole premise of liberal internationalism fell apart.

How do you deter someone who is willing to commit his own nation to total war?

The League of Nations made sense so long as the world was made up of rational economic actors, all of whom had been disarmed to the point where it was possible to deter their aggression effectively without any one nation's committing too much of its time, money, or manpower. But if the enemy had massive military forces and reserves, who would be willing to take him on, especially if the result was guaranteed to be a total war like the one Europe had just endured?

There is one way of defending against an enemy who is prepared to use total war as a deliberate strategy *of* ruthlessness, and that is to have a nation whose military strength is equal or greater that is willing to use total war as a deliberate strategy *against* ruthlessness.

This was to become the secret of the Pax Americana. America would be willing to use its entire resources, if necessary—indeed, even to suffer a nuclear attack if need be—in order to make sure that no enemy was allowed to get away with a strategy of deliberate ruthlessness. Nowhere was this policy of ruthlessness against ruthlessness better displayed than during the Cold War, when the free world faced off against the threat of a ruthless regime armed with virtually instantaneously deliverable nuclear warheads on the tips of Soviet intercontinental ballistic missiles. This is perhaps the ultimate in ruthlessness—to threaten not merely another Great War, but a nuclear holocaust. How do you call someone's bluff when they are bluffing *that*?

There was, in fact, only one solution, and it was the solution taken— the policy of Mutual Assured Destruction, nicknamed MAD with considerable poetic justice. For when approached from the point of view of any previous epoch, the policy of Mutual Assured Destruction did seem utterly irrational. If war is the deployment of violence to make an enemy fulfill our will, as Clausewitz argued, then what sense can there be in a deployment of violence that, by its very nature, destroys both our enemy and ourselves simultaneously?

Yet this was not the only "irrationality" introduced by the threat of a nuclear surprise attack, for in order to implement MAD as a plausible method of deterrence, it was necessary to transform the internal organization of the state that employed it as a deterrence. The fact that this informal transformation was officially minimized during the creation of the strategy of MAD should not disguise the extent to which it marked an enormous departure from all the previous ethical and political ideals of the United States. It was, like the Bush administration's response to 9/11, a step into unknown territory.

Prior to MAD, ours had always been a government of checks and balances, one designed to force an automatic slowdown on any too-precipitate action on the part of any one branch of government. The president, it is true, was constituted as commander in chief, but this function was originally envisioned as requiring the deliberative approval of the Senate. With the advent of the threat of nuclear surprise attack, the United States faced a brutal and utterly unavoidable choice. Either it had to renounce any plausible deterrence against a surprise attack, or else it had to permit the president to exercise powers that were literally beyond human comprehension—not merely the power to launch a unilateral attack on a single nation but the unilateral power to annihilate vast sections of the planet.

The Constitution did not grant such power, nor could the men who framed the Constitution possibly have envisioned such power. Indeed, the mere possibility of such power would, for these men, have almost certainly spelled the demise of the system that they had envisioned, for how could anyone hope to restrain or check a man to whom such ultimate and absolute power had been given?

The advent of the threat of nuclear surprise attack left us no realistic option other than to entrust such power to the President of the United States, and to do so in the face of all our previous ethical and political ideals. The alternative was stark: it was to risk the loss of all our other ideals and values, through nuclear blackmail at the hands of an utterly ruthless adversary.

For most Americans, and indeed for most people in the free world, the choice was so obvious that it is difficult for us to see that it could have been otherwise.

But suppose we were to ask the question, By what right did President Eisenhower obtain sufficient power to blow up large parts of the world? Merely to ask this question is to see its absurdity.

Here we have the essence of the problem posed by ruthlessness in the hands of those willing to use it as a deliberate strategy: there is simply no way to know where the next such threat will come from. As our brief survey of this problem indicates, history offers us no guidance for detecting ahead of time the next great outbreak of ruthlessness. All we know is that it will come in the form of a gang, simply because this is the natural form that ruthlessness takes. The gang must be united. Its members must respond unthinkingly. They must be willing to put the good of the gang before all other goods.

And yet here we come face to face with the same problem encountered by the villagers of Kurosawa's movie *The Seven Samurai*. The only way you can deal with such gangs is to have one yourself. Only, in order to keep it from preying on you, you must have successfully learned how to domesticate it.

This, we will recall, was the great secret of Sparta. Sparta harnessed the innate ruthlessness of the adolescent gang so that it could be of service to the community, rather than a source of destruction, and it did this by forcing all potential gang members to become members of the state teams, just as, in the past, the YMCA taught potential juvenile delinquents how to play baseball as a way of keeping them off the streets and out of trouble.

People misunderstand Sparta, and the United States. The secret of

American power, like that of Sparta, lies not in its military might, as if this were an attribute that came by nature. Its secret, like Sparta's, lies in its ability to harness this might and to keep it from doing damage both to the world and to itself. *Both of them kept their soldiers from aspiring to become tyrants.*

Seen in the amplest perspective of world history, this is what distinguishes those handful of civilizations that have come to exercise inordinate military might: the code of honor that keeps in check their soldiers' hunger for more power. And it is the disintegration of this code of honor that dooms all human empires. Roman history changed the day that praetorian guards grasped that it was they who made the Emperor and not the other way around.

It is this eventual disintegration that provides the empirical basis for those great cyclical theories of history; this is why the happy pages of history are not only blank but rare, squeezed between those long and morbidly fascinating chapters that tell of the struggle for power between rival gangs.

TOWARD NEO-SOVEREIGNTY

We live in a world in which ruthlessness will triumph unless there are men who know how to deal with it effectively. Civilized life begins to exist only when men have learned how to fight ruthlessness without succumbing to it themselves, and it only exists for as long as they remember the trick of how this is done. This trick has been mastered by the United States.

Has America always acted wisely or in a purely benevolent manner? Of course not, but it must be stressed here that we are not trying to imagine a perfect world but simply trying to keep civilization alive and well in the one we have, and the best way to ensure this is for America to continue to hold its position of overwhelming military dominance, as long as the code of honor that governs those who control the means of this dominance is still binding on them psychologically.

Dominance is not necessarily domination. The whole point and value of American supremacy is not to permit America to manage the world or to impose its will or its own culture on others. Empire is most emphatically not what American power should be used for. Of what possible benefit could an empire be, economically or otherwise?

Indeed, any such activity on the part of the United States would be counterproductive to its genuine purpose, which is to deter the renewals of the strategy of deliberate ruthlessness through the world, for the good of both itself and the world. America, in short, must use its power, unilaterally if need be, to destroy and remove any group of people who are deliberately and consciously following a policy of ruthlessness, whether this group is a state against another state, a state against its own people, or an Al-Qaeda-like organization.

Much of the future of the world will hinge on keeping nuclear weapons out of the hands of men ruthless enough to use them, men who do not recognize the legitimacy of the present world order and who are willing to use whatever power falls into their hands in order to destroy it.

With 9/11 the world was shown two hitherto unimaginable possibilities. The first was the possibility of an attack on an American city by a gang of ruthless adolescents and young men employing catastrophic terror. The second was the certainty that such an act would be greeted by rejoicing in much of the Muslim world, as 9/11 in fact was. By how much of the population of that world doesn't matter. Any society that can fill even one street with people dancing over the carnage of 9/11 is to be suspected, for it takes much less than a street to pull off such an act. The gang—often composed of fewer than even the nineteen Al-Qaeda terrorists responsible for 9/11—can arise anywhere, at any time, under any circumstances.

Our hindsight is unavoidably distorted. When we think of Hitler or Mussolini or Lenin, we think of them strutting grandiloquently across the stage of history, magnified many times their original size in order to fit the huge dimensions suggested by their gigantic effect on the history of the human race. From such great effects one is tempted to deduce a great cause. But such is not the case.

They all started the same way—as small clubs attended by insignificant men, an uninspiring nucleus of fanatics devoted to the same cause. What gave them their power—aside from sheer dumb luck—was their deliberate deployment of ruthlessness. They stopped at nothing, and nothing held them back. Both agents and victims of a fantasy ideology, they transformed themselves through the power of group hypnosis into men who were able to overcome all the inhibitions of their own middle-class and often prosperous and cultured backgrounds.

To permit any group of this nature to decide the next stage of history is insane, and yet this is precisely what would happen if the United States were to disengage from the world.

AMERICA AS THE SOLE SOURCE OF
GLOBAL LEGITIMACY

Those who wish to regard themselves as on the right side of history must not permit the gang to destroy the level of civilization within the communities on which they are preying; this is the first task that must be accomplished before attempting any others. You can do no good until you get rid of the gang. For the gang destroys the very basis of trust between members of the same community, and it does this by getting them accustomed to expect violence—and lethal violence—from those *within* the community. That is why gangs do not hesitate to use the same terror against members of their own community that they use on those outside their community, as the routine execution of Palestinians by Palestinians sickeningly demonstrates.

Ruthlessness has no root causes. It is not engendered by poverty or illiteracy or a lack of education or the Muslim religion or the concept of jihad. It is a technique for gaining power. That is what it started as and what it will always be.

That is why we must beware of giving ruthlessness a reason to be ruthless. For the moment you have done this, for however noble a purpose, you have fallen into its own fantasy world, and you are seeing an act of catastrophic senseless killing as a legitimate expression of a political grievance. To mistake ruthlessness for desperation is the fundamental error of those whose sympathies are unclouded by judgment.

IT IS IN these terms that the debate over the threat of American imperialism must be addressed. The senseless and economically pointless acquisition of an empire could only impede the United States' ability to carry out its genuine mission; an empire would become a source of conflict, instead of an agent for solving it.

That is why I propose jettisoning "empire" and adopting the concept of neo-sovereignty. The principle behind neo-sovereignty may be simply stated: If a nation contains gangs who have acted with conspicuous ruthlessness, then it is not entitled to be considered a sovereign state.

For sovereignty, let us remember, is based on the real monopoly of violence and not merely one written into the constitution. Therefore, any nation that can't keep a lid on such gangs has no right to be considered a sovereign state by definition.

So what happens to it? This would depend on the attitude of the nation. If it asks for help, you give it help. But if it refuses to take action itself, or to allow others to take action, then clearly something must be done. The question then becomes, Who ultimately decides what is to be done?

The answer, in my view, is that it must be the United States.

My reason for believing this is that the United States represents the ultimate source of legitimacy in the world and that if its legitimacy is challenged, or subverted, then the world will enter into precisely the kind of legitimacy crisis that Europe entered into after the First World War, when cults of ruthlessness sprang up in the vacuum left by the collapse of four empires, and ending in the holocaust of the Second World War. All legitimacy crises in mankind's history, without exception, have provided the perfect environment for the incubation and rise of gang rule.

This point must be stressed, because intellectuals instinctively believe that for legitimacy to be valid it must be based on a reason. It is not enough, in other words, to have people believe that an authority is legitimate for it to be legitimate by the standards of the intellectual. But in taking this position, the intellectual does not realize that he has already turned himself into a revolutionary intent on subverting the accepted order of things. For this is all that legitimacy means or can mean: that those in authority are accepted by the overwhelming majority of citizens as being, more or less, those who should be in authority.

Who legitimizes legitimacy? The moment this question is even permitted to be asked, the foundation of legitimacy has been swept away, for its foundation is simple habit and custom. Once you are no longer obeying those in authority from custom and habit, what do you substitute in its place?

This is why, when an old legitimacy collapses, or is pushed over the cliff, what takes its place is always the ruthless, for they are the ones capable of fighting their way into the apparatus of power from which the old legitimacies have been expelled, precisely as the Nazis did. Can anyone seriously believe that such a gang of thugs could have created the German state, and its armed forces, from scratch? It fell into their hands, because no one else was ruthless enough to stop them.

Hence those who believe that it would benefit the world for the United States to cease representing legitimacy are tragically and dangerously deluded. They are hurrying on not the realm of perpetual peace but another squalid episode in the history of the gang.

A PROBLEM STILL remains. What happens when the antecedent takeover by a gang brings about a total loss of any memory of legitimacy?

What is so terrible about gang rule is not just what happens while the gang rules, but what happens after it is gone. Witness the aftermath of the Soviet Union, and that of Iraq. Where gangs of ruthless thugs have ruled, they have made it virtually impossible for anyone else to rule except another gang of thugs. In every case, they have killed the legitimate ruler, and usually his entire family with him, as the Bolsheviks did, so that there is no going backwards; yet because they must rule by terror and cannot rule by custom, they never really learn how to rule at all.

This is a challenge facing the world and not just the United States, and not just in Iraq. How do we get societies started again when they have been infected with the pathology of ruthlessness, whether by the agency of what was jokingly called a state, under Saddam Hussein, or by the agency of terrorist organizations such as riddle the Palestinian people? This is not an American problem but a world problem. How do you fix communities long afflicted by ruthlessness?

This is the task the United States faces today. If we are justified in taking out ruthless gangs who are using the state for their own profit and gain, what happens then? Honorific states can be created wholesale, by fiat, but genuine states, exercising real sovereignty, cannot be made this way. And that leaves only the following three choices:

Take out the ruling gang, and hope that something better comes along.

Take over the country and rule it yourself, which is the way of empire.

Train the country in the ethos of the team.

Here we have a problem, for most of us aren't terribly sure what this ethos even is, though we have been embodying it all our life—speaking its prose fluently, like Molière's Monsieur Jourdain, without ever knowing it. Therefore, our first task is to understand what we have that is so important but which we have utterly failed to appreciate. For if the world is going to move upward in the next stage of history, rather than downward, it will be through the dissemination of the ethos of the team and not through its retreat.

We are now living in a world where decent and sincere men and women attack the United States for removing Saddam Hussein, the archetype of the ruthless gang leader, who brutalized twenty million human beings for three decades. They condemn the United States president for declaring a war on terrorism—which is simply the contemporary form of the age-old war on the cult of ruthlessness, a cult that is the enemy of all the diverse and distinct cultures of mankind.

Here is a good way to tell whether you are standing on the right side of history. Do you want to see the rule by gang go the way of slavery and be driven from the face of the earth, or do you believe that rule by gang is a natural right? Those who argued that the United States should not attack Saddam Hussein's Iraq because of the sacred right of national sovereignty should perhaps remember the reputation today of those who in the past justified the property rights of slaveholders. What is the difference, except scale? There may be good conservative reasons for preserving a wicked status quo, but there are no liberal progressive ones. And while it may well be prudent in some cases to try to contain ruthless gangs that are in power rather than to remove them, this can at best be an act of expediency, and never one of morality.

MOST INTELLECTUALS TODAY, both in America and in Europe, will vehemently disagree with this perspective, claiming that they hold a monopoly on the right side of history. From their point of view, it is America that is on the wrong side of history—and, indeed, that it is America that is the obstacle to any forward progression. For them, the next stage of history, if all goes well, will bring an end to American hegemony and the establishment of the liberal cosmopolitan's vision of "the community of all the men and women on the planet," as the American philosopher Martha Nussbaum has characterized this political ideal in the influential essay, "Patriotism and Cosmopolitanism."

But this vision is deeply flawed. It is the attempt to construct Kant's realm of perpetual peace out of a world of liberated individuals, each free to follow his own bliss, in Joseph Campbell's memorable phrase. Yet if each individual in the cosmopolitan community is at liberty to pursue his own autonomously selected moral vision independently of the ethical standards chosen by other liberated individuals, the result will not be community, but chaos.

This, it should be noted, was not a problem that arose in Kant's own original vision of perpetual peace. Beginning with the realistic assumption that the ordinary human being "encounters in himself the unsocial characteristics of wanting to direct everything in accordance with his own idea," Kant argued that there could be no "universal cosmopolitan" community, unless all the members of this community were prepared to extinguish their own individuality and to transform themselves into virtuous automatons, each equally a slave to duty. How else, after all, could the universal cosmopolitan community be free from the kind of ethical conflicts that have from time immemorial generated violence and war?

However, the modern liberal cosmopolitan rejects Kant's moral absolutism as anathema and, like Martha Nussbaum in the essay mentioned above, traces the origin of liberal cosmopolitanism back to the radical individualism of the ancient Greek philosopher who first coined the term *cosmopolitan*. But this effort to found a cosmopolitan community on the radically liberated individual is unfortunate for two reasons. First, it creates the mirage of a political alternative where none in fact exists: it is impossible to construct even a village out of individuals who are all busily pursuing their own bliss, let alone the community of all the men and women of the world. Second, the existence of this intellectual mirage diverts energy and resources that could be better used in making genuine living communities more cosmopolitan in the ordinary sense of this word—that is, more open to diversity, more tolerant, more inclusive.

These two conflicting senses of the word *cosmopolitan* are at the heart of the conflicting visions of mankind's future that we have been examining, and until we can understand them we will not be able to make sense of the issues that are confronting us, nor of the dangers that arise from the misplaced pursuit of utopia.

7

TWO TYPES OF COSMOPOLITANISM:
LIBERAL VERSUS TEAM

ACCORDING TO Martha Nussbaum's influential essay "Patriotism versus Cosmopolitanism," the original founder of liberal cosmopolitanism was the ancient Greek philosopher who lived in the generation following Socrates, and who subsequently became a by-word because of his lantern-guided search for an honest man—or, more correctly, for another honest man. Diogenes, known as the Cynic, was the first man determined to be an absolutely liberated human being.

One fine day, according to legend, Diogenes, upon being asked by a stranger to give the name of the city-state in which he had been brought up, responded that he was a citizen of the world—*cosmopolitikos,* from *cosmos,* the Greek word meaning "the word," and *politikos,* the Greek word meaning "citizen."

Commenting upon this celebrated remark, Martha Nussbaum argues that Diogenes, in declaring himself a citizen of the world, was signalizing his refusal "to be defined by his local origins and local group member-ships, so central to the image of a conventional Greek male." Yet, while this observation can hardly be disputed, Nussbaum makes a further claim about Diogenes' statement for which there is simply no a shred of histor-ical evidence—namely that Diogenes is disowning his local attachments in order to identify himself "in terms of more universal aspirations and concerns."

The implication here was that Diogenes, in repudiating his local community, was affirming a larger one. But a glance at the other anecdotes that have come down to us concerning the life of Diogenes would be sufficient to dispel such a strangely anachronistic importation of our own Enlightenment-derived categories back into a world that would have found them alien and incomprehensible. Diogenes did not spurn his fellow citizens of his native polis in order to embrace his fellow citizens of the world. He spurned them all, with equal contempt. Indeed, even in our own time it would be difficult to find someone who better illustrated Rousseau's famous dictum that the cosmopolitan is a man who claims to love humanity in order to avoid having to tolerate his neighbors, except that Diogenes never pretended to love humanity. His "cosmopolitanism" was simply the flip side of his fundamental cynicism, and in order to understand the one, we must first understand the other.

The Greek word from which we derive *cynicism* is *cynos*, which simply means dog, and the term *cynic*, as used by both Diogenes and his detractors had no trace of its modern significance, and certainly did not mean a man who knew the price of everything and the value of nothing. Rather, the cynic was the man who, abjuring the artificial constraints imposed by social custom, decides to model his standard of conduct on the natural lifestyle of the dog. If a dog does not need luxury to live, then neither does the cynic. If the dog can wander the streets and sleep in a tub, then so can—and did—Diogenes.

Indeed, Diogenes pushed his countercultural lifestyle to the point that would make even the most extreme of modern anarchists or libertarians blush. When observed masturbating openly in the agora, Diogenes, upon being reprimanded, replied, "Ah, if one could only make the pangs of hunger disappear by rubbing the belly."

The logically consistent cynic—which Diogenes undoubtedly was—applies the same hypernaturalistic principle to all his ethical obligations, especially the all-compelling ethical obligation that virtually every Greek felt toward the community that had educated and reared him—the very ethical obligation, it must be remembered, that Socrates felt he owed even to the city that had condemned him to death and that he used as his justification for refusing his friends' offer of escape.

Would a dog have behaved like Socrates? Obviously not; nor, presumably, would have Diogenes, had he been confronted with the same choice. Just as the dog had no ethical obligations to the city he happened to be scavenging off of, so too the cynic had no ethical obligations to whatever spot chanced to provide him with a temporary place of rest and sustenance. Rather than being a rejection of ethnocentric particularism, this was simply a rejection of ethical obligation altogether, and that is what explains the true significance of Diogenes' use of the term *cosmopolitan*. Diogenes consents to be a citizen only of a nonexistent and purely ideal community simply because there is no danger that such an abstract entity will ever make an actual concrete demand on him. The *world* asks nothing from him; he owes it nothing in return.

At first glance, it is hard to imagine an ethical outlook that is more at odds with the political ideals that Martha Nussbaum—and so many other liberal intellectuals—wish to promote. To the neutral observer, if Diogenes may be said to represent any contemporary political position at all, it would appear to be the most paranoid forms of the survivalist mentality embraced by those normally found at quite the opposite end of the political spectrum from these intellectuals.

Yet this first glance is misleading. There is indeed a reason why the intellectuals who embrace liberal cosmopolitanism freely acknowledge their inspiration to the first cynic, who was also, in a very genuine sense, the first intellectual as well. Fanatically insistent on retaining complete autonomy over his own values and conduct, Diogenes represented the concrete incarnation of the Sophist's liberation from traditional thinking. Like all modern intellectuals, Diogenes thought for himself, devised his own plan of living, made his own ethical choices. Unlike Socrates who was notoriously faithful in carrying out the various ethical obligations imposed on him by the city-state that had raised and educated him, Diogenes swept them all aside: they were other people's affairs, and not his.

But once this is understood, it becomes apparent that Diogenes' cosmopolitanism had no positive political context, but was in fact only a vehicle that permitted him to repudiate all the various duties that bound "the conventional Greek male" to carry out his various familial and civic roles. It was, to use the language of the 1960s, a cop-out, a way of allowing Diogenes to do precisely what he wished, when and where he wished to do it—that, and nothing more.

For Diogenes, in short, the claim to be a citizen of the world was not the blueprint for a world community, but a manifesto of radical individualism—the repudiation of all ethical commitment, and not the search for a higher form of it.

In which case we must ask how such a purely negative attitude could possibly become the basis of a serious political position—a position, moreover, that preens itself on its superior ethical standards and that invariably claims to occupy the moral high ground in any political debate.

Normally this claim to the moral high ground is based on the contention that the liberal cosmopolitan ideal is morally superior to the various forms of ethnocentric particularism that have plagued mankind, perennially dividing it into warring sects and tribes. Hence, by analogy, those who subscribe to this ideal are morally superior to those who are content with the ethnocentric particularism that they have merely inherited.

If we examine this claim, however, we can see at once the fallacy behind it. It is based on the notion that one can compare a moral ideal, taken in complete abstraction, with the actualized values embodied in a living, breathing community of real men and women. But this is not comparing apples and oranges; it is comparing applesauce and ambrosia—the imaginary nectar of the gods against the prosaic pulp of a domestic staple.

Utopias are always preferable to actual communities—they are designed to be. And hence it is easy to argue that the liberal cosmopolitan's "community of all the men and women on the planet," in Martha Nussbaum's words, would be superior to any actual community, however tolerant or inclusive or liberal this community may be, *if in fact such an imaginary community really existed.*

But what kind of claim is this? Isn't it a bit like saying that the novel I intend to write one day will be far superior to *War and Peace* because of my intention to make my novel perfect?

In the final analysis, the ultimate harm done by the modern liberal formulation of the cosmopolitan ideal is that it sends mankind on a wild goose chase. By urging us to devote ourselves to an imaginary "community of all the men and women on the planet," it keeps us from focusing our precious energies and resources on the only practical solution that lies on the historical horizon.

The historical choice confronting us is not between cosmopolitanism and ethnocentric particularism, but between actual historical communities that embody the values of liberal civilization to a high degree and those that do not; or, to put it another way, between the narrow sectarian, tribal, and racial particularism that has long divided and bloodied the human race on the one hand, and the *team cosmopolitanism* first devised by the Romans, and later adapted by the modern West and by the United States, on the other.

This second sense of cosmopolitanism was not the result of philosophic speculation, but of hard-nosed practical experience. Because the Roman *imperium* stretched across the known world, those who were called upon to rule it were required to deal with all manner of outlandish peoples, each with different customs, folkways, and gods.

Being called upon to rule, however, and being able to rule successfully are two quite different tasks, and while many have attempted it, few have succeeded for more than a hiccup of time, and none with the permanency of Rome.

Why? This is something of a mystery, though there is one clue to it in the story that the Roman historian Livy tells of Rome's first great spurt of growth. The Romans, he said, being then few in number, threw their underpopulated city open to all the outcasts and misfits in the surrounding regions, to all who had nowhere else to go. The result, according to Livy, was the formation of a society that was composed exclusively of males, and of males who shared no common parentage or family line. Curiously, Livy states explicitly about the origin of Rome what we can only speculate about the origin of Sparta.

Did it really happen like that? There is, needless to say, no possible way of proving this one way or the other. We lack anything approaching the kind of evidence that would allow such a determination of empirical fact.

But we aren't dealing here with empirical fact, but rather with the way a certain people, the Romans, *imagined* themselves. There is no reason to think that Livy is putting forward a scandalous or revolutionary theory of the origin of his own society. This, in other words, is how Romans of Livy's time imagined themselves coming to being, and the antifamily character of this myth is overwhelmingly obvious. In fact, we read just a bit earlier in Livy how Romulus had murdered his brother Remus—much as Cain murdered Abel—indicating that the Romans' political sense of the fraternal was less surely anchored in biology than in the "blood brother" status of one's teammates.

Hegel, in his *Philosophy of History*, accepts Livy's story as historically accurate. To Hegel, the founders of Rome were simply a gang of thugs. Like the so-called Dorians who invaded Greece, the original Romans were simply an antique variation on our modern phenomenon of urban street gangs. Or, to draw on other historical periods, they were like the pirate bands that have sprung up in every historical context in which they have been possible—from the Caribbean to the Sea of Japan and everywhere in between.

The gang may formulate its own rules and traditions, but there will always be, at least in the origins of the gang, an awareness that these are rules that the members have created and chosen and not simply the law of heaven that has come to them from immemorial generations.

This fact explains why those cities whose culture or myth reflects a gang origin—such as Sparta, Athens, and Rome—also have a legendary law giver who is cast as a historical figure, Lycurgus for Sparta, Draco and later Solon for Athens, Numa for Rome. The law giver devises the law, and he gives it to his community, which accepts it from him, but the reason for the acceptance lies in the acknowledged wisdom of the law, not in the tradition-based authority of the law giver. This marks a dramatic change in human consciousness.

In societies caught in the cake of custom, whatever is done is done because there is no other conceivable way for human beings to do it. But in the type of society we are examining, there is an explicit awareness of its difference from the ways of other societies. Other people do it their way, but *we* have been taught by our law giver to do it this way—which is superior. In short, we do it not because it is the only way but because it is the right way. Thucydides, for example, in discussing the Greek custom of exercising in the nude, remarks matter-of-factly that the barbarians are incapable of such conduct and that nudity is an indication of the superiority of the Greek ethos over that of other peoples. And in this peculiar quality, we can detect the origin of that characteristic that Samuel Huntington finds so deplorable about the West—its sense of superiority to the rest of the world.

There are two ways of thinking that you are superior. First, you think you are the only person of any worth in the world, and so you pay no attention to anyone else's claims about their status. They are beneath your notice. This is how the Chinese felt about the rest of the world, and it explained the decision of the Chinese to discontinue their tentative voyages of discovery, despite the fact that their navy had ships in its fleet vastly superior to the Portuguese caravels that, nearly a century later, would visit the ports of China. It is the way that people with an overly lofty sense of their own splendor refuse to take seriously the tastes or the thoughts of those of lower status—economic, educational, or social.

The second way of feeling superior is exhibited whenever someone takes seriously the other person's claim to superiority, if only in order to prove to him just how wrong he is. This is agonistic superiority, the kind that permits antagonists to thrash out competitively who is actually superior to whom. This is what the Greeks had, and it is one of their legacies to us. To think that a Western civilization could exist in the midst of other societies as the Chinese did, feeling so smugly superior that it refuses to dispute with any other culture, is to suppose what is flat-out impossible. It is the essence of the West to wish to prove its superiority to others—not to impose it, and certainly not to dismiss its potential rivals as beneath contempt. The West acknowledges the Other and is willing to compete with him; other civilizations would prefer that he not exist. It is the West that has gone to study the East, and not the other way around.

But to think that your way is superior to the ways of others is to think that the two ways are commensurable—that they can be measured on the same scale. This may, of course, be an illusion, but the West's belief in it is sincere and unfeigned. Certainly this attitude is an immense improvement over so looking down on another people that you regard them as having nothing in common with you, so that you alone are the "humans" and they are altogether something else. Furthermore, it is the inevitable by-product of thinking and reflecting. If we live differently from everyone else, the Spartans insisted, it is because a wise man taught us how to live this way. It is, therefore, a wiser way of living than the way you live.

Such thoughts can never go through the head of people who have simply followed the tradition of the Family, for this is a tradition that changes only superficially around the world, one in which each sees himself simply as continuing the normal cycle of organic life.

If there is wisdom, then there is a wise way of doing things, as well as an unwise way, and who would ever have tried to become wise if it made no difference in the life he lived? And if the wise don't live better ways—if they just live different lives—then what is the point in trying to gain wisdom? It is utterly futile to try to create a reflective and thinking culture if you tell your children that there is no point to thinking and to reflection—a truth that many of our academic literati have somehow forgotten, perhaps at an eventual tragic cost to our society.

These questions were, of course, exactly the ones that the generation of the Sophists would ask in mankind's first culture war, and it is obvious that the mere posing of such a question can have a disturbing impact on a society that is guided by the team principle. For if wisdom and reflection are of no value, if everything is relative and any man's opinion is as good as another, then what is the point of the team?

If one opinion is no better than another, then what is the point of a meritocracy? If no man has greater talent or ability than another, why make so much fuss about finding the right man for the right position? Or looking at merit or virtue at all?

NONE OF THESE problems much disturbed the far less speculative Roman mind. Just as Greece was destroyed by the individual's coming to dominate over both the team and the family, so Rome prospered and throve because it was able to curb the individual and, even more important, to blend both the team principle and the family principle into the amazingly stable concoction that was the civic ecology of the Romans.

In particular, while Sparta displayed an almost infantile refusal to abandon the gang principle. Rome did not. Rather than enslaving its neighbors, as the Spartans had done, Rome intermarried with them and inevitably annexed them. Whereas Spartan society was xenophobic and inward-looking, Roman society became expansive and outward-looking.

This was precisely the achievement embodied in the Roman concept of *patria*. A *patria* can only exist as the target of the loyalty of a self-conscious team, that is to say, of a group of men who are able to redirect their primordial loyalty from their family and tribe onto a totally new object: not a piece of land or turf, but the team itself, and not the team as this particular collection of men, but the team as an ongoing structure of ethical habits capable of reproducing itself from generation to generation.

The Romans did not merely carry on the team principle that had first been discovered by the Spartans and which had been disseminated through the Greek world by the organizational arms race. Instead, they took certain features of the team principles and managed to fuse them with certain features of the family principle, while leaving behind those aspects of both that did not serve their purpose.

From the family they took over the idea of hierarchy, but they purged from it all traces of its original biological moorings in kinship and blood ties, while from the team they took over the idea of One for All, and All for One but purged from it all traces of its original moorings in their inherently unstable adolescent gang.

The persistence of the gang principle had condemned Greek society to remain in a stage of perpetual adolescence. It simply could not grow up. The original gang ethos out of which it had emerged still contaminated the ideal of the team: as a result, the Greek city-states were never able to cooperate effectively, despite the threat first of Philip of Macedon and his son, Alexander the Great, and then the final threat of Rome. That sense of inviolable turf that had produced the first embodiment of civic freedom, the embryo of patriotism, made those who had achieved this stage understandably reluctant to move beyond it. To give up civic autonomy was simply too difficult for those who knew how rare an achievement it was.

Furthermore, Greek pederasty differed from all the other forms of transgenerational homosexuality found among civilized people in that it was—to put it in its crudest formulation—a system of son-swapping. This meant that wherever it flourished, namely in the aristocratic warrior culture of Sparta and other oligarchies, it inevitably led to the destruction of paternal authority, which in turn proved to be the fatal weakness in the system.

There is no clearer way of illustrating the difference between the Spartan and the Roman systems than to compare the way a Spartan child was brought into the community with the way Roman child was. The Roman mother set her child on the bare earth in front of her husband, at which point the husband had a choice: he could lift the child from the ground, and thereby signal its acceptance into the family, or he could leave it where it lay, indicating that the child was to be abandoned. In Sparta, as we have seen, the father was required to take his newborn child to the elders. If the elders decided that the child was not fit to be a Spartan, his fate was sealed, and there was nothing the father could do to alter it.

Even Sparta's famous "communism," that is, its refusal to permit the acquisition of wealth by individuals, was a direct result of the same relentless logic. What better way to cancel and annul the paternal authority than to make the father economically irrelevant to his biological son. The father could not protect him as a newborn baby, nor provide for him as an adolescent or young adult. There were no purse strings to be cut between the Spartan father and his son. Nor did the father provide his son with the proverbial roof over his head. From an early age, the son was housed and fed by the team. When a Spartan boy thought of an authority figure, the last image he would have conjured up in his imagination would have been his own biological father. Instead it would be the team, whether represented by the elders or by his teammates or by the age-cohort of boys above him is irrelevant.

Here is a case of two different cultural systems in which the existence of one drove out and undermined the existence of the other. Dorian pederasty excluded paternity; paternity excluded pederasty. To promote the one was to destroy the other.

This truth was neatly encapsulated by the cycle of Greek myths that told the story of Oedipus. According to the myth, Oedipus's father, Laius, the king of Thebes, was the "inventor" of pederasty. When his wife, Jocasta, gives birth to their son, Oedipus, an oracle predicts that the boy will grow up to murder his father and marry his mother. Horrified, the parents decide to expose the infant, but the shepherd given this task takes pity on the child and permits him to live. Later, after he has been adopted by another royal couple, Oedipus hears the same oracle that his biological parents had heard, but he mistakenly thinks that it applies to the couple who have adopted him—who, of course, have never told him the truth about his origin. Immediately Oedipus sets off on his wanderings, in order to put as much distance between himself and his adoptive parents as possible. One day, in his travels, Oedipus comes to a crossroad at the same time as another traveler. They begin to dispute who has precedence, and Oedipus kills the other man, who is, needless to say, his own biological father.

The dispute about precedence is an event that would have been unimaginable in the world of *homo hierarchicus,* where every human being had his unique place in the all-encompassing cosmic order and there could never be any question of who should go first. It is a symbol of the continuous strife and rivalry, the inescapable agonistics, that was Greek life: every position of authority was open to challenge. And how else could it be in a pederastic culture? If the father was devoted to boys other than his son, while his son found authority figures in males other than his father, how important could a father be to his biological son, or the son to his father?

We must add the disturbing fact that the heavily idealized image of the fidelity of the boy to the older male, represented by Achilles' loyalty—and certainly not his sexual passion for—the older Patrocles in *The Iliad,* while the stuff of heroic poetry, was increasingly not the stuff of real life. In the poetry of Theognis of Megara, it is apparent that this classic prototype of the pederastic relationship was being contaminated by money considerations on the part of the boy, as well as by a purely sexual motive on the part of the older male. Even in the speeches in praise of pederasty that Plato puts into the mouths of the guests of *The Symposium,* if read with care, make it apparent that this was an institution in serious trouble and coming under increasing attack.

IT IS IN this light that we can understand the full significance of the Roman concept of *patria potestas*—the power of the father, the foundation of the Roman social order. It was exemplified in the ceremony of taking a newborn child into the family described earlier, but equally and even more formidably in the law that permitted the Roman father to punish his sons—and indeed any member of his family—with death.

Rather than seeing in this authority a relic of a primitive stage, we must grasp that *patria potestas* was an advance. It was by means of this peculiar institution that the unruly spirit of the gang could finally be exorcised from the principle of the team. It was, in short, the victory of paternity over pederasty, and it changed the world forever.

The ruthlessness of the father was a defense mechanism against the ruthlessness of the gang, a way for paternal authority to crush adolescent rebellion. The Romans, in short, completely transcended the gang by purging it of all trace of the anarchy that it had originally let loose on the placid and unchanging world of the family. The result of this "domestication" of the gang was something entirely new.

The Romans created a civic ecology in which, for the first time, the team and the family principles were brought into a synthesis and harmonized, rather than being at loggerheads with each other, as had been the case in Greece, where the aristocratic warrior class inevitably represented the team and the agricultural class inevitably stood for the family—a contrast neatly symbolized in the clash of cultures between Homer's *Iliad* and Hesiod's *Work and Days.*

The Roman patricians would preserve the team spirit among themselves, but they would impose hierarchy on the rest of their society and eventually the world. Indeed, the rest of the society could even be organized by the team principle, but the relationship between these teams would itself be governed not by the team principle but by that of hierarchy. There would be a chain of command, modeled on that of the Roman father's total power over his son; it was to be absolute and not subject to dispute or controversy. If you were told to obey by the person over you in the hierarchy, you obeyed. The Romans, in short, would have executed the pouting Achilles for refusing to follow orders and certainly would not have written a long poem in his praise.

The Romans recognized that there had to be someone whose commands could not be questioned if there was to be any order in a society, especially during a time of crisis. This became the job of the Roman office of dictator, a person appointed for a limited period, and only during a time of national peril. But their greatest of all inventions was the concept of an office in and of itself. For it was this innovation that permitted the Romans to take over the team principle without the risk of destabilizing their social order.

THE PROBLEM OF LEADERSHIP

The problem of deciding who was entitled to make executive decisions would inevitably be the chief drawback to the gang ethos. The leader of the pack exercised authority by virtue of his personal merit or charisma. His leadership therefore rested in some characteristic that was peculiar to him as an individual—his courage or his cunning, for example. But since all the qualities that might possibly count as charismatic were qualities that other individuals could also manifest, there would inevitably be challengers to the position of dominance assumed by the leader of the pack.

Early efforts to solve this problem, without relapsing into tyranny, included the device of having two kings, as the Spartans did, or two consuls, as in the Roman Republic. To divide the command in a time of crisis, however, would always be to court disaster.

This is the great advantage of biological hierarchy: there can be no contenders for the position of patriarch. In any family, biology determined the executive authority. The trick then was to take over the principle of hierarchy but to free it from its biological base and to fuse it with the meritocracy of the team. A person's individual merit qualified him for the position of leadership but did not entitle him to this position.

The difference is the difference between being the World Champion boxer and being the President of the United States. The World Champion can only hold his title so long as he is prepared to defend it against anyone who can credibly challenge his claim to it; if he refuses to face a challenger, he must relinquish his title. But the president, so long as he is in office, does not need to defend his title against those who might wish to challenge him. There may be and usually are many individuals who would be quite as fit to serve as president as the one who just happens to be in office, but those personal qualifications make no difference. The president is the president because of the office he holds, not because of his own personal charisma, however this might be measured.

Yet the only way that this system could come about was if the society had figured out a method by which it could produce lots of people who could competently hold executive office. The only way to free a community from the need to rely on the rare gift of charisma in this or that exceptional individual was to devise a method whereby individuals with the necessary gifts for leadership could be produced routinely and in sufficient quantities to permit a choice among them.

For example, in a world in which few are willing to risk their lives in the face of almost certain death, a man who is able to do this reliably will have an immense edge over his competitors for leadership if his community is looking out for a brave man to lead them in battle. The same will not be the case in a society, like Sparta and Rome, where men are brought up to fear shame far more than physical death. Here there is no charisma attached to a lack of fear, nor does it single any one person out for any particular merit. Rather it has become routine and expected.

This fact had profound consequences, since it meant that virtually anyone in the society could hold the position of the leader. Because everyone had transformed his natural personality through the discipline imposed on the members of the Roman community, it became conceivable for anyone—at least within the class of men who had been trained in this way—to fulfill the duties of the leader in the time of crisis, as the Roman legend of the farmer turned temporary military dictator, Cincinnatus, made clear. Alexis de Tocqueville would make the same point about America. True, he wrote, it was not a nation led by exceptionally great men, but this was because it did not need to be.

In a society of this nature, it follows that even the office of military leader, commander in chief, could become one office among others and one that various different individuals could fill equally well. No Alexanders, Caesars, or Napoleons need apply. In short, routinization of character formation meant that the social order no longer had to depend on the charisma of this or that particular leader. Thus it became possible to select the man to fill the office, to debate which one should serve, and even to vote him in and out. Even more importantly, it meant that, for the first time, a person's commands would be obeyed not because of who he was as a person—or who his family had been—but because of the office he filled.

THE ROMAN INNOVATION meant that hierarchy was no longer a biologically anchored principle but could be employed to organize nonbiological relationships. It liberated hierarchy from its embodiment in a chain of command that depended on any particular set of persons and permitted it to be used to organize total strangers. In this, it resembled the team principle; yet it was exempt from the gang element out of which the team principle had emerged, since it was not strictly egalitarian. Yet it preserved the team principle insofar as it permitted anyone to occupy any position on the hierarchy purely by virtue of his merit and not because of his kinship position. Thus it gave rise to the corporate principle.

The corporate principle automatically achieves a number of things. First, it provides for greater stability in any community that adopts it, because it permits the position of leadership to change hands without the necessity of conflict. The new consul, for example, does not need to prove himself personally in order to tap into the loyalty of those who are required to obey his commands, just as the President of the United States gains his authority from his office and not from his individual charisma. Thus, in a time of crisis, or when a leader falls or dies, the community is not thrown into discord and disarray over the question of who should step into the vacated office. Whoever has been officially designated in advance to be the new leader will in fact be obeyed, and since the new leader will able to count on this, he does not need to resort to any extralegal measures in order to coax the community to follow him, such as bribery, intimidation, or terror.

A whole new mode of legitimacy emerges—one that can survive a change of individual leaders but which does not rest on the natural hierarchy of the family, as the passing on of kingship to the eldest son does.

This, in itself, is revolutionary, for it implies a way of keeping team-modeled societies from falling prey to the lure of charisma in the dangerous individual. After all, this, we need recall, is what the Greek thinkers, including both Plato and Aristotle, condemned about all democracies in Greece—that they were prone to degenerate into tyrannies, whenever one man became the leader of a faction.

Second, it creates a new tolerance, because in order to discharge an office, it is only necessary to be qualified to perform the duties of the office in question. Whether or not you are a member of the same family or tribe no longer matters, only whether you are "the man for the job." This detribalization also puts a new emphasis on the individual: he may now rise from obscurity by his own merit. He can work his way up the hierarchy, instead of being born into it.

Obviously, this was always true of any gang-style organization, but with the qualification that whoever worked his way to the top had to be someone who was either sufficiently ruthless or a big risk taker or, most likely, both. This requirement clearly tended to favor leaders who possessed these qualities as personality traits, so your only salvation as a society arose from the unlikely chance of finding a leader whose complexity of character permitted him to act like a brutal thug on his way up the mountain and like a wise king once he got to the top. Hence the enormous advantage of being ruled by people who have proven themselves to be good team players on their way to power, and indeed it is a fortunate society where the criterion for being trusted with power is having been a team player even when it was a challenging and difficult role to play.

This is one of the secrets of American stability, one that has permitted it to remain a free society despite the power of the media to manufacture the modern incarnation of charisma, namely glamour. The men whom the two mainstream parties permit to run for the presidency are men who have proven their status as team players far beyond the call of duty. This will be true as long as the two parties retain their power, and it is impossible to imagine any political party eclipsing them which had not done so by being a better team, and thus productive of even better team players.

The ability to unite mindlessly for a common cause is the secret of power. For if people unite only about things they care deeply for, you would have a society made up of a multitude of minuscule parties, each with some very small and very angry agenda. If you wish to have an effect on the world, you must put aside all your unique passions and be prepared to back something for no better reason than that no one on your side can see any reason not to.

The third and perhaps the most important new possibility opened up by the corporate principle is its potential for expanding immensely the size and scope of any community that adopts it. The family was limited by its biological base: the team by its insistence on consensus, and the principle of blackballing. As the Roman Empire exhibited in its epoch, and as capitalism has demonstrated in ours, the corporation has no intrinsic limits to its possible growth.

The ability to expand was implicit in the whole concept of a hierarchy based on considerations of merit. A person could start at the bottom—as an apprentice, as a beginner—something one could not do on the team without violating its egalitarian ethos. With the advent of the corporate hierarchy, new members could be brought into the organization on a provisional basis. They could be trained up to the standards of the corporation—as happens today with new employees at any business—and this new gain of personnel could come about with minimal risk to the stability and well-being of the corporation. One rotten apple may spoil the barrel, but it does less damage when it is at the bottom.

This critical distinction between novice and adept was extended by the Romans to include citizenship. You did not have to be born a Roman to become one, as Saint Paul proved. Rather, you could make yourself one by adopting the Roman ethos and making it yours.

THIS BRINGS US back to the Roman ideal of cosmopolitanism, which we can now see as a synthesis of a purified team principle and a purified hierarchy principle.

This form of cosmopolitanism we will call *team cosmopolitanism*. It may be said to exist in any community in which membership is given to anyone who is prepared to accept and internalize the ground rules of this community, regardless of their particular ethnic backgrounds. Team cosmopolitanism does not aim at creating a community of all the human beings on the planet but at creating a society where membership is open to all who wish to embrace the team ethos of their new community.

Team cosmopolitanism is, and has been, the fundamental organizing principle of the United States. In this case our Roman heritage is no mere heirloom but a living force that still animates us; it has successfully managed to form a powerful bond that today unites a nation of nearly three hundred million people.

This indeed is the peculiar form that the United States' sense of superiority takes. As a nation we believe that the values of the team (liberty, fraternity, and equality) are better values than the values of the family (blood kinship and hierarchy).

In this sense there has never been a society less profamily than the United States, where those who believe that they are defending the traditional family are in fact defending a radical departure from this tradition.

The innovation represented by the classic American nuclear family was the inevitable by-product of the immigrant experience in every American's past—in coming to the new world it was necessary to leave behind the extended families of the old—not only of the flesh but of the imagination. Here people could no longer think of themselves in terms of remote, and speculative, chains of consanguinity, but only in terms of such palpable immediacies as father, mother, daughter, son—and perhaps grandparents. No one here is interested in avenging the honor of third cousins twice removed.

In the United States, membership in the club of citizens is not denied to anyone because of mere nature or because of his status in anything anyone might care to call the natural order. This is a law that seems to have the irresistible force of gravity, but on a much slowed-down time scale. It is precisely this superliberal feature of our society that permits something that warms the heart of every American patriot and conservative—America's enormous strength in the world, which arises not from her military hardware or her technology, or from her ideals and much less from any ideology, or even from her dynamic capitalism, but rather from the miraculous civil ecology that has no example to rival it, with the sole exception of Rome.

Here it has come about that the team has transcended all limitation of scale. The various teams operating in the United States, from small businesses to schools to universities to government agencies, make up a honeycomb network that provides immense stability to the system—so immense that there is little need for the state, either in the local or the regional or the national form, to meddle and interfere in the lives of its citizens.

"Need" in the sense of the amount of interference necessary to maintain the level of liberal civilization to which the citizens have become accustomed and that they could reasonably expect to be maintained. This does not mean that there may not be much more interference than is needed, as there undoubtedly is. But much of this interference is caused by the pathology that inevitably overtakes any democratic social order, the desire to meddle with the lives of the less enlightened or, as often as not, the less revealed to.

These questions do not affect my main argument, which is that liberal civilization has become almost instinctive with us, and that this is the prime source of our forgetfulness. We can see now that it is this forgetfulness that is responsible for the popularity of liberal cosmopolitanism among so many contemporary intellectuals. In this case, what is being forgotten is that it is simply impossible to construct a whole social order, from the smallest grouping to that of all the men and women on the planet, solely in terms of the individual and without any assistance from the family or the team. Just as the Indian caste system represents a society based almost exclusively on the family, and Sparta represents a society based almost exclusively on the team, liberal cosmopolitanism projects a society based almost exclusively on the individual.

I say "projects" because of the simple fact that this is all the liberal cosmopolitan can do with his ideal—to make it a project, never a reality. The reason is obvious: it is impossible to create even the tiniest community simply from individuals, without the intermediary of the family and the team. You would have to bring children up in such a way that they could never begin to form loyalty to their family, or their playmates, or their neighborhood, or their religion, or their language. You would have to teach them only to feel loyalty and allegiance to a community that you would never be able to show them as a concrete thing—a community with no language, no customs, no patriotic lore, no flag, no color, no race, no ethnic food, no national music.

We have seen this idea before, in Plato's *Republic*. It came in the form of his all-too-ingenious device to wean children away from personal loyalty and love for their biological parents. If a woman was twenty-three when she gave birth, her offspring was taught to call "mother" any woman who was exactly twenty-three years older than he was, and ditto for "dad."

The family, like the team, divides the world into us and them. The liberal cosmopolitan, however, pays no attention to where this dividing line is drawn. The family draws it in biology. The team draws it in human conduct: behave yourself like one of us, and nothing else matters. The youngest son can inherit the family business. The third girl may get married before the first. She may even be the president.

This tolerance was the gift of the team. Nothing else in the world has ever produced it. Not all the speeches and noble orations, and surely not all the philosophic treatises on justice. It was the team that drove out biology, and with it the evils of racism and prejudice of every form.

Still, all these blessings come with a price tag. You must be loyal to the team. When it is in a fight, you will mindlessly take its side. When it is spoken poorly of, you will resent the slander intensely and make your resentment clear to the party responsible. You must, in short, always take its side in a quarrel.

The cosmopolitan thinks he can live in a world where he never needs to take a side, but the only way you can have a world where you don't need to take sides is to create a world without conflict. But what will you do with the people who want a world *with* conflict, if only because they don't want the world without conflict that has been imposed by you? Men will always have something to fight about, and when the community of all the men and women of the planet has been finally formed, what they will fight about is who is to decide how this community is to live.

As Sancho Panza once wisely said, "When two men mount a horse, one must ride behind." It will be just as true in the community of all the men and women of the planet as it was in Sancho Panza's Spain. The struggle for superiority is not simply the manifestation of a psychological pathology, such as narcissism, but an unalterable aspect of the human condition. It is wired into our nature, not through the instinct of aggression or territoriality, but because the very logical structure of the world demands it.

If this is a truth that was manifest to Sancho Panza, how has it come about that almost all intellectuals of our time, both on the Right and the Left, have so completely forgotten it?

How, in short, did reason go wrong?

8

HOW REASON GOES WRONG

The bane of philosophy is pomposity: people will not see that small things are the miniatures of greater, and it seems a loss of abstract dignity to freshen their minds by object-lessons from what they know.

—WALTER BAGEHOT, in *Physics and Politics*

ROBERT CONQUEST has rightly called the twentieth century the "ravaged century." But if it has been ravaged, it has been ravaged by the intellectual, for the past century was unique in that for the first time in human history intellectuals sought and gained power, with catastrophic results. No other identifiable social class in mankind's history had ever initiated horrors on the scale of the Nazi holocaust and the Black Book of Communism. Nor does it serve any purpose to deny the title of "intellectual" to the likes of Hitler, Mussolini, Stalin, and their cronies on the pretext that they lacked *true* intellectual eminence. The world is full of intellectuals who lack such eminence.

But the twentieth century might also be given another rather pejorative title—the Century of Dead-Ends. Since this is not a generally accepted philosophical concept, let us pause for a moment to examine it.

A historical dead-end occurs when a set of abstract ideas or ideals can no longer find anyone to *embody* them, that is, to animate them with their private passions. They cease to have buyers—like a stock that has fallen out of favor. The theoretical writings that originally spawned and explained the idea remain on the library shelves, but they no longer move men to action or inspire creative innovation.

All dead-ends share another trait in common: They were all the work of a highly educated coterie keen to remake the world according to its own superior design. They all issued in programs. They all envisioned vast and complicated projects, like Husserlian phenomenology or the logical empiricist's unification of the sciences, all designed to set aside or overthrow the existent chaos of individual disciplines, with their own *ad hoc* and homespun methods. Or else they issued intense manifestos proclaiming new and universal principles by which music or art or architecture would be re-created *de novo:* Schönberg's serialism was not intended as a personal style, suitable to his own tastes and talents; it was a virtually mandatory program for all future composers to follow. The International Style in architecture declared its scope and purpose in its very title, and the resultant "universal and homogenous" buildings seemed equally to fit in—or clash—in whatever locale they were commissioned. Activated by the fury of a Byzantine iconoclast. Clement Greenberg, the reigning aesthetician of abstract expressionism, wished to abolish the representational image from all future canvases. There was, generally speaking, to be no turning back. Art had to march stolidly ahead and, like Lot's wife, was forbidden even so much as a glance at what had been left behind.

These revolutions all ended the same way. They went nowhere. In the relatively harmless case of Husserlian phenomenology, its "presuppositionlessness" quickly disappointed expectations, while the logicist project did succeed in offering a stunningly convoluted derivation of the "occasionally useful" proposition "$1 + 1 = 2$" in Russell and Whitehead's *Principia Mathematica*—an awful lot of very hard work in order to establish an embarrassingly trivial truth. Academicians here and there compose dodecaphonic music to be reviewed by their peers, but the International Style, which requires lots of money, is dead as a doornail—though a great deal more conspicuous.

Much less harmless were mankind's forays into creating a new humanity from scratch. At the root of all these programs was the same maniacal drive to make a clean sweep of things. And behind this urge was invariably a group of intellectuals who believed that the world had been waiting for their appearance in order to set itself right.

Here again we will turn to Hegel to help us out. For Hegel this impulse

is all a manifestation of *Verstand*—an unexotic German word that is usually translated, by convention, as "understanding," but this rendering is
no more helpful than Hegel's original choice, which, like its English
equivalent, carries no special distinction. If anything, the English word
understanding, with its hint of sympathy, leads us away from Hegel's
meaning, for the kind of thinking he has in mind is at the other end of
the spectrum from sympathetic identification with an object: it is the
cold, classifying, pigeonholing activity that is the special province of the
scholar and the intellectual—so much so that probably the best transla-
tion of the German word is abstract reason.

Why does abstract reason manifest itself in this way? The short answer
is provided by Hegel at the very beginning of *The Encyclopedia of the
Philosophical Sciences:*

> The severing of actuality from the Idea is particularly dear to the
> Abstract Reason, which regards its dreams (i.e., abstractions) as
> something genuine, and is puffed up about the "ought" that it
> likes to prescribe, *especially in the political field*—as if the world
> had had to wait for it, in order to learn how it ought to be, but is
> not. (Italics mine)

The error of abstract reason is, in short, forgetfulness. It forgets that its
abstractions are designed to try to capture the infinitely elusive real. It
begins to use these same abstractions as yardsticks by which to judge the
real.

Yet although abstract reason may be said to be the intellectual's reason, or the reason with a capital R of the Enlightenment, the Reason
that was forever teaching men self-evident and undeniable truths, it was
most emphatically not Hegel's idea of reason, which he called *Vernunft*,
and which we will call *concrete reasoning*—using the gerund to represent
the idea that such reasoning always involves making a concept and not
merely taking it over as a finished product.

It is a mistake to see these two different forms of intelligence as if they
were two mysteriously different faculties of the mind, which each of us
possesses in equal degrees, like will and intellect. More accurately, they are
different ways of organizing and relating to experience in general, and furthermore, they tend to be historically and culturally embodied in distinct
social groups and even classes—a fact of the most immense importance

for both the theory and practice of politics. This is because a politics of abstract reason will be implacably hostile to a politics of concrete reasoning. While abstract reason wishes to prescribe to the world, to tell it how it ought to be, concrete reasoning does the very opposite. It exists to understand the world—in the belief that by understanding the world it will come to find itself already present in this world—and in the social and political world just as much as in the natural world. This, after all, is the sense of "rational" that Hegel was referring to when he made his famous declaration. "The real is the rational and the rational is the real"— a statement which Hegel acknowledged to have been shocking to his contemporaries, and which is no less shocking to ours.

The best way of grasping Hegel's distinction, I think, is by drawing on an analogy to human language.

To begin with, when Hegel speaks of a system, he means not a deductive system like Euclidean geometry—he is quite explicit about that—but rather the natural "system" that one finds in a human language. What is systematic about a language is certainly not that it is derived from a set of explicitly articulated definitions and axioms. On the contrary, a language simply comes into being through a complicated ad hoc, hit-or-miss, random, scattered, unpredictable process, and yet once it is there, it is identifiably and even systematically one particular language and not another. For example, if you know English, you are able to generate an infinite number of English sentences, as Noam Chomsky has reminded us; what is more, you are able to recognize whether any given set of sounds is a sensible English sentence or not, and all this despite the fact that there are only a few speakers of English who are able to parse correctly the utterances that come out of their very own mouths. Yet this grammatical ignorance in no way prevents these same people from being able, without a moment's hesitation, to detect a grammatically incorrect sentence as "sounding wrong," even though they may be utterly incapable of explaining why it is wrong in terms of the conventional categories of grammar.

An example of this difference between implicit and explicit knowledge may be found in Plato's dialogue, The Euthyphro. Here Socrates, in order to make a point in his argument, must first devote over two full pages of discussion in order to make Euthyphro grasp the difference between passive and active verbs—a difference that we now routinely acquire in what was once, rather significantly, called grammar school, with the difference between us and Euthyphro consisting in the fact that we have been able to profit from the work of those early Alexandrian grammarians who first began to identify the parts of speech, and whose repertoire of conceptual distinctions has come down to us over the centuries in neat and tidy packets of predigested information. It is not that Euthyphro could not use the active and passive constructions of Greek in his actual speech; he, like all other Greek speakers, obviously could. It was rather that he had no explicit way of recognizing or designating this distinction.

This means that Plato himself was utterly ignorant of grammar and would probably have been perplexed about what such a thing could be. He had, of course, mastered the Greek language, but the idea that someone learned a language by mastering a subject called grammar would have struck Plato as nonsensical: language was a skill and a technique of doing, like swimming or riding a horse—or, even more appositely, like mastering a team sport.

For the Greeks, knowledge was what they discovered for themselves without the aid of tradition. For them to get the idea of something, they had to go directly to that something and figure out what it was; they could not first see how it was defined in a book or summarized in an encyclopedia. This is what gives them their eternal freshness. They were like adolescent boys figuring out things on their own, without Dad to tell them how to do everything the right way.

This is the significance of Hegel's statement in the preface to *The Phenomenology of Mind* that "as far as factual information is concerned, we find that what in former ages engaged the attention of men of mature minds, has been reduced to the level of facts, exercises, and even games for children; and, in the child's progress through school, we shall recognize the history of the culture of the world traced, as it were, in silhouette."

Formal education, based on abstract reason, while indispensable to modern civilization, becomes, by virtue of its very success, a danger to the civilization that formal education itself has created. This observation is a variation on the same theme that Jean-Jacques Rousseau explored in his first epoch-making essay, "The Discourse on the Progress of the Arts and Science." The danger of formal education is that it begins to drive out the very intellectual qualities that are necessary in order to achieve original and innovative thinking—the very kind of thinking that it is the whole point of formal education to pass on as rote learning to the next generation. This is how Hegel puts it, again in *The Phenomenology of Mind:*

"The manner of study in ancient times differed from that of the modern age in that the former was the proper and complete formation of the natural consciousness. Putting itself to the test at every point of its existence, and philosophizing about everything it came across, it made itself into a universality that was active through and through."

The difference is the paradigmatic distinction between the figure of Socrates and that of the academic intellectual. Socratic wisdom had an appalling degree of vulgarity about it: there was absolutely nothing that was unworthy of philosophical contemplation. Had he lived in our age, Socrates would have been fascinated and enthralled in contemplating all manner of things that most intellectuals will normally not even admit to recognizing the existence of; reality TV would have provided him with a whole host of topics of philosophic speculation, for example. When Socrates said the unexamined life is not worth living, he most certainly did not mean something as trite and transparently shallow as "Question authority." Rather he meant that we should ponder the vast richness of actual concrete life directly and without any intermediary. For Socrates the examined life was a life spent going out into the world and thinking about what passes before you—developing insight into reality by handling it and kicking its tires, so to speak, and not by merely reading other people's thoughts on it or attending their lectures.

According to Hegel, however, all this has changed with the triumph of formal education, since "in modern times, the individual finds the abstract form ready made; the effort to grasp and appropriate it is more the direct driving-forth of what is within and the truncated generation of the universal than it is the emergence of the latter from the concrete variety of existence." Translated a bit more into English, this means that in formal education our ideas do not come from working out a solution of our own, during which process we will be made aware of the purely makeshift status of such do-it-yourself ideas, but rather they are presented to us as finished and done with, in which case our job is simply to copy them, like a schoolboy copying a set text—which is indeed the fundamental model of learning for abstract reason.

In modern education, we do not begin figuring out what a concept is by first looking at the world in which this concept may or may not be instantiated, and often instantiated in quite different forms, but focus rather on the definition of the concept in isolation from the world. We grasp it as a disembodied ideal—very much in the sense that Plato argued that the forms *(eidoi)* were unchanging and eternal entities, radically separate from the flux and turmoil of the actual.

Even if we grant that this is true of such entities as numbers and circles and straight lines, is it equally true of all abstract terms, and most important, is it true of those great principles that we appeal to when we are making political judgments—principles like democracy and equality, liberty and tolerance? Is there a perfect model of these abstract entities residing somewhere outside the human mind?

At first glance, this might seem to be itself an abstruse and rather unworldly problem for ivory-tower metaphysicians to pursue—like the question, If a tree falls in a wood and no one hears it, does it make a sound? But such a conclusion would be a terrible mistake. The belief that our abstract political ideals exist apart from the world in some eternally unchanging Platonic form is a source of genuine danger to any civilization that has become forgetful of the actual and practical source of all such ideals.

The danger here is that posed by "the fanaticism of abstract thought."

This is a phrase coined by Hegel in a passage in *The Lectures on the Philosophy of History,* where he is analyzing the violent efforts of the French revolutionaries to impose their own ideals on a social order whose structural underpinnings had only recently collapsed. Hegel's point is that violence is inevitable once people have set out to reshape the world according to their own ideals—ideals that turn out to be nothing more than a kind of intellectual make-believe. The resultant complex is a fantasy ideology, one in which those promoting this complex will stop at nothing simply because they have convinced themselves that they—and they alone—have been chosen to advance the ideals that they hold dear.

This fanaticism is not an incidental characteristic of those who become mesmerized by abstract ideals, but the result of any educational system that requires the mastery of a set of abstract symbols rather than immersion in concrete and practical life. It is the result, in other words, of that training by which modern men and women come to count themselves as educated. It is, therefore, an inevitable consequence of being an intellectual in the widest acceptation of this term, and this means, in the United States of today, a very wide acceptation indeed.

The logic behind this fanaticism is childishly transparent: The world does not live up to my ideals of it. Therefore, it must be changed to fit these ideals. And since it is entirely the world's fault that it does not come up to my ideals, the world is in the wrong, and my mission is to set it right by any means necessary. This does not entail, of course, that every educated person is a victim of ideological delirium, but it does mean that all are potential victims.

9

TOLERANCE: A CASE STUDY

ARLIER WE SAW that mankind broke through Gobineau's biological barrier through the acquisition of tolerance, for clearly, as a community becomes less and less addicted to violence, it acquires the trait of being more and more tolerant. But which came first? Did men first begin to *believe* in tolerance and then decide to act on this new ideal? Or did they first break their addiction to violence, only to discover that they had invented the ideal of tolerance, as if by accident?

This question is important, because if we assume that men first glimpsed a pure ideal of tolerance, which they then imperfectly embodied in a concrete community, the first thing that strikes you about it is how poorly they succeeded. This is often the attitude taken toward the seventeenth-century English philosopher John Locke, who in his 1667 "Essay concerning Toleration" argued the case for religious tolerance—and yet not for the kind of religious tolerance that we take for granted today. By tolerance Locke meant tolerance of all the various competing Protestant sects, but not—quite emphatically not—the toleration of either Roman Catholics or atheists.

This exclusion, by our contemporary standards, is not merely inconsistent but hypocritical as well. How easy to tolerate those who agree with you, we smugly think, and how hard to tolerate those who don't—a sentiment derived from our conviction that if we are to be *truly* tolerant, we cannot pick and choose which sects will be tolerated and which won't, but must be willing to tolerate all religious sects and groups, including those who have no religion at all, such as atheists and agnostics.

This modern critique of Locke makes the large, if unquestioned, assumption that Locke began with the idea of tolerance *as such,* and that it was from this abstract idea that he derived his own specific version of tolerance, but that for reasons which were purely personal or arbitrary— for example, because he was an anti-Catholic bigot—he was unable to follow through logically or consistently in his own formulation of the ideal of tolerance.

This modern criticism of Lockean tolerance is an example of what we will call the Platonic fallacy at work—a fallacy that haunts the mind of every intellectual precisely insofar as he is an intellectual and which is a habit as hard to break as any compulsive addiction. It is the nature of the intellectual to always begin with an idea—with the idea of democracy, for instance, and not the actual thing that doesn't quite fit anyone's definition of it. But why on earth should this idea have a higher status than the real, messy thing that is held to fall short of the ideal?

To see where this fallacy begins, and where it goes wrong, requires careful examination. And while the same point can be made concerning any other of the sacred abstractions beloved of modern intellectuals, the example of tolerance is singularly apposite, because we have already seen the critical role that the achievement of tolerance plays in the foundation of our idea of liberal civilization. In short, if the intellectuals have gotten this one wrong, then they have gotten the whole idea of civilization wrong as well.

THE PLATONIC FALLACY

First of all, let's go back and try to understand what we mean when we talk about Locke's concept of tolerance. In other words, when Locke uses the word *tolerance,* what did *he* believe he was referring to?

For the modern mind, religious tolerance is simply a normal function of the liberal state—liberal in the hallowed, old-fashioned, nonpartisan sense of this word. We naturally expect an enlightened state to tolerate sects, and for us it is a matter of relative indifference what sects it tolerates. For us, the only restriction on tolerance would arise if a particular sect wanted to violate the laws of the society.

For Locke, on the other hand, tolerance was made up of two quite distinct aspects. First, there was the empirical fact that a large number of sects had themselves actually elected to tolerate the existence of other sects within the state. Secondly, there was the state's decision to tolerate those sects which had decided to tolerate each other—a decision predicated upon, and even derived from, the previously achieved social tolerance that was already functioning quite well in Locke's England.

The difference is that *we* no longer pay any attention to what in Locke's time was a necessary condition of tolerance, namely, the willingness of the various sects to abide by the ideal of tolerance, whereby they relinquished all desire to have their own sect impose its faith on the state as a whole.

The reason we no longer pay any attention to this is that, in America, it has been a long time since we needed to. All the religions practiced in our society have long since agreed to behave like those early English Protestant sects whom Voltaire admired for their willingness to set up shop alongside their competitors, as opposed to burning them at the stake. As a result, in America there are Protestant Jews and Protestant Catholics and even a few Protestant atheists—the ones, namely, that don't insist on having everyone share their lack of faith.

Viewed historically, Lockean tolerance was an achievement that presupposed a previous achievement, the willingness of most sects to tolerate each other in practice. Without this achievement, the state could not have implemented its own policy of tolerating these sects, and the reason for this should be obvious: a society whose religious sects were committed to a life-and-death struggle for dominance would have created a state of affairs that would have been literally *intolerable.*

Once this is understood, it becomes quite obvious why Locke felt compelled to draw the line at the toleration of the Catholic faith: it was because he believed, quite rightly, that the Catholic Church was not as yet willing to abide by the principle of tolerance that the Protestant sects had elected to follow. It was not merely the Catholic Church's own intolerance that was the problem but the fact that the Catholic Church had a real chance of triumphing over all the Protestant sects. Had it done so, the Protestant ideal of tolerance would have been history and not the wave of the future—including, ironically, the future of the Catholic Church itself. For, paradoxically, it was only through the Protestant intolerance of Catholic intolerance that the latter was eventually brought to an end— a good example of how a confessed "double standard" actually ends by serving the cause of liberalism by preventing others from undermining it. Thus the exclusion of Catholics, though undertaken simply in self-defense, ended in compelling Catholicism to an acceptance of the principle of toleration, a totally unanticipated result.

THE EMERGENCE OF TOLERANCE

It is important not to see Lockean tolerance as a compromise, not even as a necessary compromise forced by adverse circumstances. Instead, we must learn to see the ideal of tolerance as beginning out of the concrete practice of small groups that, piecemeal and bit by bit, learned to adjust their own claims against others and to achieve a practice of mutually collective trust, in limited domains and under specific circumstances. The "ideal" of tolerance, in other words, is not imposed from above but rather emerges from below. It is first glimpsed in the form of concrete social customs and routines, and little by little it is extended by analogy until the same underlying principle becomes the basis of the social interaction for larger and larger collections of people.

Tolerance is not cut from a pattern but grows from a seed.

In our discussion of ancient Greece, we saw that the strange seed from which tolerance grew was in fact the boys' adolescent gang, with its willingness to form a society composed of young males who had no blood connection with each other and who, in essence, agreed to tolerate each other's behavior for the sake of the team, setting the groundwork for the spirit of compromise and negotiated settlement that would evolve into the *polis*, the Roman *patria*, the Christian church, and the modern business corporation.

Clearly the first boys who were willing to join together in a project, despite coming from different families and even tribes, were not consciously modeling their behavior on the ideal of tolerance. They were rather creating a pattern of cooperation from whole cloth, and they made this particular pattern because it was the only one available to them. Outcast boys who have no family have no other choice but to cooperate for their survival in an inhospitable world and to reimagine the primordial division between us and them to run along the lines determined by their gang and not their forgotten families.

But where exactly is the concept *then*, that is, before it is articulated in a symbolic or abstract form? What, to use philosophic jargon, is its onto-logical status? It is not in anyone's head, after all. None of the boys went around thinking, *My, isn't tolerance a lovely ideal?* Indeed, it is possible that none of them even liked the newly innovated prototolerance very much. It may have been imposed on them by their own leader, in order to strengthen their gang. It is even possible that the first germ of the concept of tolerance started out merely as a truce between two gangs. However it occurred, no one can be credited with self-consciously inventing the ideal. Rather, this form of social interaction was accidentally hit upon, and it had, as its serendipitous, unintended consequence, the fact that some people were able to cross the biological barrier and join together in a common purpose, even if this common purpose was simply plunder or escaping death.

In sharp contrast, the Platonist starts with the pure ideal of tolerance and then tries to actualize it in the real world, just as the Demiurge in Plato's *Timaeus* struggles to impose the ideal Forms onto the recalcitrant and unwieldly material world, like a skilled potter working with gravelly clay.

Once you have accepted the Platonist's basic metaphor, however, you are confronted by the fact that there is a disturbing gap between your ideal and its concrete realization—a gap which appears due entirely to the defective nature of the concrete approximation of the ideal and which therefore cries out for redress, a gap that forever discloses the superiority of the ideal over the "merely" concrete and real.

THE FANATICISM OF ABSTRACT THOUGHT

This is the Platonic fallacy and the ultimate origin of what Hegel called the fanaticism of abstract thought—an intellectual pathology that is traceable to abstract reason, with its insistence on the priority of the abstract over the concrete, a pathology that Hegel saw as the cause of the Jacobin Terror, and, indeed, of all forms of fantasy ideology and revolutionary fanaticism.

Hegel's cure for this pathology consists of rejecting the basic metaphor underlying the Platonic fallacy and replacing it with one consciously drawn from Christian doctrine, so that for Hegel, *the ideal exists primarily in its incarnation,* in the flesh and blood of concrete practice between human beings in face-to-face local encounters, in consistent and predictable patterns of behavior. The abstraction of this ideal from the real is, therefore, a secondarily and wholly derivative phenomenon.

For Hegel, the concept of tolerance—what tolerance really is—cannot be grasped all at once but rather appears, step by step and stage by stage, like the development of a flower. If you ask me to point out a flower and I point to a bud, you are apt to conclude that the flower is nothing more than the bud. You would be wrong, of course, but how can I explain that you are wrong if you do not know what a flower in bloom is? And yet, once I have also shown you an actual rose and not a rosebud, you will be able to grasp at once that your belief that the bud was the flower was indeed wrong, and yet only half wrong. The flower is also contained in the bud, so in a sense, if you were to try to show what a flower really is, you would have to show both the bloom and the bud—and indeed the seed as well.

The essence, or in Hegel's language, the concept of a flower is like a faithful transcription of this unfolding, where at each stage of development we can say, "Yes, partly a flower, but not quite completely a flower," but where at no stage can we say, "Finally, there it is, the real flower," simply because the real flower is inseparable from the whole process that produced it from the seed stage to the bloom stage.

For Hegel, the situation is no different when it is a question of the essence of tolerance. Here again we must watch it grow—grow as a human practice blindly and implicitly before it can ever emerge as a conscious and deliberately chosen technique for patterning our social organization.

Tolerance does not begin as tolerance, any more than a rose begins as a rose. At first it is nothing but men chancing, for whatever reason, to come to live with strangers without killing them, and only afterwards does this fact get noticed. But it is the actual arrangement of living together that is primary. Only later is an attempt made to explain in words what exactly this arrangement means, and for Hegel, *it is this process of making the concrete arrangement intelligible to us in abstract terms that is the always defective approximation.* For Hegel, it is our abstract ideas that fall short of reality, not reality that falls short of our abstract ideas, and the only way to make the two fit is to continue to force our ideas to be confronted with the reality, instead of trying to force reality to fit our ideas. This is why the path of abstract reason is what Hegel calls "the path of despair": the abstract ideas provided by abstract reason are constantly challenged by their own inadequacy to articulate the real.

If Hegel is correct, then those who subscribe to the Platonic fallacy are transformed from idealists trying to improve the world into utopian fantasists bent on turning it upside down, all in the pursuit of their illusionary goals. For at the heart of this illusion is belief that the concrete world is still waiting for its redemption through the imposition of abstract ideals onto its own resistant and defective clay.

This view implies a radical critique of the role of the intellectual in the social order—and again, not of the Left-wing intellectual or the Right-wing intellectual, but the intellectual precisely insofar as he is an intellectual. For the danger is that the intellectual, of whatever persuasion, will end by elevating his own particular subjective ideals—which may well be nothing more than whims or caprices or even fantasy daydreams—into a destructive and all-consuming fantasy ideology. For fantasy ideology is the preserve of the intellectual; unless he is very determined to fight against this natural tendency within, this is the risk that he will invariably run when setting about to improve the world. Such improvements are always characterized by one essential quality: they are improvements that the intellectual wants but that the world believes it can do without, as it has done without all such improvements for so much of its not altogether unsuccessful career.

Is this because the intellectual is by nature deranged or evil? Not at all. The problem is rather that the intellectual, simply by being an intellectual, automatically assumes the logical and moral priority of abstract ideas, so that he never thinks of challenging the validity of his own fundamental conceptual categories but always assumes that any misfit between his ideals and reality must be the fault of reality, and nowhere is this more dangerously true than in political thinking.

But where does this tendency come from? We already know the answer to this question: this tendency is entirely due to the fact that the intellectual is the product of modern formal education. To be an intellectual is to have acquired abstract ideas *in their finished and completed form*—a finished and completed form that naturally implies a process of finishing and completing, where this process may have taken several millennia to obtain its goal.

Thanks to the economy of modern formal education, this arduous process of struggling to arrive at conceptual clarity is no longer evident in the finished product, just as the various rough drafts of a novel are no longer present in the completed manuscript. It is this economy, not any besetting intellectual laziness, that makes the intellectual forgetful of the very conditions of the clarity that he simply copies and reproduces, just as a child learning to subtract does not need to repeat all the various missteps occasioned in the history of mathematics due to a lack of a concept for negative numbers. For the child, the existence of negative numbers is a given; negative numbers are not elaborate *constructs*, but simply things like trees and frogs and the moon, and this means that he has no reason to suspect the revolutionary innovation that such numbers represented at the time of their introduction into mathematics—an introduction, it should be noted, that was occasioned by the discovery of the need for such numbers in the concrete practice of accounting. The child acquires the concept of a negative number as a ready-to-hand tool and sets to work with it as soon as he has acquired it. Indeed, he will probably be much more efficient in his use of this tool the less time he spends reflecting on how this tool came to be put into his hands, in the same way that it is easier to learn to *do* calculus than to understand its logical basis as reconstructed by nineteenth-century analysis.

ABSTRACTION AND SUBVERSION

Unfortunately, the intellectual does not limit himself to passing abstract judgments on the past but also actively pursues his critique in the world immediately present to him. In contemplating the social phenomenon called the United States of America, for example, he will, quite unconsciously, automatically see in this immense and staggering complexity of social interactions a set of clear and distinct ideas, such as democracy and capitalism. Instead of beginning with the whole complex mess as it manifests itself in the world, he will replace it with what he regards as a simplified model that contains only the essentials. But this model is itself constructed entirely out of those abstract ideas that he has been given in the course of his education, whereupon he will then either criticize the social phenomenon called the United States of America for its failure to come up to his sacred abstraction of democracy ("What democracy *really* means"), or if he is conservative, he will spend equal intellectual energy in bemoaning the failure of the United States to come up to the standards of small government. At no point will it occur to him to turn the tables on the sacred abstractions and to ask of them, "Why on earth should you have priority here? Why do I judge the United States by you? Instead, why don't I judge *you* by the United States?"

The intellectual might defend himself by saying, "You cannot derive the *Is* from the Ought, or the Ought from the Is. We are concerned with the Ought—with the ideal. Therefore, your critique is not valid."

All the intellectual is saying is, "I don't like the way things are, and I want them to be completely different," which is fine, provided you know that this is what you are saying. But this fact is hidden from the intellectual because he cannot break himself of the habit of seeing the Is as a defective form of his Ought. If the United States ought to be a democracy in his sense, then its failure to be one means that something must be done in order to rectify this shortcoming. For Hegel, on the other hand, the matter was quite different. If the United States is in fact a society that you feel is good—or as good as it can be under the circumstances—then it follows that whatever it is that the United States does to bring about this good is something that it *ought* to do. But this leaves open the question of what it is about the United States that is *in fact* productive of the good that we find in it, and on analysis and reflection we may well find that this good is produced not by its close approximation to your or my ideal of democracy or small government but *by its deviation from this ideal.* There is no a priori reason, in other words, why the venality of Tammany Hall might not have been more conducive to civilized life in New York City than an incorruptible administration run by reformers who alienated the potentially unruly multitude that made up Tammany's political base. Rather, this can only be decided, *if it can be decided at all,* by empirical analysis. The same argument can be applied against every such a priori moral judgment on political questions, for if our standard is a concrete phenomenon and not an a priori abstraction, then it is by the former that we must judge the latter and not the other way around.

From this perspective, it becomes easy to see why intellectuals can be counted upon to play a subversive role politically, and this is equally true whether they spring from the Left or from the Right. Charles Maurras's vision of a monarchist revival in France circa 1900 was just as much a utopian pipe dream as any socialist blueprint for paradise. To use a more contemporary example, consider David Stockman's *The Triumph of Politics,* in which he and other young "Reaganite" intellectuals thought of themselves—and not altogether facetiously—as Bolsheviks of the Right. For Stockman, the Reagan *Revolution* was no quaint metaphor but stood for a genuine ideal.

This denigration of the political—where "political" means what politicians, and not political philosophers, do—is a characteristic and absolutely natural consequence of the Platonic fallacy. Intellectuals of both Right and Left remind us that the reason that we do not have heaven on earth is the willful refusal of politicians to allow the pure and unalloyed realization of the ideal. Politicians talk, trim, hedge, barter, cajole, fix, quarrel, but above all, they compromise.

For the intellectual, compromise is inherently flawed. It is always the compromise of the better with the worse, of the ideal with the contingently existent. Compromise is always an attempt to copy in a defective material some ideal and perfect object, like attempting to reproduce Rembrandt's *Night Watch* in finger paints. This, according to Hegel, is perverse. Compromise is reason in and of itself, both in terms of the *process* by which the compromise is achieved and in terms of the *result* achieved by this compromise. What will always be defective are our own mere subjective ideas about how things should be, and these include even our most cherished ideals, if in fact they are merely our ideals. If a million men dream the same dream but do not act on this dream, it remains just as much a dream as if only one person had dreamt it, and so it is with our subjective ideals.

There is only one way to cure our ideals of this defect, and that is to have other people challenge them. For it is out of this challenge and clash of our subjective ideals against the subjective ideals of others that something real may at last emerge from the cocoon of mere abstraction. No matter how patched up or riddled with logical consistencies this emerging compromise may appear to a disinterested third party, this does not change the great single fact about such compromise—namely, that it creates a new form of reality, one in which what before had been merely ideal and abstract has now gained a foothold in the concrete and practical. This new form of reality not only allows people to work together in terms of the newly created reality, but it also allows them to use this previous compromise as a pattern on which to model other compromises, where what is at stake are ever more serious clashes of our ideals. Such compromises end by creating institutions, if this word is stretched widely enough to include every kind of persistent organizational form. And it is here, in these persistent organizational forms—whether these be Roman legions, Renaissance academies, Dutch drapery guilds, British political parties, or American corporations—that Reason becomes the Real: a claim that Hegel acknowledged was shocking even in his time, but which is no doubt even more shocking in ours. Imagine claiming that General Motors is a better example of rationality than the mind of the solitary philosopher.

At this point it is important for us to recall where this principle of compromise began—namely in the sense of team that emerged with the Spartans and which they passed on to the other Greeks, and to the Romans, and to all the fundamental institutions of the West, without exception. Thus, whenever intellectuals attack those institutions that have continued to embody the spirit of the team, they are attacking the very foundations of liberal civilization—the very thing that permits us to live in peace with one another, even when we disagree over ultimate values and final truths.

To hate compromise is to hate the team. To hate conformity is to hate the team. To permit individual liberty to trump all other considerations, bar none, is to destroy the very possibility of the team—and with it the possibility of a genuinely liberal social order.

That is when the intellectual becomes an enemy of civilization. To merely tell people how admirable tolerance is, rather than training people to conduct themselves in a tolerant manner, is to make tolerance impossible. The same is true of all the sacred abstractions that the intellectual holds dear. For men do not keep in communion by meditating on the virtue of community but by doing things in common, just as the value of cooperation can only be taught by making men cooperate.

YET MAKE NO mistake, the intellectual is also an inevitable by-product of man's struggle to escape the savage mind, and the only way mankind can keep from falling back into this state is through the aid of precisely the formal education that is the source of the intellectual's chronic forgetfulness. It is only through education that mankind is spared the necessity of having to start all over again from scratch in each generation; this means that the further an individual has come from savagery, the greater must be the stock of concepts and skills that he must be required to master in order to keep up to the same level of achievement as the previous generation, and this is assuming that he has no interest in transcending this previous level. But this inevitably means that more and more of what is valuable and necessary knowledge must be presented in a finished and completed form. Who could ever learn modern physics, for example, if he had to refute centuries of arguments for the Ptolemaic system?

We are stuck with the intellectual and with intellectualist habits of thinking. There is no way to go but forward. To try to rid ourselves of the intellectual would plunge us back into savagery. Yet it is not certain that unless we can free ourselves of him we will fare much better. And, of course, by *him*, I really mean all of us.

The only choice is for the intellectual to undergo a kind of conceptual therapy, one that allows him to understand how a concept like tolerance actually grows through compromise and trial and error from an isolated concrete practice into larger and larger patterns that repeat this same concrete practice at higher and higher levels of social organization. Or, to use another metaphor, what is needed is *a critique of Abstract Reason*—a critique that, analogous to Kant's, asks, How is it possible for us to have acquired seemingly ready-made abstract ideals like tolerance and democracy, justice and equality, law and equity, and so on down the list of the sacred abstractions? Once we have asked this question, we will at least not be quite so quick to take these abstractions as things but will begin to see them as processes, as an endless emergence from the implicit into the explicit, a process made up of various stages, all of which, at the time they emerged, represented the very latest triumph of organizational reason.

THE ULTIMATE IRONY of the intellectual is that he becomes an enemy of civilization by refusing to accept the idea that civilization can have an enemy, by dreaming of a world in which men will no longer be driven by what Francis Fukuyama calls "the irrational desire to be recognized as greater than others."

But is it always irrational to wish to claim superiority? If a man is the pilot of a jet airliner and has had many years of experience flying airplanes, is it irrational for him to claim superiority over someone who has only flown several hours of solo flight? Or someone who has never flown at all? If you have staked a claim to a gold strike that you have discovered after years of prospecting, is it irrational to insist that your claim is superior to those who just happened to notice your strike?

To deal with these questions, we will now turn back to Hegel once more, only this time we will take a look at his master/slave dialectic in order to discover what it is really all about. We will discover that it is not at all about a struggle for pure prestige but rather about the price of staking any claim to anything of value in this world—the price being that you may have to defend your claim against those who refuse to recognize it.

10

THE ORIGIN OF THE ENEMY

PHILOSOPHERS HAVE LONG PUZZLED over the origin of the state. As a way of making their ideas clear, they proposed a world in which there were no organized societies—no states or government, simply men wandering about very much on their own—a world which was said to constitute "the state of nature," a state under which human life merited Hobbes's condemnation as being nasty, brutish, and short.

In his seminal "Essay on the Origins of Inequality" (also referred to herein as the Discourse on Inequality), Jean-Jacques Rousseau argued that Hobbes had gotten it wrong. In fact, according to Rousseau, Hobbes did not back go far enough. His men were already recognizably human and were clearly motivated by what Rousseau thought could only have been a later development, namely, *amour propre*—the narcissism of civilized men in pursuit of prestige and rank, attention and admiration.

For Rousseau the true primitive would be quite different from that—in fact, quite different from anything we were likely to come across in our already highly socialized world. Rousseau's explanation of this difference turned on a distinction that he felt was absolutely critical—the distinction between what he called *amour de soi-même* on the one hand and *amour propre* on the other.

* * *

AMOUR DE SOI-MÊME is the love of self that Rousseau says—and the French in general agree—is good and should be, if not encouraged, at least indulged. It is the source of joy in *joie de vivre*. *Amour propre*, Rousseau tells us, is the root of man's misery. This is because, unlike *amour de soi-même*, *amour propre* does not focus on the pleasure of possessing but on the status that possessing is imagined to give us in the eyes of others.

That is to say, if a man drives a BMW because he genuinely enjoys the feel of a good car, he manifests *amour de soi-même;* if he drives it because it is a status symbol, he manifests *amour propre*.

But even with such a metaphor, it is still possible to misunderstand the nature of *amour propre*. It is not the crude, boisterous pride of mere possession, such as the rich man might feel on showing off his Mercedes to someone who drives a beat-up Honda, but something far more insidious. It is the feeling of the man who cares much less about having an eighty-thousand-dollar car than about having one that costs a hundred dollars more than his neighbor's—anything, so long as it ranks just a little bit higher in the infinitely graduated status hierarchy that is the backdrop for all exercise of *amour propre*. It is not the desire to have what others have, which is covetousness, nor even the desire to have more than you have now, which is simple greed, but the desire to have more than others, without which no more amount of moreness is sufficient to avert misery.

Rousseau's primitive, however, would be preoccupied only with *amour de soi-même,* and he would be completely innocent and ignorant of *amour propre*. He would, in short, be like the wild child who was discovered in France nearly a century after Rousseau had originally imagined him in his essay:

> Who does not see that everything seems to remove from savage man both the temptations and the means of changing his condition? His imagination paints no pictures; his heart makes no demands on him. His few wants are so readily supplied, and he is so far from having the knowledge which is needful to make him want more, that he can have neither foresight nor curiosity. . . . *His soul, which nothing disturbs, is wholly wrapped up in the feeling of its present existence, without any idea of the future, however near at hand: while his projects, as limited as his views, hardly extend to the close of the day.* (Italics mine) (Discourse on Inequality)

What Rousseau describes is a virtual state of autism. In fact, men at this stage of their development are so cut off from any awareness of other men that they are utterly indifferent to what anyone else may think about them. There is thus no *amour propre,* or vanity, or ego, in our sense of the word. Men bump into each other and that is all.

Of course, sometimes they bump into one another very hard. Rousseau was under no illusions about the fact that in such savage circumstances violence would occur, but it would simply be the violence of two animals quarreling over food, not violence over questions of precedence or rank. For what rank could there possibly be in this world? Even brute physical strength would be of only temporary value, merely a useful way of dislodging a particularly attractive and juicy rabbit out of the hands of someone who had gotten to it first; it could secure no human prey. At least, not for very long. Rousseau observes:

> I hear it constantly repeated that, in [the state of nature], the strong would oppress the weak; but what is meant here by oppression? Some, it is said, would violently domineer over others. . . . This indeed is exactly what I observe to be the case among us; but I do not see how it can be inferred of men in a state of nature. . . . One man, it is true, might seize the fruits which another had gathered, the game he had killed, or the cave he had chosen for shelter; but how would he ever be able to exact obedience, and what ties of dependence could there be among men without possessions? If, for instance, I am driven from one tree, I can go to the next; if I am disturbed in one place, what hinders me from going to another? . . . Should I happen to meet with a man so much stronger than myself . . . [he could] compel me to provide for his sustenance while he himself remains idle; [but] he must take care not to have his eyes off me for a single moment; he must bind me fast before he goes to sleep, or I shall certainly either knock him on the head or make my escape. That is to say, he must in such a case voluntarily expose himself to much greater trouble than he seeks to avoid, or can give me. After all this, let him be off his guard ever so little; let him but turn his head aside at my sudden noise, and I shall be instantly twenty paces off, lost in the forest, and, my fetters burst asunder, he would never see me again. (Discourse on Inequality)

But if this is in fact the true image of our first state, then we are back to the question with which we began: How did we get to be the way we are now? How is it that we became organized into societies and states? Rousseau offers his explanation with this oft-quoted passage:

> The first man who, having enclosed a piece of ground, bethought himself of saying "This is mine," and found people simple enough to believe him, was the real founder of civil society. From how many crimes, wars, and murders, from how many horrors and misfortunes might not any one have saved mankind, by pulling up the stakes, or filling up the ditch, and crying to his fellows, "Beware of listening to this imposter; you are undone if you once forget that the fruits of the earth belong to us all, and the earth itself to nobody." (Discourse on Inequality)

This is what I am choosing to call the Myth of the Cunning Imposter. It is the idea that human societies arose out of an original act of theft perpetrated by the clever upon the guileless.

The Myth of the Clever Imposter has taken many guises. They all possess the following set of features:

First, since it was the few who imposed upon the many, the few could not retain their control simply by their own collective resources of physical strength—not without enlisting the help of the many, or at least a good number of them, to aid them. And this help was, naturally, obtained by fraud and could only be obtained by fraud. The duping of the many will always be a necessary condition of the rule by the few.

Second, since there were far more of the many than the few, the many could crush the few in a contest of brute force, having many more bodies available to them. This meant that the present system was in fact *less natural* than one in which the many ruled.

Third, the unnaturalness of the present artificial order is what has produced the specific character of human violence—wars, murders, crimes. As we noticed earlier, Rousseau believed that human beings in a state of savagery could injure and even kill each other, but all such action was purely incidental. This state of affairs was guaranteed by the fact, emphasized by Rousseau, that there was no need for a fight to the finish: if one man threatened another, or even licked him in a fight, so what? This other man could simply go to the next tree or cave, and that would be the end of it. In other words, in a state of nature, there was no need for a life-and-death struggle that might always be avoided by flight to another location.

Fourth, the *amour propre* that, according to Rousseau, "leads each individual to make more of himself than of any other, causes all the mutual damage men inflict one on another" and "arises [only] in the state of civil society." In short, *contra* Hobbes, "in the true state of nature, *amour-propre* did not exist."

For Rousseau, *amour propre* is the result of man's "original sin" of property, not the cause. It begins when human beings start to see themselves in relation to others, and hence it can only exist *after* human beings have left their primitive autistic stage, for the autist is supremely indifferent to how he measures up in the eyes of others, simply because in the stage of autism he does not understand what an other is.

The scene that Rousseau paints may seem both too idyllic and far too solitary. After all, when we think of savages, we may be far more apt to imagine cannibals than the noble savage so often associated with Rousseau. Furthermore, we know that mankind has never been solitary but has always been found in tribes or herds. Yet this does not change Rousseau's point in the least.

You can imagine the savages as vicious cannibals who roam in great packs. You may permit them to have all the ties of blood and kinship imaginable. And, lastly, you may even imagine them as having quite elaborate hierarchies based on biological relationships, such as father and son, mother and daughter, uncle and nephew—both actual and merely fictitious.

What you may not have any of them do is to take an order from someone who is not tied by blood to them. What Rousseau is after is how *political* inequality arose—that is, the difference in standing between two groups where this difference cannot be reduced to a biological relationship. How did one group of human beings come to command and another to obey, in those cases where the superiority of those who command is not reducible to a principle of biological seniority?

This is a critically important question. If we look upon this superiority as constituting the essence of injustice and the source of all oppression, wouldn't it be worth our while to discover how such a reversal of the *nat-*

ural order could occur? Here again we return to the question that Gobineau raised, but in an inverted form. Why did some tribes break out of the tribal cake of custom, while the vast majority did not?

The myth of the cunning imposter completely answers the question of the source of human misery. The answer is, in Francis Fukuyama's words, "The *irrational* desire to be recognized as greater than the other." (Italics mine)

TO UNDERSTAND THE master/slave drama of Hegel, we must begin at this point. Our culture trains us. It teaches us what to be ashamed of, what is permissible to do in front of other people and what is not. It teaches us how to show respect and deference, how to indicate that we have a peaceful intent, how to assert ourselves without offending others, and in general how to behave "properly" with others in our interactions with them.

Hegel calls this *Bildung,* which actually does have an etymological link to the English word *building.* Often translated as "education," this term leaves a totally misleading impression of Hegel's meaning, so I will use the phrase *character-building* instead, with as much stress as possible on the architectonic metaphor. Character should always be thought of in the original Greek sense of the word, as a hard, metal stamp that imposes its shape upon the world.

Just as a tall building needs deep foundations and will demand a certain logical pattern in its construction, the first floor coming before the second, the second before the third, so too does the building of human character. But the essence of character-building, like any building, is that it is an event not in nature but outside of it—and indeed *against* it. It is artificial and productive of what would otherwise be highly unlikely. The whole point of character-building is to create human beings who are capable of controlling their impulses, of displaying the quality of self-mastery, of demonstrating that purely practical sense of autonomy that we associate with Jefferson's sturdy yeomen and the solid burghers of Rousseau's *Social Contract*—written, by the way, as a profound second thought to the Discourse on Inequality.

The reason that I have gone on at such length about character-building is that for Hegel it is something that man could not have achieved as long as he remained a child of nature. For whereas Rousseau in his Discourse on Inequality saw all the ills that civilization had brought into existence, Hegel, looking beyond these, also saw those beneficial qualities which could not have been achieved unless men had left the state of savagery and of nature.

If we were to flesh out the dramatic stage setting for the struggle for recognition at the heart of Hegel's master/slave drama, we might describe it this way: The characters in our piece have reached the point where they have mastered the skills required to control, with some degree of success and confidence, the satisfaction of their appetites by means of such techniques as settled agriculture and small-scale animal husbandry. Idyllically isolated communities that were merely extended families would illustrate the scene in history that this stage represents. All human relationships would be manifestations of the family principle.

Now, according to Rousseau's scenario, one day the cunning imposter decides to stake out his parcel of land and say to everyone else in his community, "This land is mine." The problem is, if this trick is going to work, everyone else in the community must understand what "mine" means. But how could they? Remember this is the first time that the word "mine" has been used about land or territory. Therefore, if the people the cunning imposter is trying to trick are to be tricked, they must recognize the meaning of the word from some other context. Where would the community have learned this word?

For example, suppose a member of the community had simply said to the others, "This pot of rabbit stew is mine," or possibly, "This rabbit is mine." Shouldn't he really be the one to bear the blame of being the cunning imposter?

Suppose he has caught the rabbit while he was out hunting and has mixed his labor with its dead body. Indeed, let us suppose that he has diligently been tracking this rabbit for several lean and hungry weeks. So let us imagine him bringing it back and boldly declaring, "This rabbit is mine!"

What sense will his community be able to make of this, if they have never heard the word "mine" used before? How will he be able to convey to them what he is trying to express, namely, his rightful claim to be the owner of this particular dead rabbit and, by implication, his right to make a stew out of its meat that will be consumed by him and him alone— unless, of course, he decides to give others the right to share it with him.

What is it about the rabbit that the hunter can point to in order to demonstrate its "mineness?" Clearly, "mineness" is not what David Hume would call an "immediate and sensuous" impression, or what we might call an empirical quality of the rabbit: the tribe could easily devote weeks and months to passing the rabbit around and examining it from nose to tail, and yet never would it come across the occult quality or characteristic that the hunter claims to have discovered in it.

So where does this strange property of "mineness" come from?

Let us try another Arcadian scenario: the hunter is on his way back to his home carrying his rabbit. He crosses the path of another hunter, one who belongs to a different family. This second hunter has caught nothing that afternoon, and he sees that his fellow hunter has been more successful, and not having eaten for several days, he adroitly grabs the rabbit out of the original hunter's hands. The original hunter in a moment of world-historical inspiration cries out, "Stop! That rabbit is *mine.*" The other hunter, not having a clue to what this might mean, continues to run off with what is now quite clearly dinner (proof, by the way, of Hegel's thesis that it is utterly pointless for individual genius to try to leap ahead of its particular historical era).

Let's have one more try. This time, however, at the point where the first hunter cried, "Stop! That rabbit is mine!" let us have him clobber the second hunter as he is trying to run off with the rabbit. The first hunter then goes over and tries to retrieve the rabbit but discovers that the second hunter is equally unwilling to give it up without a fight, whereupon he proceeds to slug it out with the first hunter, until at last one of them is in a position to run off triumphantly with the rabbit under his arm.

The drawback to this scenario is that no one said the magic word: "The rabbit is mine." They didn't need to. At this point, they are embodying in their actions the behavioral foundations of what will come to be recognized as the meaning of "mine," but only after it has been established by the ongoing repetition of this pattern of behavior. In other words, at some point in time one of two hunters will make use of some expression that will indicate to the other hunter that what he has in his hands he will defend with his fists, and whatever word this is will come to mean "mine." For in point of fact, within the present context, this is all that "mine" can be: *a communally identifiable signal of a willingness to fight to order to keep possession of some desirable physical object.* The complex action by which such a signal is given to other potential rivals is what I will call, for the sake of simplicity, the act of *staking a claim.*

Hegel, using his own language, addresses this issue in *The Philosophy of Right:*

> A person puts his will into a thing—that is just the concept of property and the next step is the *realization* of this concept. The inner act of will which consists in saying that something is mine must also become recognizable by others. If I make a thing mine, I give it a predicate, 'mine', which must appear in it in an external form and must not simply remain in my inner will. It often happens that children lay stress on their prior *willing in preference to the seizure of a thing by others.* But for adults this willing is not sufficient, since the form of subjectivity must be removed and must work its way beyond the subjectivity to objectivity. (Italics mine)

In other words, the seizure of the thing takes precedence over the mere willing, because in seizing it you have stepped from mere subjective intention or willing out into the objective world: your subjective state cannot be recognized, but your physical acts can be, and no physical act is subject to quicker recognition than the act of knocking someone in the head. This has important consequences, for it means that, *contra* Rousseau, the concept of property did not begin when the unilateral claim "This is mine" was accepted by the simplicity of others. It began because such a claim was *not* accepted by others, simple or not. More precisely, it began when such a claim was met with a counterclaim, made by someone who was just as insistent on standing up for his claim as his counterpart was insistent on standing up for his.

This is an unforeseen and unintended consequence of staking a claim: *you are also claiming that you are willing to stand up for it;* if you are not willing to do this, then you have no business staking the claim in the first place. To put it another way, if you are not willing to stand up for the claim you have staked, then you are not the kind of person you claimed to be when you staked your original claim. For every claim has a twofold nature: by staking the claim you are claiming a certain physical object—a stream or a cave or a pasture or a rabbit—but you are also making a second claim, indeed, a meta-claim: you are claiming that you are the kind of person who will *in deed and act* defend this claim against all comers. In the process of staking your claim you are simultaneously claiming a special status for yourself—the status, namely, of someone who is dangerous to cross because you can be relied upon to cause physical harm and suffering to anyone who challenges your original claim. But—critically—if you are not able to deliver on this meta-claim, then you have been exposed as a *bluffer*, as someone whose claim-making activity is not to be taken seriously by others.

The hard, cold logic of the situation requires that if you wish to keep your rabbit—or your stream or your fields—you must be willing to fight to protect and defend them against all comers. Naturally this does not mean that you actually have to fight; it merely means that any challenger must believe that you are willing to fight, and this belief must be enough to dissuade him from challenging your stake.

But this fact has a peculiar result. In addition to getting to keep your rabbit by knocking someone over the head, there is another way of keeping it, and that is to convince someone else that you will knock him over the head if he attempts to take your rabbit. This fact permits the possibility of a feigned defense—a threatening show performed solely as a means of avoiding an actual fight.

This throws a complication into our scenario, for it means that it is perfectly possible for someone to develop defensive strategies in which threats and boasts are used in order to frighten off would-be assailants, and equally possible for these strategies to be devised or imitated by those who in fact are merely bluffing and who have no intention of putting themselves into genuine danger in defense of their rabbit or their fields.

Such behavior, of course, is common in the animal world: cats and dogs both engage in threatening behavior in defense of their territory, and this fact by itself shows that we have still not reached the genuinely and distinctly human level, since the whole point of the threatening display of animals is to get to keep what they want, without incurring damage to themselves.

Let us try to imagine a world of human beings in which all conflict was limited to this kind of thing. If someone wished to keep his rabbit, and someone else wanted to take it, the two parties would engage in all manner of screams and shouts; they would jump up and down as ferociously as possible; they would make absolutely terrifying faces at each other; they would swear to inflict on the other the most blood-curdling cruelties.

In a world where *everyone* is bluffing, the only difference would be that some bluff better than others, so that the winner will invariably be he who bluffs best. In such a world one might even allow *some* carefully measured blows—the antagonists could slap each other's face; they could kick the other in the shins; they could pull each other's ears—indeed, they could tap all the various resources of *nonlethal* combat that have made pro wrestling such an exciting spectator sport, and all for the purpose of making your opponent *believe* that you are serious.

HERE WE NEED to stop the drama and to reflect on the significance of the scenes we have witnessed. We have arrived at the point that we have been looking for: the stage at which, if mankind had only stayed at it, the human race would never have fallen into the horrible habit of oppressing others, and insisting that these things were mine and not yours, and all the other ills connected with inequality. All these woes and ills derive from one single act: someone—just once, somewhere—decided to call the other person's bluff.

That is all it took to start mankind on the path to ruin. Someone said, "Oh yeah? You and what army?" and *meant it.* At that very moment the enemy was born.

Before we must take this fatal step, let us examine the world that we are about to leave, to see if there is any way that we could continue to go on dwelling in it forever.

Now, obviously, the bluffer's world would have some peculiar characteristics. For example, those who bluffed best and who were in turn hard to bluff would dominate over those who bluffed badly and were themselves easily bluffed. It would mean that the easily bluffed could, in fact, be bluffed out of their very existence: that is, when given a choice between calling the bluffer's bluff and dying, the easily bluffed would simply choose to die. The only alternative the easily bluffed would have, aside from rolling over and dying, would be to call the bluffer's bluff *at all costs.* But the moment you have done this, the logic of the bluffer's world—its fundamental ordering principle—is destroyed, and that world collapses into the all-too-real *real* world. There is only one way a person can be determined to call someone's bluff at all costs, and that is to be willing to die.

When I was a child, someone told me about the game of chicken played by teenage boys with their hot rods. The setup was simple: a long stretch of straight road and two cars at either end barreling down directly on each other, where the first to swerve was called chicken and where the one who didn't became the winner.

It was obvious to me, on a little reflection, that there was a surefire way to always win at this game—refuse to swerve under any circumstances. Of course there was a problem with this: the strategy failed if the other player also followed it. The moment it was adopted by two players, there was a problem.

To see how this works out, let us raise the curtain again on our own interrupted Arcadian drama. Only now we are ourselves playing the dramatic personae.

In the neighborhood where we live, there is a vicious-looking fellow whom we call Gog, and it is Gog's nasty habit to go up to anyone who has some tempting morsel of food—such as *your* rabbit—and to demand that it be turned over to him, for his personal consumption. Moreover, Gog is always prepared to back up his demand with a threat, and in this case the threat is, "I will rip your head off unless you give me your rabbit."

Now, by the rules of the bluffer's world, Gog must be the kind of person who can credibly make this statement: he must appear to you to be in such physical condition that this claim does not seem laughable. A good bluff must seem plausible, and Gog's—alas—does.

At first, you respond in kind. You boldly say that you will eat Gog alive if he takes your rabbit, and again, we must assume that this threat has prima facie credibility in Gog's mind. That is, he must size you up as someone who could in fact at least *try* to eat him alive.

For the bluffer's world to be preserved, the fate of the rabbit must be decided by the fact that either you or Gog will, at some point, be intimidated by the other's bluff—emphasized by those nonlethal blows mentioned above. One of you must be willing, on this basis and this basis alone, to call it quits, just as in our game of chicken, the surefire strategy will work only if the other side does not adopt it.

But in our present scenario it has been decided that you are going to stand up to Gog's bluff. You are determined to call Gog's bluff *at all costs*. The bluffer's world will now be irretrievably shattered if Gog, like you, decides that he too is determined to call your bluff at all costs; in this case both of you are committed to fighting until one or the other of you is dead.

Let us step back for a moment and look over the shoulders of our two combatants. We have seen that the logic of bluffing leads one inevitably to the realization that the only proof that one is not bluffing is to stake one's life—and, of course, to be willing to kill one's opponent as well. This does not mean that anyone is necessarily willing to reach this point: again, it is possible to imagine a world in which, each time one came to the very brink, one party always yielded, simply in order to avoid death. There is nothing, in other words, in the logic of bluffing that compels anyone actually to go to the point of dying in order to demonstrate the credibility of his threat. So why would any human being ever elect to call someone else's bluff *at all costs?* Or to put the matter another way, what could possibly bring someone to stake his life on a rabbit, his or someone else's?

The answer begins in the bluffer's world. Imagine what would happen to this world if one day someone, perhaps Gog's older brother, Org the Ruthless, were to come across the following strategy: Org, when he wants something, wastes no time making idle threats. He simply kills the person who has what he is after and then takes it from his corpse. No fuss, no bother—just sheer and immediate killing.

You will note at once that this strategy does not suffer from the drawback seen earlier: Org the Ruthless, in killing a bluffer, is not staking his own life, for he is perfectly aware that the bluffers are only bluffing, and the fact that he is able to kill them proves this to Org. Org is not one to be greatly troubled by the choice between "Your rabbit or your life," which, of course, is quite different from "Your rabbit or my life." Org, in other words, has hit upon a revolutionary strategy that allows him to have your rabbit *without risking his life.*

And this is the fatal weakness of Bluffer's world. It is at the mercy of the first Org who devises a strategy of kill first, then take.

In a world full of bluffers, the ruthless will rule.

Furthermore, Org's strategy has an interesting by-product. When word of Org's methods spreads, it soon becomes possible for Org simply to approach any bluffer with a rabbit or some other goody, and yell, "Hand over that rabbit," whereupon the bluffer, grateful to escape with his life, tosses the rabbit to the approaching Org.

The bully scenario, as we shall call it, allows us to imagine yet another world. In this case the Orgs of a region can expropriate anything that they want or need, and those who are unwilling to fight Org to the death will simply have to relinquish their status as persons capable of staking claims on anything, because, from the moment Org appears, those claims are immediately seen to be mere bluffs.

But the bully world is fragile in the same sense that the bluffer's world is fragile: the ordering principle of Bluffer World required that no one is willing to stake his life at all costs, while the ordering principle of Bully World requires that *no one else* is willing to stake his life at any costs— which means, conveniently enough for Org, that Org does not need to stake his life either.

This last point is critical to the stability of Bully World: for the moment someone is prepared to stake his life against Org in combat, then Org too must stake his life, and with that, the logic of Bully World abruptly collapses. For now it is possible to determine something that could not be discovered previously: namely, whether or not Org was merely bluffing. In a world in which no one called Org's bluff, how could it be decided whether he was really staking his life or not? After all, if instead of docilely tossing Org his rabbit, you stand your ground and tell Org that you are willing to fight him to the death, what choices does Org have? He can turn tail and run off, thus revealing himself to have been bluffing all along. Or he could try to prove to you that he was not bluffing. Either way, the moment you are willing to stand up for your rabbit, Org the Ruthless suddenly is made aware of the downside to his previously flawless strategy—namely, that unless you are sure that you are dealing with bluffers, you face the real possibility that your opponent may kill you before you can kill him.

The problem from *your* point of view is this: How can you discover whether what you have before you is Org the Bluffer or Org the Bully? There is only one way and that is to continue to fight Org as long as he continues to fight you, and this means that—unless Org is bluffing—the fight *must* be a fight to the death. Either he must die, or you must die, or both must die.

You and Org are now both prepared to stake your life and to kill the other—over a rabbit! And this would seem to imply that something has gone terribly wrong in your and Org's analysis of cost-benefit ratios. Are you both, in fact, willing to die over a rabbit—or even, to make the matter a bit more plausible, over a cave or a well-stocked stream?

WE HAVE MET this ruthlessness before, but we can now grasp it in its pristine and primordial form. Ruthlessness is an infallible strategy to use in a world in which no one is willing to fight to the death to defend his stake in something—be it a rabbit, an orchard you have planted, a social order, or a civilization. This is why the enemy can never be exiled from among us: he exists wherever human beings find it important to stake a claim.

To stake a claim is to say that there is something that I must have my way on and that I will not give in to you. It is to resist oppression. But this means that the only way that human beings can resist oppression is to be willing to fight and to die. Otherwise, they are making public confession that others may do with them as they will.

The savage tribes who simply flee when attacked, and who seek out new corners of the jungle in which to hide, demonstrate the truth of this principle and are behaving as Rousseau says savages should. If you are prepared to give up everything, you will not have to fight. Provided, of course, that you are prepared to give up your own will and to become the slave of the ruthless.

This is the climactic scene of the drama. Those who are not prepared to risk their lives—or simply lack the capacity to do it credibly—must accept their fate and become the slaves of the master. Instead of fighting each other to the death, one combatant, hereafter known as the *vanquished,* must elect to submit to the will of the other combatant, hereafter known as the *victor.* But the defeated combatant, by this very act of surrender, automatically relinquishes all claims to the status of someone who is entitled to make and defend first-order claims on the world. He can claim neither property nor even his own person. In behavioral and operational terms, he has surrendered all claims to be recognized as "free" and has thus become the slave of the victor, just as the victor becomes his master. The vanquished from now on will accept the victor's claims unconditionally, whatever these claims may be.

But does this really solve the problem that Rousseau posed in the Discourse on Inequality when he asked how in the state of nature the strong can ever manage to subjugate the weak? What is to keep those who have been temporarily defeated from simply moving somewhere else? To find another cave, or stream, or rabbit? What difference would the struggle over recognition make to the vanquished, if he could simply lick his wounds and slink off somewhere else, thus freeing himself from the servile status to which the victor wished to condemn him?

This is why it is essential to stress the connection between *property* and *the struggle over recognition:* for Hegel, they are merely the two sides of the dialectical coin. The victor is the victor in the battle for possessions by virtue of the fact that he proved himself indifferent, and thus superior, to mere natural possessions. By displaying his willingness to die in a contest for mere things, he was able to convert these things into property at the very same time that he confirmed his claim to a free status, for a consequence of the actualization of this claim is that he is now able to control property (i.e., to defend it effectively against all comers). *Property,* in short, arises only when men are willing to die for their *things.*

In *The Philosophy of Right,* Hegel makes the connection between freedom and property explicit. "If emphasis is placed on my needs, then the possession of property appears as a means to their satisfaction, but the true position is that, from the standpoint of freedom, *property is the first embodiment of freedom and so is in itself a substantive end.*" (Italics mine)

After the struggle for recognition, it is only the victor's freedom that is allowed to embody itself in property; it is precisely in relation to this issue that the vanquished have been vanquished. This entails that, at the end of the battle, the vanquished has accepted the victor's claim to have the sole title to assign, distribute, and generally control all forms of property ownership; the vanquished has accepted this claim because he must accept it. At exactly the same time, by accepting his servile status, he has accepted the status of someone who has no right to claim property in his own name; thus, by his defeat, he loses not merely this or that particular thing he happened to possess: *he loses the title to claim anything whatsoever as his.* And that is precisely what constitutes his servile status—the fact that he cannot make and sustain claims on anything whatsoever. At this point the slave recognizes both the master's claims to status and to property, but the status of the slave is such that no claim of his will be recognized by anyone.

By his willingness to stake his life, the master has confirmed that he is in fact the one who is qualified to defend and protect the holdings of those whom he accepts as his own. His action in the life-and-death struggle confirms his status as someone who can "actually defend" his community's holdings "by force of arms." And the recognition given to him by the slave is the recognition that he is in fact the one who both is *and should be* in charge of the defense of these holdings.

We must be careful in using the word *property,* for in fact what we are really talking about, when a group makes a claim to territory, is something on the order of the gang's turf, or the Greek *polis,* or the Roman *patria.* Underlying all of these ideas is a common theme—that a team has staked its claim to this piece of territory and that it is prepared to defend it against any who would challenge this claim. Here also, in embryo, is that principle of civic freedom—the freedom of the team not to live as the servants or slaves of someone else—that is the first and most fundamental of all senses of freedom.

Ruthlessness founds the state, for only those who have mastered ruthlessness can defend themselves against it. This does not mean that they will necessarily have to resort to ruthlessness in their self-defense but simply that they must know how to do so if called upon to defend against those prepared to use it. And this is why, for Hegel as for common sense, the violence that goes into the founding—and the preservation—of the state must be radically distinguished from violence that is only the assertion of one man's subjective will. In *The Philosophy of Right*, Hegel writes, "Once the state has been founded, there can no longer be any heroes. They come on the scene only in uncivilized conditions. . . . The heroes who founded states . . . did not do this as their recognized right, and their conduct still has the appearance of being their particular will. *But as the higher right of the Idea against nature, this heroic coercion is a rightful coercion.* Mere goodness can achieve little against the power of nature." (Italics mine)

Violence or force is both legitimate and justifiable but if and only if it is used to establish a civilized order (i.e., a state, or to defend an already existent one against attack or internal dissolution). In short, not all violence is equal. The violence which is used to create, defend, and protect the whole social order is rational and legitimate, and this means that violence used to disrupt this social order, to pit one class against another class, to advance the interest of one section, or one ethnic group or minority, cannot be justified and is not legitimate.

Thus the double standard in respect to violence, so deplored by many of our contemporaries, is an unavoidable condition of civilized existence. If the violence of the ruthless is equated with the violence of those who are defending themselves against the ruthless, then the distinction between civilization and de-civilization collapses.

Although we have been discussing cartoon caveman and their rabbits, the issues here are quite serious ones, for contained in the master/slave dialectic is a profound critique not only of Hobbes but of liberalism in general. In his *Leviathan* Hobbes had argued that it was possible, in principle at least, to create a stable and peaceful social order exclusively on the basis of the enlightened self-interest of the individual members of that social order. Each man would see that it was to his advantage to renounce violence as an instrument for his own self-aggrandizement and to permit a monopoly of violence in the hands of a single authority. That was the whole point of entering into the covenant.

Here we see exposed the Achilles' heel of all forms of liberalism, from Thomas Hobbes to John Rawls: the tenet that all men have the exact same proportionate fear of violent death, and that because such a fear is equally distributed, men all have the exact same motive to renounce violence, namely their equal fear of violent death at the hands of their neighbors. But the point of the master/slave dialectic is that all men do *not* have an equal fear of violent death, and that those who have less will rule those who have more. This means, when translated into social and cultural terms, that the social order that instills in its young an ethos of ruthlessness will eventually dominate those social orders that fail to do so.

The historical warrior cults, such as those of Sparta and the Apache, represent the historical manifestation of the basic underlying logic sketched out in the master/slave dialectic. They are flesh-and-blood incarnations of the dilemma inherent in the working out of the logic of staking claims: those who have trained themselves not to fear death, by mastering ruthlessness, both toward themselves and others, are the ones who will rule and dominate, as the Spartans ruled and dominated the helots around them.

BEFORE THE ADVENT of the modern liberal world order, only those cultures that taught contempt of death were in a position to stake a claim to a particular piece of territory, while those who were unwilling to pay such a price invariably found themselves pushed from whatever region they may have temporarily settled in, like those wandering tribes that are forever crisscrossing the pages of Roman and Byzantine history. The only way a people could obtain what the Greeks called a *polis* and the Romans a *patria* was by a willingness to fight and die defending it against those who would take it away.

This is a point illustrated nicely by a passage in Robert Southey's famous *History of Brazil.* Describing Sebastian Cabot's exploration of Brazil, Southey explains how in 1527, as Cabot was navigating the Paraguay River, he came across a tribe of "an agricultural people." Most of the indigenous tribes that Cabot and the other earlier explorers of Brazil had encountered had been very much like Rousseau's savages, of whom they were probably the original model, namely, hunter-gatherers with no fixed abode. But the tribe that Cabot came across "four and thirty leagues up the Paraguay" was not like these others. According to Southey, "as these people cultivated their lands, so also they knew how to defend them. Property had produced patriotism; they had something to fight for; and so well did they fight, that having slain five and twenty of [Cabot's] men, and taken three, they prevented him from advancing."

Mankind faces two alternatives: staying at the same cultural level of Rousseau's savages, and of those who roamed and wandered through the Brazilian jungle, or becoming civilized. Civilization can be reached only by those who, like the tribe that Cabot encountered up the Paraguay, are willing to defend their property—their *patria*—at the risk of their own lives: by those, in short, who have become masters by mastering their fear of death and so transcending their natural attitude. This dilemma confronts classical liberalism with a paradox. Those who renounce violence will have no property or *patria* in which to establish their liberal community. But how can you achieve a liberal community unless everyone who lives within that community has previously renounced the use of violence, since a liberal community is precisely one where all parties covenant to abjure violence as a means of satisfying their needs and desires?

The master's overcoming his fear of death is thus an essential link in the development of human freedom. The master rules because he is the one—and the only one—who is in fact *fit* to rule since he is the only one *able* to rule in a Hobbesian world. The authority of the Leviathan cannot emerge out of enlightened self-interest but only out of an education that instills an absolute fearlessness of death on the part of those who possess the Leviathan's authority. This is the simple reason why both the Greek city-states and the Roman *patria* counted as its citizens only those who were able to bear arms in its defense—and who were able to do so because they had mastered in themselves the savage who wishes to flee in the face of certain death. It was not because they were arrogant, phallocentric male chauvinists. Rather, it was because this was the only possible way in which men could be free in such a world—and the only way that their dependents could avoid being the slaves of strangers.

* * *

THERE IS ALWAYS something touching about claims that invoke natural rights or moral rights. There may well be such things, just as there are transcendental numbers, in some Platonic realm, but they are incapable of settling disputes even with those who are your friends and who subscribe to the same belief system. Your enemy could care less. For him what counts is that you have staked a claim and cut him off from something that he wants, and that is all he needs to know.

Reason and reasoning, in this case, are pointless: you will have your reasons and the enemy will have his. At bottom, all that counts in staking a claim is that one is prepared to fight and die for something.

The moment people have found something worth fighting for, the enemy comes into existence. The enemy is the person who refuses to honor and respect the stake you have claimed; he is your enemy, and you are his. Thus, if civilization is born with the staking of a claim, then it must be concluded that the enemy comes into being at the precise same moment.

Civilization and the enemy are born linked together. They are like the twins Romulus and Remus, concerning whom Livy reports the following legend: "Remus, by way of jeering at his brother, jumped over the half-built walls of the new settlement, whereupon Romulus killed him in a fit of fury, adding the threat: 'So perish whoever else shall overleap my battlements.'" To found a city is to make a mortal enemy; such has been and will be the fate of all civilization.

DOES MIGHT MAKE RIGHT?

We have watched how the master emerged out of the inevitable drama of staking a claim. His ruthlessness, directed both at himself and at others, is the key to his dominance, and it is the slave's lack of ruthlessness, in respect both to himself and to others, that condemns him to his condition as someone who can stake no claims of his own.

Is this just? Certainly not by the standards of the liberal cosmopolitan. Is it avoidable? No, because if we follow the dialectic step by step we can see that this was the only way man could possibly emerge from his original savagery. As Hegel says, "Mere goodness can achieve little against the power of nature."

Does this mean that the master has come to dominate the slave by brute force? No, this formulation is a parody of the true relationship between the master and the slave. The Spartan, for example, did not dominate the helots because of brute force, but rather because he had organized an entire community in which citizens were trained to think nothing of facing death in battle. That is not brute force, but something quite different: it is character-building on a communal scale. The Spartans, after all, had no advanced technical gadgets or wizardry; their material was themselves, and from the moment of birth the Spartan was subjected to a rigorous and often even vicious mode of discipline and training, the sole purpose of which was to ensure that Spartans would live free and subject to no one but Spartans. Their walls, as they so often boasted, were themselves, and it is a boast not without the deepest significance.

To call this "Might makes right" is a typical misunderstanding brought about by abstract reason, for in falling back on this slogan, we are once more committing the cardinal sin of forgetfulness. We are focusing on the result of Spartan might, while overlooking what was involved in the creation of this result.

History shows that when a crisis comes, it is dangerous to try to create samurai from scratch for the purpose of fighting against the new practitioners of ruthlessness. Yes, you may equip your defenders with authentic samurai swords, and dress them up in samurai robes, and even give them lectures on the samurai code of honor.

But lectures on a code of honor can never suffice, because a code of honor can only be acquired through character-building techniques that must begin when you are a child and that cannot be taught from a book. A code of honor, if it is to protect you from those whom you have entrusted to protect you from your enemies, must be hardwired into the nervous system of your particular samurai, so that it becomes absolutely unthinkable for any of them to violate it.

Sparta was the first society that was able to implant such a code of honor in those who were the defenders of the city, and all societies that have been able to successfully overcome the addiction to violence *within* their communities have found it necessary to reproduce the Spartan technique.

A society that has paid no attention to this problem runs a serious risk, not only of being unprepared to defend itself against the emergence of new agents of ruthlessness, but of being forced to entrust its fate to men who have not been brought up to be worthy of that trust. And that is why every society that has been able to keep violence from engulfing its own community has needed to address the question of how to create guardians who may be trusted in a time of crisis not to take advantage of the weakness of the social order that has turned to them for its salvation.

Bonaparte rose to power in precisely this way. France, weary of unending revolutionary turmoil, turned to him to protect it from the next outbreak of ruthlessness on the part of this or that political clique, or to use our terms, gang. In appealing to him, however, they were appealing to a man who had no code of honor and who sought only glory and prestige for himself and his family. Thus played out the pessimistic cycle that we observed earlier: the Bourbon family dynasty was destroyed by a gang takeover, after which the gangs fell to disputing with one another, so that the general population was more than happy to hail the coming of a savior, who proved to be a tyrant and who ended by trying to establish a family dynasty that would be perceived as legitimate. And, oh yes, each gang had its own pet fantasy ideology, and there are people who, even today, take their intellectual content quite seriously, but each ideology was merely a technique for making this or that particular gang feel that it was on the right side of history, so that it could pursue its own agenda with the requisite ruthlessness.

This is why fantasy ideologies have been the number-one enemy of civilization since their emergence out of the French Revolution. For their purpose is, above all else, to undermine and subvert the code of honor that governs civilized life, so that it becomes impossible to trust those whom we have always trusted. Their job is to make men feel unashamed of doing what they were raised to feel ashamed for merely imagining.

Indeed, the pivotal event of the French Revolution was the moment that the soldiers of the king, sworn and trained to obey his commands unthinkingly, began to think about those commands. From the second that the French officers asked themselves, "Why should we obey *him?*" the king and the monarchy were doomed.

A code of honor is essential to the survival of civilized values in a community, and it is most indispensable in the class of men who are the leaders of that community. Enlightened self-interest cannot replace it, nor can all the abstract ideals and values in the world. The code of honor must rather be embodied in the deepest customs of the society and ingrained into the character structure of its leaders; anything that threatens this code of honor is a threat to the survival not only of a community's values, but of its very existence as a community.

This is a truth, that no society, including our own, can afford to forget.

11

THE RARE VIRTUES OF THE WEST

LET ME BEGIN with a modest proposition.

When someone says that he wishes to live in a society that upholds certain values, what he means by this is that he wishes to live in a society that actually practices and observes these values and not merely in one that pays lip service to them, just as we all prefer to deal with a man who is actually honest in his transactions rather than a man who merely pretends to be honest.

If you agree with my modest proposition, you are like me and most other people. We prefer the genuine to the sham, the practiced to the preached. But how far are we willing to go down this path?

For example, imagine a world where no one espoused the *ideal* of honesty, where even the very concept of honesty was lacking, so that there were no words for it. One might think of this as a land stumbled upon by Gulliver in his travels—a land where no one stole or lied, simply because it didn't occur to them to do so, a land where honesty was an unthinking and automatic habit, so deeply embedded in the folkways that it appeared as much a phenomenon of nature as gravity. In this land, consequently, there were no sermons or speeches praising the value of honesty, no ideology to moor it up, no philosophical principles to offer a metaphysical foundation for it. It was simply what "everyone" did, and because it was what everyone did, there was no problem in assuring the

181

social reproduction of this value: people simply picked up their habit of honesty just as they picked up their language, by spontaneous and untutored mimetism, that is, simply by doing what others did.

Now suppose Gulliver is called upon to leave this happy land—which we shall call Happy Land—and suppose that his ship is knocked off course, so that he is stranded on the beach of yet another terra incognita. Here he is met by a host of well-dressed figures, each of whom represents a learned discipline—theology, philosophy, law, political science, and so forth—and these worthies proceed to entertain Gulliver by a number of very stirring set speeches, all of them in praise of honesty. Gulliver soon learns, however, that things are not what they seem in this new land, and shortly discovers that the same worthies who lectured him on honesty have—while his back was turned—plundered his shipwrecked vessel of all of its valuables and left him without a cent or a sail.

This land—which we shall call the Not So Happy Land—is one in which everyone praises honesty but no one practices it. Of course, they all want to practice it very badly, and they spend most of their time—when they are not off stealing and plundering—in long philosophical disquisitions on the value of honesty, in the vain hope that by contemplating honesty as a Platonic ideal, they will one day be able to go into their friends' homes and not exit with the spoons up their sleeves.

What makes the difference between Happy Lands and Not So Happy Lands?

If you wish to live in a society in which specific values are genuinely embodied, then you must recognize that there are certain necessary conditions that this society must meet before it can successfully embody the kind of values that you wish for it to embody. In point of fact, in order for a society to embody liberal values, certain quite illiberal conditions must first be met, without which there can be no liberal values at all.

This is because every liberal society needs shame. Shame is a force superior to reason because it is rooted in the deepest of our fears—the fear of being abandoned. Shame always contains the threat of expulsion from the community, be it that of the family or the team—the threat of being condemned to the primordially wretched status of the outcast and the pariah, to be marked as the internal enemy, the ultimate bounder. This is why shame is a reflex long before it is a subject of reflection—a crucial fact that has both good and bad consequences.

It is bad because shame is utterly shameless. It is without principles.

It does not begin with a set of ethical axioms, from which it proceeds to deduce all the specific applications of these axioms in our daily living. On the contrary, the shame system makes up lists and inventories of forbidden conduct, like the code in Leviticus, where there often seems to be neither rhyme nor reason guiding the selection. It follows no apparent method and makes no connection: it just piles one thing on top of the other.

There is nothing that men cannot be made to feel shame for. Shame is value-free: it can be attached to acts of altruism as easily as it is attached to acts of the vilest egotism. It may mandate murdering strangers or providing them with shelter. It may make us reach out to take care of another man's child or force us to abandon our own. It serves equally well the purposes of civilization or of savagery.

Yet shame systems are essential to civilization because there must be high levels of what is called simple pride among citizens. For what else is simple pride than the acceptance of the shame system of one's community as an ethical obligation to which one has voluntarily bound one's self, thereby translating these obligations from the realm of the arbitrary and accidental into that of the essential and deliberate?

But if this is true, it follows that it is through shame that even our most liberal and generous sentiments—and values—are anchored. It is through shame, ultimately, that we develop the tendency to treat other people decently, and with fairness, and to judge them according to the "content of their character and not the color of their skin," in Martin Luther King Jr.'s famous words. It is thanks to shame—paradox of paradoxes—that we are enlightened.

Hence, if you wish to live in a society that embodies liberal values and does not merely give them lip service, it is essential that these values be anchored at the visceral level in our automatic and mechanical sense of shame and pride.

This means that those who wish to live in a world that embodies liberal values must recognize that their own ideals cannot be actualized in the community without having been previously moored in the shame system, and that any attempt to circumvent this system, or abolish it, is doomed not only to failure. It is also doomed to betray the very values that it is attempting to secure.

This, of course, is the truth that every religion has instinctively grasped. It explains why religious education has always consisted of instilling a set of automatic and mindless prohibitions in the child's nervous system, long before any effort is made (if any effort is ever made) to convince him of the truth of this or that article of faith. It also explains why every religion has taken such pains to make the individual feel ashamed to depart from the shame system of his community and why all sorts of devices have been employed to bring him back to the fold, from stoning to excommunication to mere shaming. It also explains why the clash of cultures—especially those that have radically different shame systems—can take on such ferocity: the conduct of the Other is all too often conduct that, by our lights, is shameless.

Once again we find that the rationality of the social order is dependent on what appears to be an underlying irrationality, for no shame system can be acquired by means of a social convention to which people may freely ascribe. Rather it must already have been instilled and implanted *before* we are capable of achieving the consensus that would be necessary to found the system on a social convention. Yet without this illiberal and universal inculcation of shame, no community would be able to achieve the trust system that is indispensable to all liberal societies.

A trust system functions by ritualizing possible occasions of conflict in such a way that they are less likely to lead to outbreaks of violence and disorder, and it does this by instilling in each of the members of the community in question an automatic and instinctive respect for the rules of the game, so that each actor would feel ashamed to violate these rules, even if doing so gave him a better chance to win the prize that is at the heart of the conflict. It may accomplish this through good manners, as in "polite" society, or through informal teasing and ribbing, as in a blue-collar shop; or through the elaborate protocol of peer review among scientists; or through good sportsmanship among professional baseball players.

This fact explains why loyalty to a trust system, whether it be your school, your team, your shop or your corporation, or even your country, is held by common sense to be intrinsically, and not merely derivatively, valuable. All these forms of team loyalty, including patriotism, are not merely means to an end—that is, instruments for achieving a specific goal or objective; they are also ends in themselves. This is the great secret of any truly successful team, be it a Baptist church, a gay community, a blue-collar business, a well-run high school, or a whole society: to wit, that those who enact its interaction rituals must be uniquely proud of their particular team. They must believe that there is some special quality that makes them a team, much as lovers believe that fate has brought them together.

Without such communal enthusiasm the fluency and naturalness of the trust system's interaction ritual will begin to dissipate, and people will become conscious that what they are doing is simply the same old routine, and they will no longer feel the magic in it. This is precisely what happens when the sense of legitimacy essential to any healthy team—its feeling of rightness to those who obey its rules—is challenged by those who wish to subvert or destroy it.

Despite the advantages of the shame system, there is one thing that it cannot do. It works by making people ashamed to behave in a certain way because they are afraid of how other people will react to them. But this in itself limits its ability to control behavior. For what happens if there is no one around? What if a man were given the famous Ring of Gyges that rendered him invisible and thus able to escape the scrutiny of the public eye? What becomes of your trust system then?

This is a challenge that would not be met until what Hegel regarded as the third and final stage of human freedom had emerged in northern Europe, approximately a thousand years after the collapse of the Roman Empire in the West. And the key ingredient in this new mode of human consciousness was the concept of the conscience.

THE WEST—or more broadly, as defined in this book, civilization as a whole—does not have a monopoly on shame, or trust systems, or codes of honor. We must add ingredients on top of these to discover what in the West is so precious and worth defending.

The Protestant Reformation began by demolishing the traditional method by which the human race was able to assure itself of having done the right thing, namely, appeal to an external authority, one that resides in either the social or the religious order. At first glance, this would appear to be an open invitation to moral and social anarchy. If the ultimate law was God's Book, and the ultimate authority on this law was you, who was in a position to contradict you? So what if other men thought you were misguided or wrong or even dangerous; who were they to judge?

The priesthood of every man is the most revolutionary doctrine that the world has ever known. The Greek Sophists, in comparison, had merely argued that man was the measure of all things, which simply meant that no man could claim to have more than mere opinion on any matter. But this produced only a democracy of uncertainty: we were all equally unqualified to speak for the Absolute. The Protestant doctrine held, however, that every man could know God's will in every particular case that came before him.

This claim was made all the more extraordinary because it was accompanied by a rejection of the trustworthiness of human reason. Reason for the first Protestants was not merely the slave of passion; it was its whore. It could not offer the individual any guidance, since it was notoriously corruptible; every blandishment of secret selfish pleasure could lure it from the straight and narrow.

Thus at a single stroke both authority and reason were cast aside as guides to human conduct. What did that leave?

The answer, of course, was conscience.

With the coming of the Protestant Reformation, whole generations that had been raised under the authoritative teaching of the Roman Catholic Church suddenly questioned the validity of those teachings, despite the fact that many of these had no doubt become part and parcel of his being. The Protestant experience of conversion was the triumph of conscience, for all at once the entire stock of a person's internalized system of values— the superego, if you will—was thrown open to question. Things that people had been trained and taught to regard as right were now seen and felt to be wrong. No wonder then that the Catholic Church thought that the Protestant idea of conscience was simply the old abomination of pride, the primordial sin that drove Adam and Eve from the realms of Eden.

Certainly the Catholic Church was right, in that pride was part of it all. Only proud people are capable of entertaining the illusion that they, and they alone, might be entrusted with the keys to the secrets of the universe. This was not the pride merely of the individual, however, but a new kind of pride—a collective pride that resided in the whole community. Furthermore, it was the pride of a completely independent people, of successful citizens who had made it on their own—and not on their own as separate individuals, but as a team.

The doctrine of conscience could only occur to people who have long since been making almost all of the decisions about their own affairs, people for whom there was no powerful agency that required either their intellectual or their spiritual submission or subjected them to its guidance and manipulation. The doctrine of conscience was, in a sense, a "rationalization" of what was already present in the Northern European urban middle class, the sense that they could handle things themselves, without the intercession of any higher authority.

The independent burghers of Germany had learned to handle an enormous complexity of human interactions without the continual appeal to the decision-making authority of some outside agent. This was an immense achievement. What happened was that one day, in their great pride at their achievement, they noticed what they had done, and they decided to turn their spontaneously evolved ethos into a consciously articulated and explicitly confessed principle.

They had discovered conscience.

The prosperous German middle class had invented a system for spontaneously resolving disputes without the intervention of a third party. It had worked so well for them that they decided to make an issue of it, that is, to turn it into a principle that could be applied more generally, in regions far beyond the original application. This means that it is an error to ask whether Protestantism caused capitalism, as Weber argued, or capitalism Protestantism, as Marx argued. Rather, the ethical habits that permitted the rise of capitalism were the same ethical habits that were promulgated in the doctrine of the priesthood of every man, and that gave birth to modern professionalism as well.

Professionalism is different from classical courtesy, because in the latter there is a concern with the avoidance of conflict, since aristocratic manners are designed not to offend the fragile ego, the *amour propre* of others. Thus the elaborate rituals for accommodating each person's desire to be treated as something special that is so characteristic of courtesy. In contrast, professionalism is an exhibition of absolute self-control to the point of allowing the other party to determine the standard of behavior that you will follow with him. Imagine how you would feel if your doctor dressed in his bathing suit examined you while talking on the phone with his sister. You would feel outraged: he was not taking you seriously. That is what the theatrics of the professional image is all about, to induce the client into believing that he is being taken seriously.

The client has a claim to the undivided attention of the professional, and anything else is an insult. Here again, the professional cannot make up his own standards of what constitutes taking others seriously. He must adopt the standards of those whom he wishes to convince that he is taking them seriously.

In sum, to advertise yourself as a professional is to announce to others that you will behave predictably, that you will do what you are expected to do, and that you are the kind of person who can be counted on. It is to say to the world, "I renounce my own private judgment on my conduct, for I have personally committed myself to the standards of respectable conduct in everything that I do." Respectable conduct is conduct in which the community at large can find no fault.

It is critical to understand that the concept of conscience could not have come into existence in a community that did not already *embody*, and not merely give lip service to, the ideal of respectability (i.e., it had to be a community in which people really acted respectably, and hence really were respectable). The principle of conscience would be too dangerous to let loose among people who could care less what other people thought of their behavior, for in this setting, the doctrine of conscience would in practice be an invitation to anarchy.

Respectability must be a behavioral norm of any community before that community can begin to entertain even the *illusion* of conscience. Before people can take such a thing seriously, they must first be able to look around them and see a community in which more or less everyone is behaving respectably.

THE ETHICAL COMMUNITY AS THE HIGHEST STATE OF FREEDOM

Such a community may be call an "ethical community," and it is here that Hegel locates the highest form of freedom obtainable to human beings—the kind of freedom that is present when *all* men are free, which is opposed to those earlier stages represented by the two modes of human organization that we have already come across, namely the family and the team.

In Oriental despotism, the ruler was rendered legitimate by a metaphoric framework drawn from biology: the king was to his subjects what the father was to his family—a father who could, depending on his mood, be tyrannical, forbearing, loving, cruel, stern, indulgent. In a word, capricious. In the ethical universe of the Oriental despot, only one man was free.

In the Greek city-state, on the other hand, the rulers were teammates. What connected them was not kinship but a common team spirit, a feeling for what the Romans called *patria*.

Yet in this world, though there was freedom for the members of the ruling team, the price of this freedom was high—and familiar to us from our exploration of the master/slave dialectic. The freedom of the team was a result of the team's obsessive and exclusive dedication to the cult of military virtue; the team could reproduce itself only by instilling fearlessness into the next generation through a rigorous discipline that excluded even the thought of manual labor. In short, the same military cult that assured the freedom for the few, namely the members of the team, could only exist when supported by a system of slavery, or at best serfdom, for the many.

These rules no longer held in the well-ordered trust systems that were associated with the Protestant religion, where all could be free without requiring the enslaving of any.

It is important to understand that in going from the freedom of one to the freedom of the few and finally to the freedom of all, it is not that many more have the same thing, i.e., freedom. It is rather that each kind of system produces its own kind of freedom. In the despot, freedom of caprice; in the warrior, freedom from the fear of violent death; and in the Protestant burgher, rational freedom—the freedom that arises out of self-mastery.

By *rational freedom* Hegel meant nothing remotely metaphysical. Free here simply refers back to the kind of practical and everyday autonomy that was so highly valued by both Jefferson and Rousseau—the ability of the average man to take care of his own needs, to exercise mature self-control over his impulses, to look after both himself and his family, and to stay out of other people's hair.

This kind of freedom is clearly different from the freedom of following one's own bliss that is represented by the principle of liberal autonomy, for it is a freedom that can only be actualized in precisely the kind of community that is created through the constructive illusion of conscience. That is to say, it can only occur in a society where all the members trust each other to exhibit mastery, not over others, or over the fear of death, but mastery over something even harder to achieve—one's own impulses and fantasies and wayward desires—a conquest that even Alexander the Great, master of the world, could not achieve.

But this self-mastery, as we have seen, is something that can only be realized through the character-building preparation of a moral education. The result of this Protestant character-building was a group of adults who had acquired through the rigorous shame system of their culture a kind of imprimatur, a guarantee of their power of self-control—a power that permitted them to be implicitly and completely trusted.

Businessmen were able to trust each other across the continent of Europe—an amazing feat. How did men manage to trust each other enough to ever let other people handle their money?

This is an achievement reminiscent of the Imperial loyalty training given to an elite few in Frank Herbert's novel *Dune*. Once a person had been passed through this quite daunting procedure, there could never be any doubt whether he could be trusted. There was literally nothing, not the fear of violent death for either him or a loved one, that would make him betray his sacred loyalty. In the novel, such men were produced because it was obvious that having a pool of such men around is extraordinarily useful: a person who can be trusted without reservation is obviously a valuable asset for any community to have, and it is to such men that any task involving honesty or loyalty will be entrusted.

Yet, would this be any less true if the same effect had been produced not by special training but by an inherited shame system based on a religious superstition? You may believe that the Protestant doctrines of grace and predestination are absurd, monstrous, and irrational—vile superstitions without a trace of humanity or veracity in them. But this does not change the fact that the shame system associated with these ideas did in fact produce a new kind of man, the professional, the man who, like the characters in *Dune,* could be implicitly trusted by those who dealt with him.

This was the man who put his duty to the team community first—meaning that before all else, he would follow the rules of play that supported and upheld the team. All the other members of his community could be certain of his conduct; they had no need to waste any effort in wondering what his next move would be. In conducting himself in this way, the professional abandons the pursuit of his own bliss.

The famous Protestant work ethic was in fact the natural result of this professional attitude toward one's work, which invariably meant putting the task to be done ahead of the subjective wishes or caprice of the individuals assigned to doing the task.

The work ethic had a flip side to it. For in wishing to get the job done, the professional was in fact putting the wishes and desires of his client ahead of his own. The cobbler, like Hans Sachs in *Die Meistersinger,* who works late at night to finish a customer's pair of shoes, might be shallowly adduced as an example of the Protestant work ethic, a man addicted and driven. In reality his action was an example of impulse control in the service of others, though one that had been made so automatic, so fluent, that it no longer seemed remarkable either to the cobbler or to his customer.

In such communities, the professional attitude, born of the Protestant conscience, was linked with the team model of organization through the guild system, and the end result was a community that was unique in requiring as little external compulsion as is possible with a given amount of social complexity. Each member of the community saw himself as a fellow player on the same team; his sense of civic loyalty was intense and unquestionable; and each had the same level of confidence in his fellow citizens that a dancer in a quadrille has in his partners. These beliefs engendered a community in which very little was needed to maintain the "trust equilibrium" of the community. Men policed themselves, judged themselves, ruled themselves. All civic business was carried out through those mutually collective processes that we examined earlier.

This was not the moral autonomy of the isolated individual confronting a universal reason, or the liberal autonomy of the man who follows his own bliss, but an autonomy *within* the team system—a mutually collective autonomy, a self-mastery that is like the mastery of the game of basketball shown by a well-drilled squad or the mastery of the Brahms *First Symphony* shown by a great orchestra, in which each player knows when he is to play and, even more important, when he is to be silent.

This is the ideal trust system if one is interested in simultaneously reducing violence and maximizing equality; it represents, for Hegel as for Rousseau, the ideal social order as such. It is in such societies that human beings are able to maximize those qualities that are the cardinal virtues of civilization: stability, spontaneous cooperation, tolerance of their neighbors, and the abstention from violence as a way of settling conflicts.

For those who wish to live in a social order that actually embodies, rather than preaches, the virtues of peace, freedom, and orderliness, the burden of proof is upon them to show where human communities have ever existed that exhibited a trust system in which these virtues were embodied in greater abundance than in the capitalist West.

They can't. That is simply a historical fact. Most of us could have lived rather comfortably in Adam Smith's Glasgow, Samuel Johnson's London, or even Calvin's Geneva—certainly more easily than in Montezuma's Mexico City or Caligula's Rome or Ramses II's Memphis.

This fact has enormous consequences, for it means that the conditions that produce a high degree of civilization, including the shame system and the various constructive illusions required to produce and sustain it, must now be seen as necessary conditions of that civilization and not as primitive holdovers from an outmoded tradition, the product of ignorance, folly, and cupidity, designed merely to pointlessly repress the healthy natural instincts.

If such "repression" is a necessary ingredient in constructing an ideal community, then it is no longer repressive, but transformative. Repression is a shove that merely knocks something back into place; the character-building education that results from the shame system *and* conscience produces a code of honor that is one of mankind's greatest achievements, and it enables all the accomplishments that are normally listed under our "great achievements."

This is different from what the shame system by itself can produce—as anyone who had ever lived in a society governed only by shame immediately realized. This difference is why capitalism has been a progressive force in the world—indeed, by far the most progressive that has ever existed. Not because it is an efficient mechanism for producing wealth, but because those who lead such societies will under normal circumstances represent the virtues that professionals find most admirable—an avoidance of violence as a problem-solving technique, a preference for consensus over conflict, a high degree of cognitive sobriety, and reliability. Once they gain power, such leaders expect to do very much what they had done before they gained power. This is why democracies virtually never go to war with one another; it is not because they are democracies, but because they are managed and operated by trained professionals whose habits preclude taking unnecessary risks.

This, however, is not the only reason why capitalism, despite its critics, has operated as a progressive force in the world. For if you want to make a human characteristic undesirable among those in a business-governed society, make those who conspicuously display this characteristic unemployable—or even employable only at lower levels on the socioeconomic scale—and you will see just how quickly that unwanted characteristic disappears.

This is useful. Because it allows a society to collectively exercise an enormous degree of control over the behavior of its members, and in particular the behaviors of those of its members who might otherwise be most susceptible to requiring much stronger forms of social control; and here I am referring to young men. The reason why young men have been induced to work is not because they are more competent than women nor because women have to stay home to have babies. It is because if the men stayed home instead, they would soon be forming into warrior bands, such as the Apaches and the Spartans.

When men have nothing else to do, they go bad—and they go bad very quickly. It is male idleness that is the one thing that can be pointed to as a factor promoting terrorism, since this same idleness is always productive of some kind of ruthless behavior. Eliminate this idleness and you help to eliminate terror.

The more young men a society can attract to peaceful employment the better, and this is true whether the employment is useful or not. This means that if you can afford to put young men to work digging ditches and filling them in again, then you have benefitted society by diverting these young men from pursuing the way of the ruthless.

But can you?

No society has ever been rich enough to bribe all its potentially violent members—some will always aspire to be the giver of the bribes rather than the receiver. And that is why this was a problem that could not be solved until the advent of capitalism.

Capitalism discovered a way of giving young men peaceful work that was self-sustaining. Organize the young men to make things and to give services that other people will pay money for, and from the money you receive, you can pay the young men enough money to keep them from turning to violence. Note that what I am talking about here is not the violence that a starving beggar employs to kill a rich man for his loaf of bread, but the violence of gangs fighting over turf.

Capitalism then is the only known preventive for the rule by gangster and warlord; and it has achieved this quite by accident.

No one meant capitalism to do this; it was not why it spread. Its elimination of this form of social pathology was the serendipitous outcome of the desire on the part of various clever and energetic individuals to get rich quick. Businessmen, who hate uncertainty above all things, dread the rule of the warrior gang or the gangster and do all within their power to keep testosterone at bay.

* * *

THE BIRTH OF THE concept of sovereignty in the writings of Jean Bodin, during the same period as the heyday of the Protestant communities of Northern Europe, was not a meaningless coincidence. For sovereignty is dependent on a well-ordered team community in which the society's leaders, no longer guided by the warrior aristocrat's sense of honor, have developed the kind of self-control provided by conscience. The sovereign, in other words, differs from the despot, the tyrant, the king, or the emperor—indeed, any previous incarnation of political power—not by virtue of his own qualities, but by virtue of the qualities of the community of which he is in charge.

In a nutshell, the sovereign can rule as a sovereign, and not a tyrant, only if the members of the community that he governs already know how to govern themselves, as they do in the ethical community. A sovereign is only required where men have mastered the art of ruling themselves in normal daily life; they do not need the master to discipline them any longer. Yet they are also aware that no matter how well they may govern themselves, certain exigencies will arise where a collective and common policy must be determined for the whole community, such as in an act of war. In that case there must be some one unique agent that can represent the community in its dealing with other communities.

THE ART OF WESTERN LEADERSHIP

The necessary preconditions of having a sovereign are radically different from those required to have a master. First, the community must have genuine interests and objectives that are supported by "the general will" of the community, that is, virtually the entire community. These are those things on which everyone more or less agrees, such as emergency actions in time of collective disaster or common peril.

Second, there must be a tradition that holds it possible for human beings to conduct themselves objectively, in the manner of a professional or of Adam Smith's disinterested spectator. In a world full of cynics, there can be no sovereign—a high price to pay for cynicism. This too is why the team model is alone able to produce sovereignty, and not the family model. It is only the team that can even imagine human beings as capable of objectivity, for what objectivity means, in practice, is precisely the willingness to be guided by the good of the team and to not be swayed by what is good only for you, your family, or your tribe.

Third, there must be a mode of training certain human beings, like the Imperial training in *Dune,* whereby those who have been through such training can be trusted implicitly by the members of the community to act as disinterested agents in the case of conflict, so that there will be no anxiety that the sovereign will claim more power than is necessary to discharge his duties. The sovereign, in other words, must be seen by the members of the community as bound by a code of honor not to use his office in order to further his personal interests or those of his family.

Now a glance at this list of preconditions should make it quite apparent why the sovereign emerges so late in humanity's development: he could not have arrived on the scene until the successful dissemination of the Protestant conscience through the secularized code of professionalism had achieved its civilizing function.

But there is one last feature that needs to be stressed, because it is also an integral part of the idea of the sovereign: the community of which the sovereign is the sovereign must be capable of ruling itself sufficiently for the purpose of removing a sovereign who refuses to abide by the terms of his "contract."

Here we can clearly see why the metaphor of the social contract is an essential part of the concept of sovereignty and has no place whatsoever in the world of the master and the slave. It is only because, like the gentlemen whom Locke was addressing in his *Second Treatise,* the sovereign's "subjects" must be capable of acting in concert *without his guidance.* He must not be the glue that holds them together, or the tyrant who keeps a lid on their anarchy, but the agent that upholds his end of a bargain. Otherwise the freedom of the community would be imperiled.

THE LIMITS OF SOVEREIGNTY

The sovereign thus emerges as the solution to the problem of defending the ethical community without subverting it, and seen in this light, the sovereign appears wholly different from the classical tyrant or warlord. He is not proactive, but reactive. He does not dictate, but responds. He stays within limits.

In principle this means that the sovereign's interference with the life of the ethical community of which he is the sovereign may be minimalist—

the exception rather than the rule. The line demarcating what is the sovereign's business and what is the business of the ethical community may be drawn wherever the ethical community desires it to be drawn.

Wherein we can now see the final gift to the world of the Protestant conscience: the sovereign functions in relation to the ethical community in the exact same way the master functions in relation to his guild and his craft. He has so thoroughly mastered the rules, and has been bred to have such profound respect for them, that others can trust his discretion when it comes to his craft. He is allowed to bend the rules, and even to break them, because he is a master and not an apprentice.

This, in fact, is the essence of the sovereign: he can declare when the normal rules by which the free men of an ethical community govern themselves must be suspended and when an exception must be made, but only for the purpose of preserving the ethical community from a danger that threatens to subvert or destroy it. It is thus the sovereign who declares who is to count as an enemy of the ethical community of which he is the sovereign and what acts are be deemed as treason to the community. And it is the sovereign who determines what steps must be taken in order to deal with the enemy.

Yet, just as the master cannot codify ahead of time what exceptions to the rules he might be forced into making in his craft, so too the sovereign cannot decide ahead of time what exceptions he will have to make in order to preserve the rules through a time of crisis. This is actually a good thing, however, because it means that a dangerous exception can never become a fatal rule, by virtue of the fact that it is clearly and explicitly acknowledged as an emergency measure taken under abnormal circumstances, like the Roman custom of creating a one-man dictatorship during times of peril and crisis. Better a temporary dictator without a written and formal grant of power than a permanent office with one.

This is a necessary condition of defending and protecting any community from the cult of ruthlessness. There is simply no way that anyone can know in advance where ruthlessness will emerge next. Hence, unless we are prepared to permit someone to make this decision concerning the clear and imminent danger emanating from such an inherently unpredictable threat, the community will be utterly defenseless in time of danger.

That is why the sovereign must rule. For if he does not, then those who are prepared to use ruthlessness will eventually rule in his place. The sovereign's actions must be deemed legitimate, even those actions that violate the rules of the trust system in order to defend them. This is why the sovereign must constantly act in such a way as to produce consensus where consensus is possible. This is simply a recognition of the sine qua non of sovereignty and that which, once again, distinguishes it from tyranny. A tyrant may rule without consensus, but not a sovereign.

The classical sovereign was called into existence by the simple law that says larger societies have a much better chance of bending smaller societies to their will than vice versa. This entails that anyone who could manage to hold together all the components that go into making up such a large society would be a useful person to have around if you had an interest in the welfare of that society. Such a person could keep things together in a crisis—a function that was often a key to the very survival of the community.

But this fact makes it clear that you cannot simply produce the sovereign at will, and for two quite distinct reasons. First, because not every social order will accept one, and second, because not every man will be likely to possess the particular skills needed to act as one successfully.

The need for a sovereign cannot, by itself, create one, nor can the will of a few. To construct the sovereign requires what Rousseau calls *"la volonté générale,"* the general will of the whole community. Where this is lacking, the society in question is doomed, eventually, to reenact the fate of Poland that we considered earlier. Looking at Poland's dilemma from our current perspective, we are able to say at once what was missing—the appearance of someone qualified to act as a sovereign, meaning not qualified by constitutional rules and regulations, but qualified in the sense that he would be accepted as the sovereign by the Polish nobility and in the sense that he would behave like one if accepted. In short, Poland lacked the kind of collective social habits that make the sovereign *possible.*

A sovereign cannot be authorized into existence by a constitution, nor invoked by a charter. The sovereign can only appear, if he does appear, like a solution to a difficult equation that one has happened upon by chance. It is there, and it so easily might not have been. Necessity does not produce possibility.

The best analogy we can draw to the sovereign is the modern CEO. We all know what characteristics are required to make a CEO: he must be able to placate and cajole the various competing structural antagonisms within his corporation, just as the sovereign must know how to handle those conflicts between competing ethnic tribes and religious groups that make up his society. But merely knowing what makes a CEO is not the same thing as making a CEO; an entire culture, or trust system, is necessary, and not only in order to create a CEO, but also in order to create those people who are capable of working *under* a CEO.

In Poland no CEO emerged to guide the Polish state. Which factor failed here? Was it because Poland did not produce a man suitable to be a sovereign, or was it because Polish nobles were not suited to have a sovereign? Was it beyond the capacity of any man? Could Napoleon have managed it, or Washington? This may well be a question that is impossible to answer, and yet it still leads to a remarkable conclusion. The fate of a society—its very ability to survive—may well depend on the character of the human beings that are produced by its trust system, or in certain cases by the pathologies within the trust system, of which the Polish nobility's penchant for fantasy politics may well have played a role. And this brings us back to the importance of a code of honor.

A society in which children are taught to conform to the rules, as American children were taught in the 1950s, will produce adults who will conduct themselves as political agents in quite a different way than the Polish nobles who, as children, were raised with very little attention to the importance of other people's wishes and feelings. Indeed, the great evil of aristocratic societies and, even worse, of slave-owning societies is that those who dominate them have little or no use for respectability, professionalism, and all those other trust system virtues at which Americans excel and which are the main "acquired characteristic" shared by Americans of every race, ethnic background, religion, and ideological preference. Noam Chomsky, Martha Nussbaum, Jerry Falwell, George W. Bush—all of these are people who would feel shame if their children were caught butting into a line in front of other people. They all share, in ways that might shock and surprise them, the same fundamental trust system that is the social glue holding us together as a people: we are willing to wait our turn, to play by the rules.

This is the reason for America's great power—the legacy of the Protestant conscience that was diffused through the professional attitude of the businessman; the intrinsic capacity to take the wishes and needs of others seriously and to adjust our own behavior accordingly; that instinctive, mechanical, mindless conformity of the American average Joe so derided by the intellectual and the sophisticate.

But note here that by the Protestant conscience I mean an entire social system and one that need have nothing to do with the theological tenets of Protestantism. Rather, the Protestant conscience is akin to those institutions of Sparta that provided a pattern to be copied by subsequent cultures—copied not faithfully but only in essence. Just as the Romans copied Spartan training, without bringing along the pederasty, so secular Americans have copied the Protestant conscience without bringing along the Calvinism.

Hate such conformity all you wish, but do not let this hatred blind you to the values that it supports. In a world where everyone permanently followed his own bliss, in utter unconcern about the consequences to others of doing so, how limited such bliss would have to be, since it could not include the pursuit of any goal that required us to be able to count on the conduct of others.

Our own pursuit of happiness requires others not to pursue theirs—at least not during business hours. If I follow my bliss to an ice-cream parlor, I expect to find someone there who is willing to sell me what someone else had been willing to transport of what someone else was willing to make for me in the first place. Most everybody's bliss is like that nowadays. Few of us are content to wander lonely as a cloud, unless we happen to be driving in our convertible BMW while doing it.

This very conformity, the very unimaginativeness that characterizes the habits and attitude of the American business professional, is the key to understanding why only the United States is in a position to exercise what I call neo-sovereignty.

12

CONCLUSION:

THE NEXT STAGE OF HISTORY

D URING THE COURSE of its history America has devised a unique solution to the fundamental problem of politics—that of figuring out how to get people to cooperate with each other—and it has done this with an extraordinary diversity of ethnic groupings. It has created a climate of immense tolerance, and yet at the same time, it has achieved a higher degree of political integration than those societies that have used repressive techniques in order to achieve the same end. Furthermore, it has done this without the imposition of an ideology or a creed or a faith on those who wished to become Americans: they came here, and by agreeing to *act* like Americans became Americans.

The American emphasis on action over ideas is a feature of our society that has been remarked by many observers, and it is no accident that our one great contribution to philosophy is called pragmatism, from the Greek word *pragma,* which literally means "a doing." Here it is perfectly okay to believe what you want, or to have whatever values you please, provided only that you are willing to interact with other Americans by the code of honor that has worked so successfully for us—a code of honor that I earlier called team cosmopolitanism.

This code, as we have seen, has historical roots that go very far back—

back to the Romans, in fact. It has been developing, by fits and starts, ever since the founding of the United States, and it is our great contribution to the world.

That is the core idea of neo-sovereignty—that Americans have created and mastered a social technique that can solve many of the outstanding human and humanitarian problems facing the world today. We have produced a system of socialization as well as a system of organization that has been able to help us eliminate many of the deep-seated conflicts that haunt and divide the rest of mankind—conflicts of race and of religion, of sect and ethnicity. We have figured out a way of living together, and others can learn it from us, if they are willing.

Is this arrogance? If you insist on seeing it like that. But is it arrogance to think that a child can get better medical treatment from a modern hospital than from a tribal witch doctor? Or to believe that you can travel faster in a jet airplane than on a camel?

To say that we do certain things better than others does not imply that we do all things better, nor does it suggest that there are not many things—and extraordinarily valuable things—that we can learn from those who do less well what we do better. If cultural diversity has a genuine value—which it most certainly does—its value lies in the objective superiority that different cultures have over each other. What would be the point of looking sympathetically at someone else's culture if we couldn't learn from it how to live better within our own? And if it makes sense for us to learn from others, doesn't it make equal sense for them to learn from us? To force other cultures to stay permanently in the cake of custom imposed by the tradition of their ancestors is a perverse way of expressing appreciation for their humanity. It is, on the contrary, to treat them like curiosities in a museum of natural history, like those waxwork tableaux that show the casual visitor a typical scene of daily life among Paleolithic hunters or early Sumerians.

Does this mean promoting a future in which the world becomes a carbon copy of the United States? Or, worse, a future in which mankind is entrapped in the monolithic prison of the "homogenous and universal state" predicted by Alexandre Kojève's and Francis Fukuyama's end of history scenario?

To answer this question one might want to first actually take the trouble of observing what the United States looks like today and asking what part of it is to be the basis of the carbon copy. Is it to be the gay districts in the major metropolitan areas? Or the Jamaican enclaves? Or the sleepy all-WASP townships of north Georgia? Or how about a Muslim neighborhood in Detroit?

In the United States, the more we stay the same, the more we change. That is the glimpse of insight behind the concept of neo-sovereignty—a world in which there is a settled order that is recognized as legitimate by all but that exists only to ensure mutual toleration among diverse communities, all of which are encouraged to pursue their own visions of the good life within the framework of a mutually collective self-regulating order, in which each community has mastered the quintessential American trait of knowing how to get along with others. Here the new sovereign's role is simply to protect the world from having its future course determined by gangs of ruthless people, acting on the stimulus of a fantasy ideology—as has happened over and over again in the last two centuries, and which will happen again if there is no one who is willing and able to keep it from happening.

This is a far cry from the kind of totalitarian micromanaging of individual behavior, at all levels, that is the greatest enemy of human freedom—and no matter in what name it may be carried out. And it is a far cry from empire.

The United States is uniquely equipped to act as the new sovereign not simply because of its power but because of its tolerance. The conservative bugaboo of multiculturalism, far from weakening the United States' position, has made it a historically unprecedented microcosm of the rest of the world. Its diversity reflects that of the world, and this means that for the first time in world history a great power is genuinely capable of transcending the limitations to human cooperation imposed by divisions along the lines of race, sect, and ethnicity. This is a remarkable achievement, and it is only an appalling historical insensitivity on the part of the Left that makes them blind to the world-historical significance of this fact—namely, that the United States is a practical design for the next stage of human history: a utopia that works.

The great American cultural revolution that began in the 1960s and which, like all such events, had ennobling and appalling episodes, has produced, through no one's design, an America that embodies the cosmopolitan ideal far more than any other society in human history. Those who still wish to give their allegiance to a purely hypothetical community of all the men and women on the planet are not only indulging in a

fantasy, they are being downright reactionary. By failing to support the
United States in its effort to offer liberal values to the rest of the world,
and preferring instead to place their hopes in the fantasy of a community
that will never exist because it could never exist, the liberal cosmopolitan,
as we have seen, betrays both liberalism and the cosmopolitan impulse—
that is, the desire to treat all human beings as of equal moral worth,
regardless of any accident of birth.

Indeed, today there is an enormous danger that the Left has lost the
ability to offer a genuinely useful critique of America's emerging role and
has degenerated into what is dangerously close to a full-fledged fantasy
ideology. The danger here is the danger that arises with any criticism that
has become too obviously tendentious or even merely spiteful: it stops
being listened to. Under the present circumstances, this is a risk that the
Left has been running more and more, both in America and in the world
community, with the result that the culture war threatens to position the
American academic Left not as a constructive critic, or even as a usefully
carping one, but rather as an outright enemy. This was apparent both
before, during, and after the Iraq war, so strikingly that it even led one liberal Left critic to write an astonishing article, in which he confessed to the
Schadenfreude he felt at each apparent hint of a prospective disaster for the
forces of his own country, made up of his fellow citizens.

The problem with this reaction is that it represents a radical imbalance
in our civic ecology: if criticism is to push in the right direction, it must
not seem to be coming from those who have absolutely nothing in common with us. When the Left-wing intellectual seems to have contempt for
everything that the average American holds dear, how seriously do you
think his advice will be taken?

That is why the intellectual, conservative, liberal, or radical, must submit his own "natural" point of view to the same kind of critique that
Marxists have traditionally applied to all other forms of ideological distortion and disguise. For it is not only our economic class that colors how
we see the world, but our particular vocation within that class.

Nor should this surprise us. Different kinds of work privilege certain
metaphors by making them more ready to hand to the person who performs
them. If you are a farmer, your dependency on the unpredictability of the
weather inclines you to see the cosmos as unpredictable and beyond your
control; if you are an engineer, your world will tend to be seen as orderly and
subject to your control. The same principle applies to the intellectual.

The intellectual, for example, places overwhelming emphasis on the value of certainty: the essence of the Cartesian project, after all, was to be certain about everything. But will not this emphasis almost certainly entail a reluctance to accept both risk and ignorance as inherent and insurmountable limitations of human action? Will the intellectual not instinctively prefer any intellectual system that claims to give certainty about everything, no matter whether it emanates from Karl Marx or Ayn Rand? And might this same trait make him judge more harshly those inevitable glitches that plague even the most competently carried out enterprises, seeing as stupid what is merely human?

Furthermore, because it is easier to do something on paper than in reality, there will be a systematic inability to evaluate the gap between what works in theory and what works in practice. This was a lesson that I learned as a child when I decided to draw a suspension bridge that stretched across the English channel and showed it to my father. He said it was theoretically possible, and when I asked him to tell me what this meant, he said, "It works on paper." Much works on paper that does not work in life.

Much of Left-wing ideology is transparently self-serving of the intellectual class—meaning those who make their living by their claim to privileged knowledge. The only reason that this fact has not been more widely observed is that conservatives don't normally read Antonio Gramsci and Louis Althusser. If they did, they would recognize here all the characteristics of the concept of ideology that was developed by these two twentieth-century interpreters of Marx. According to both Gramsci and Althusser, it is a mistake to think that ideology is a deliberate and self-conscious mask put on merely to mislead and deceive other people. Rather, it is part of one's own way of imagining the world.

This finding is nothing more than the application of postmodern relativism to Marxism. If all of us live within an ideological box of our class or group, and it is impossible for us to judge objectively between the boxes, then each box—according to Marx's theory of ideology—will tend to distort the real world in a way that flatters our self-interest. The intellectual, like every other vocational type, will distort the world in accordance with the basic metaphors through which he interprets it. Everything in the world will add up for him perfectly.

But there is a problem here, for such a conclusion would appear to deny the possibility that anyone can ever escape from the ideological box in which he is trapped, and this implies not only ethical or cultural relativism, but the relativism of all forms of knowledge, scientific as well as moral.

To draw this bleak conclusion, however, is to make a serious error, for it overlooks the fact that we can escape from our ideological boxes, but only if we are willing to admit that we may not be certain about what we claim to know. Those who believe that they have the truth are condemned to live in an airtight box from which no escape is possible. It is their smug sense of knowing everything that has them trapped there.

This was the lesson of Socrates. Wisdom begins with a confession that we are certain about nothing and that every statement we make risks being found to be wrong at a later date and is subject to revision by us in light of this finding.

This is postmodernism with a vengeance: it is pushing it to the point at which it undergoes a dialectical reversal and becomes something quite different from what we previously thought it to be.

The person who accepts the risk that he may be wrong, and that his box may not be the last word, has already stepped outside his box: he has transcended his limitations simply by knowing them. In this process he has gained a higher perspective than that offered by anyone who remains adamantly locked inside his airtight system, from which no error escapes and into which no novelty enters.

Hegel made the exact same point about Kant's critique of reason. If you have pink lenses implanted in your eyeballs, your vision of the world will be distorted, but you will not know it is distorted. You will go through life mistakenly thinking that the world is pink. But the moment you realize that you have pink lenses implanted in your eyeballs, and therefore cannot see the world any other way, then you at least know that the world may be some other color. That is not knowing much, by itself, since after all there is no way of knowing what color the world really is; it may even be pink, for all you know! So what is the advantage gained?

It is enormous. Because now that you know that you are not seeing the world as it really is, you will begin a search to discover what it really is, and if you have any sense, you will begin by asking other people how they see the world.

In the ancient parable of the Hindu blind men, there were seven blind men who had never encountered an elephant and so knew nothing about one. Each touched a different part of the elephant and drew his conclusion about the nature of the beast from the idea that immediately sprang into his mind. Each idea was a metaphor that allowed him to think that he understood what the elephant really was. One touched the huge ear and thought it must be the front of an immense palm tree. Another grabbed the trunk and concluded that it was a huge snake. A third touched the tusks and said that they were sharpened spears, another the elephant's legs, which he thought must be tree stumps, and so on.

If these men had been truly as wise as they claimed, before deciding what the elephant was, they would have shared their conclusions. But they didn't. And because each of the blind men insisted that he had the whole truth, they all went astray. If each had simply accepted that the others might be onto part of the truth, it would have been possible for them to compare notes, to assemble their differing perspectives, and to combine their different metaphors. The end result would still not add up to an elephant, but at least it would recognize the fact that an elephant is not a snake, is not a tree, is not a plant, is not a spear.

Such negative knowledge is the foundation of objectivity. To know that cancer is not caused by demons or by the evil eye is not the same thing as having a cure for it, but it is a step in the right direction, even an indispensable condition of ever discovering a cure. We must know we are wrong before we can start to be right. The history of scientific thought, as it has unfolded in the West, is a history of errors seen through. Far from being the steady accumulation of facts, it has been a series of imploded boxes—each one of which was seen through, and discarded.

Yet to look upon this process as merely negative, as proving that everything is subjective or relative, is to miss its point entirely, as every human being, once he has reached a certain age, can see for himself if he looks back on his life. If he has gained any wisdom at all, it will inevitably come in the form of disillusionment. Yet—if he has indeed gained wisdom—he will see that this disillusionment, however difficult, permitted him to see a truth, however painful, that he could not otherwise have seen.

When the Austrian economist and thinker Joseph Schumpeter coined the superficially oxymoronic phrase "creative destruction," he was using it to speak of the historical impact of capitalism—how it tore up much of the old, in order to bring in what could not have come into being otherwise—but he could just as easily have been talking about the history of Western science or, for that matter, the autobiography of any thoughtful man or woman.

Creative destruction is also the heart of Hegel's dialectics, and is characteristic of the dialectical reversal. For Hegel, each discarded box represented a stage in mankind's collective growth and development. In the Preface to *The Phenomenology of Mind*, Hegel compares this progress to the organic process by which a flower springs from a bud. "Conventional opinion gets fixated on the antithesis of truth and falsity . . . it does not comprehend the diversity of philosophical systems [i.e., boxes/paradigms] as the progressive unfolding of the truth, but rather sees in it simple disagreements. The bud disappears in the bursting-forth of the blossom, and one might say that the former is refuted by the latter; similarly, when the fruit appears, the blossom is shown up in its turn as a false manifestation of the plant, and the fruit now emerges as the truth of it instead."

To ask which stage represents the *true* plant—the bud, the blossom, or the flower—is to ask one of those questions that make a correct answer impossible, like "Have you stopped beating your wife?" If you begin by insisting that one and only one of these is really the plant, then you are logically driven to conclude that none of them is really the plant, since equally strong claims can be put forth for each of the different stages—the bud, the blossom, and the flower. You end up by wondering how you can possibly decide among the different claims—at which point you are only a small step away from the conclusion that everything is relative and that it is simply a matter of this or that person's subjective opinion.

All of human development can be seen in exactly the same way. Take, for example, the life of an individual. Today people often live their lives jumping from one fad to another, pursuing this lifestyle for a while, then dropping it all at once to pursue another. Each episode of such a life—the early Zen period, followed by Scientology, followed by an enthusiasm for saving the whales—is self-contained and as unrelated to what went before as to what came after.

Such restlessness must not be confused with creative destruction. It is rather a purely pointless destruction, a kind of serial nihilism, the outstanding characteristic of which is a profound lack of seriousness. In place of genuine commitment and the risk attendant upon it, there is an attitude that might best be described as an ideological consumerism: you pull an idea off the shelf, see whether you like it, and dispose of it if you don't. No risk, and a money-back guarantee.

"If the fool would persist in his folly he would become wise," according to the English poet William Blake; so too would the consumer of ideologies and spiritual fads. But he doesn't persist and so never becomes even a tad bit the wiser. There is no disillusionment, just dissatisfaction, and boredom is the only motive for moving on.

Compare this to the agonizing process by which a man who has been totally committed to a faith or to a cause gradually comes to see its limitations and shortcomings. Read Saint Augustine's *Confessions,* John Henry Newman's *Apologia Pro Vita Sua,* or Whittaker Chambers's *Witness,* and you step into a different world, one that echoes the words of the Greek tragedian Aeschylus when he wrote that "the gods have so ordained it that man gains wisdom only by suffering." To change our beliefs because we are bored with them is radically different than to change our beliefs because we despair of them, and it is only the latter process that provides us with wisdom.

This is a difference that is hard to explain to those who are caught up in the frivolous pursuit of intellectual fads. Yes, to them everything *is* in fact subjective, because they never permit it to be anything else. They hold ideas about the world based on whether they like the ideas and not on whether the ideas are adequate to the world. They want to believe that by visualizing world peace they are making the world more peaceful, and they regard as warmongers anyone who does not want to believe the same fairy tale.

If all that matters is what you believe and not whether what you believe is true, then why shouldn't you believe whatever you like to believe—that is to say, whatever makes you happy when you believe it? Why not replace seriousness of thought with wishful thinking?

The fashionable doctrines of subjectivism and relativism turn out, on this analysis, to be the ideological rationalizations, in the classic Marxist sense of this word, of a mentality governed by an irresponsible consumerism that has been extended to every aspect of human existence—a consumerism in which all of life is seen in terms of options and nothing in terms of commitment. Our religious faith, our family, our country—these are all transformed from the center of our being into lifestyle choices. We can take them or leave them or replace them at will. All has become fungible.

Precisely the same frivolousness is present in the sham multiculturalism that dominates so much of Left thinking today. Each "culture" is seen as if it were merely a wholesale consumer option, as if each had been selected by the participant in that culture from out of a wide range of our possible cultural options, much the way sophisticated Americans can chose to eat Greek or Thai or Ethiopian.

This is not how the world works for those who are born into cultures that rigidly insist that there is one way, and one way only, to do everything—cultures in which "the cake of custom" is more like cement, hardened by long use and by a systematic suppression of any slightest hint of novelty or deviation from the norm.

Of course, it may be quaint and interesting for us to visit such a culture, and instructive and amusing to compare their folkways to ours and even to notice those points where they have the advantage over us. But to forget that in many of these cultures those born into them are trapped without hope of escape is to ignore the obvious.

Sham multiculturalism forgets the fate of the individual. It makes people the property of their culture and permits the airtight box of this culture to dictate their often very limited range of choices—a range that in certain systems, like the Indian caste system, provides them with no choice whatsoever.

To respect the culture of other people is genuine multiculturalism—or what used to be called good manners. To make that culture more important than the people who live in it is sham multiculturalism—or what used to be called racism.

Racism is an explanation of culture that holds that it is an emanation of race. The reason why people behave in a certain way is that they are programmed to do so. It is in their blood, as Gobineau might have argued, or in their genes, but whatever metaphor is chosen, it is something that cannot be altered. Therefore, if an individual is a member of a culture, this is not an accident of birth that can be altered, but it is the consequence of his belonging to the racial group of which the culture is merely the expression. In other words, the tendency of the individuals of a culture to behave in a specific way—for example, cannibalizing their neighbors or sacrificing their children to appease the god or selling their brothers and sisters into slavery—is not a product of cultural conditioning but a consequence of their biological constitution, and hence it is hopeless to try to change either the individual or his culture.

Thus the British in India could be of two minds about whether to abolish the practice of suttee—that is, the immolation of widows on the funeral pyre of their recently deceased husbands. Either you could save the woman, even against her wishes, or you could let her die, against your conscience. The former position was taken by those who believed that to abolish such a practice was to push the indigenous culture of India to a higher stage of civilization; the latter position was taken by those who believed that this culture was the product of the racial inferiority of the Indians, and hence it was utterly pointless to try to change it. The leopard cannot change his spots, nor can a race change its culture. Hence any and all such improvements would only be temporary and liable to disappear the moment the anti-suttee policy was not enforced by British arms.

The logic of this debate is still with us today. The only difference—though from our perspective, a telling one—is that those who argue that we have no right to impose "our values" on another culture do not use explicitly racist language to justify their position. In fact they regard themselves as being completely free from the taint of racism.

Yet isn't it racism to regard as "our" values such things as respect for the individual, due process, freedom of speech and conscience? In what sense, after all, are they ours? If they are ours because we have adopted them, and if we have adopted them because they help us to live better lives as individuals and as communities, might they not for the very same reason become "their" values too? If you have a better idea than I do, what is to keep me from discarding mine and adopting yours? In which case, what is the point of saying that the idea is yours, after I have chosen to make it mine?

As we have seen, our civilization has discarded one idea after another, in the process of creative destruction that we have observed earlier. But why on earth should we believe that this is a process of which we alone are capable?

The only reason for assuming that this is the case is racism. If other people are incapable of taking over certain ideas and values because of their racial or genetic incapacity, then yes, it would certainly be wrong—and futile—to try to get them to adopt these ideas and values. But if they have failed to adopt these ideas and values simply because they don't know about them, or because they conflict with their current culture, then who is to say that those who are being brought up within this culture might not prefer to be brought up in a culture that does embody these ideas and values?

To demand that another culture not undergo change and to do so in the name of multiculturalism is utterly indefensible. It is to treat the members of this other culture as if they were children and to condemn them to live in a kind of cultural wildlife preserve. To argue that other cultures cannot change because their members are incapable of embodying the values that we hold dear is racism.

Yet, without any question, the danger posed by this sham and racist multiculturalism arises from its refusal to recognize that there are certain things on which all cultures have agreed, and chief among these is the rejection of de-civilization, that is, the rejection of those who deliberately try to undermine and subvert the level of civilization of whatever culture they are attacking. Indeed, even when a gang has seized control of a society, it quickly acts to legitimize itself, often by murdering those members of the gang who proved unwilling or unable to make the transition, just as Adolf Hitler ordered the murder of Ernst Roehm, the leader of the SA and a pure representative of the tradition of the adolescent gang, including even the pederasty. The cult of ruthlessness is sui generis. It is both the creator of all civilizations, and their destroyer. It is the incarnation of the negative component of Hegel's dialectic, whose working out in the historical world produces one embodiment of human community only to shatter it by means of a superior embodiment. It is Schumpter's creative destruction. It is Mother Kali pulling one child from her womb while dashing out the brains of another. It is Shiva, whose dance brings old worlds to an end in order to bring new ones into being.

For us, the only question is, Whose world is ending, and whose is just beginning?

TOWARD THE END of Fareed Zakaria's essay "The Arrogant Empire," the title of which refers to the United States, comes this observation: "In a global survey taken last year, the most intriguing—and unreported— finding was that large majorities of people in most countries thought that the world would be a more dangerous place if there were a rival to the American superpower. Sixty-four percent of the French, 70 percent of the Mexicans, 63 percent of the Jordanians felt this way."

Why should this be? If, as Zakaria has argued, most of the world fears and distrusts American power, shouldn't the citizens of France, Mexico, and Jordan, among others, be looking for a knight in shining armor to put us in our place? And would this have been the result of a similar poll if the Soviet Union had won the Cold War? Or if World War II had ended in an Axis victory, permitting Nazi Germany to dictate the terms on which the remainder of the twentieth century had run its course?

Probably not. We have to wonder, then, what explains this difference. If they fear and distrust us so much, why shouldn't they want us to have a rival?

There is a way of solving this riddle.

Suppose we lived in a city that has always been ruled by gangsters. One gang had followed another, and for as long as anyone can remember, there had been gang wars, with much killing. Suppose that, after many generations of enduring such gang violence, one particular gang had come to dominate all others, so much so that it no longer had any rivals. In such a situation, it is entirely possible that we might distrust and fear the dominant gang and yet be reluctant to see a revival of the gang warfare through which we had pointlessly suffered for so long. Indeed, it would be the counsel of prudence.

This, however, does assume that the gang that now dominates our city also rules it without excessive violence or oppression. It may not be exactly what we would like to have, but we know that it is better than the alternative—which is another round of gangland killings. At the same time, such an attitude is perfectly reconcilable with distrust, ill will, dislike, suspicion, and all sorts of negative feelings toward the gang that has achieved dominance.

Nor is this necessarily a bad thing. Indeed, so long as none of this negativity translates into support for the emergence of a rival gang, then it may in fact even be constructive. For the dominant gang does have too much power, and hence it is a good thing for those who must live under it to do everything that they can do to make sure that this power is not used in ways that are harmful to them. But one thing they cannot do, if they are prudent, is to reduce the power of the ruling gang beyond what is necessary for it to rule *alone,* because then they are back in the quandary from which they had just escaped—namely, internecine warfare between rival gangs.

It follows that there is nothing at all puzzling about the world's response to the position of dominance that America has achieved since the Cold War. On the one hand, there is a sense that this is far better than the alternative from which we have emerged—that is, a world divided between two rival camps, where conflict between them had the potential of threatening the lives of every man, woman, and child on the planet.

On the other hand, there is an understandable reluctance to trust any one nation with absolute power.

Zakaria argues that there is something unique about the Bush administration that has brought about the fear and distrust and that this would not have happened under a different administration, such as Clinton's. He overlooks the simple fact that, no matter who sits in the White House at this point, it will be someone whom the rest of the world will have good reason to fear and to distrust, because whoever it is, he or she will control more power than any single human being has controlled since the dawn of time, and there is simply no way to disguise or to sugarcoat this.

Needless to say, anyone in this position should use as much tact as he or she possibly can, but we must recognize that there are limits to what tact can achieve. Diplomacy is of inestimable service when two parties are both desirous of a compromise, but it is of no avail when one side adamantly refuses to budge; even Bill Clinton, with all his great personal charm, could probably not get a car salesman to sell him a Cadillac at thousand dollars below cost.

This is the burden with which any President of the United States, and any administration, will be saddled into the foreseeable future: the horrible problem of being the dominant power in a world that has every reason to be fearful and distrustful of any power at all, much less the staggering degree of power that the United States currently possesses. In short, it is not because of *who* we are but *what* we are.

To see what I mean, imagine that your wife comes home one day with a man and introduces you to him as her new boyfriend. Will you like him? And if you don't like him, will it be because he is lacking in tact or diplomacy? Will you feel that somehow you could have accepted him if only he had been Bill Clinton and not George Bush?

That is how the world feels. It is absurd to think that the world should be jumping up and down with joy that there is one overwhelmingly dominant nation, even if you happen to believe—as I do—that there has never been a nation whose track record of humanity and generosity can even come close to matching our own.

On the one hand, we do have too much power. On the other, we cannot have any less. This is the paradox that not only we must somehow learn to live with, but so must the world.

And yet, if we think about it, this is the paradox at the heart of the concept of legitimacy, for the best way of explaining the paradox behind the poll cited by Zakaria is to put it in these terms: The world accepts the legitimacy of American power in the sense that it does not want it to be challenged by a rival. Yet this, far from being a puzzling curiosity, is the key to understanding the present world order.

There is much confusion about what legitimacy means; put simply, it is to accept that those in power should be the ones to have power, not because they are perfect or all-wise or even because we agree with them, but simply because we recognize the cost of removing them from power, and we have concluded that it is not worth paying.

Thus there are many Americans who did not like Clinton as president, and many who do not like Bush, but only a handful disliked them so much that they would have preferred to see them removed from office at the cost of a civil war. This is how much of the world feels about the United States today. They bash us, and yet they recognize our legitimate authority. And while they may not put it into words—and, indeed, use their words almost exclusively to denigrate us—their actions speak otherwise.

Looking at this period from the amplest perspective, what is cause for astonishment is not how much they distrust and fear us, but how freely and confidently they are able to express this distrust and fear. Indeed, the world is beginning to show toward us that cynical disrespect for authority that has always been one of the hallmarks of our national character. Just as George Washington's enemies attacked him for wanting to make himself king, so our enemies attack us for wanting to make an empire, and with equal absurdity. But this is fine, so long as the world is also displaying the other great hallmark of our national political character, which is to accept the legitimate authority even of men we can't stand.

In short, contrary to Zakaria's analysis, what we are seeing is not the result of the incompetence of the Bush administration but the absolutely inevitable unfolding of an entirely new epoch in human history, one in which there is, for the first time, not an empire—arrogant or otherwise—but a uniquely positioned nation, the United States, that is capable of exercising dominant power in the world, but which, despite much fear and distrust, is nonetheless regarded as the one and only legitimate power in the limited sense in which I have been using this word.

But is this kind of "Oh, well, it could be worse" legitimacy enough?

In fact, it is enough, and it has always been enough to secure the stability of those individual nation-states that have reached this point within their own boundaries, for it is the point that is reached whenever people in a society are prepared to trust men to rule who are not the men that they personally wished to have rule.

Only, for the first time, this same "Oh, well, it could be worse" legitimacy is being extended toward a single nation within the entire world order. It is this fact that demands our undivided attention, and one for which we may search history in vain for precedents. This is why the invocation of empire, either to justify or to deride America's present policy, is such an obstacle to comprehending what is unique in the current situation. It is a bit like describing Wal-Mart as a mom-and-pop store.

THE CIVILIZATION THAT the United States is now called upon to defend is not America's or even the West's; it is the civilization created by all men and women, everywhere on the planet, who have worked to make the actual community around them less addicted to violence, more open, more tolerant, more trusting. Civilization, in this sense, is Chinese, American, African, European, *and* Muslim. Those who are working for this purpose are all on the same side, and we all have a common enemy. It is an enemy whose origin goes back to the dawn of history, and indeed, the enemy that began the whole bloody and relentless cycle of violence and war, the eternal gang of ruthless men.

Someone must be prepared to fight them whenever they threaten to enter into history and threaten thereby to change even the very possibilities in terms of which we are, forever after, doomed to imagine our future.

Those who wish to help the Third World must see that the source of its poverty lies not in the capitalist system but in the rule of the gang that has blighted it for millennia. Where the family rules, the team cannot prosper, and if the team cannot prosper, then neither can the society. It is not capitalism that creates democratic liberalism but the peculiar team sense of community that arose out of Protestant Europe, one combining team and conscience to produce individuals capable of making their own way in the world while being ever mindful of the needs of others.

One's approval of this system may be due to cultural bias or distortion; here again, those who wish to argue that this system does not in fact produce these goods are flying in the face of the evidence. The West got rich and free because it followed this pattern: the East remained poor and unfree because it continued to be immersed in the family.

There is no reason on earth why a person may not choose to live in the intimate and reassuring world of the family and fight tooth and nail against any encroachment upon the world that he and his ancestors have created—a world full of beauty, poetry, significance, and value, rich and irreplaceable. But he must not pretend that there is not a cost to living in this world, just as there is a cost to living in any one social order rather than another. Not all goods and values can be embodied in the same community or even in the same world. Compromise can achieve wonders; the worldly success of the spirit of the team demonstrates this quite well. Yet there must always remain that with which no compromise is possible, because it refuses to compromise itself.

AT THIS JUNCTURE in history, it is in the interest of civilization, wherever it is found, to keep the legitimacy of the Pax Americana intact. But this will require the simultaneous avoidance of three distinct perils.

First, the United States cannot permit itself to become the arrogant empire that its critics fear, or, indeed, an empire of whatever kind. It must be first, but first among equals. It must adopt the psychological finesse of a George Washington; that is to say, a style of a leadership where the leader is far more concerned with preserving consensus among his followers than with asserting his authority over them—not because consensus is good in itself, but because it is an indispensable precondition of strong leadership. If the leader is not trusted by those whom he must lead, he will be incapable of exercising the kind of leadership that is most necessary in a time of crisis and peril: He will not be permitted to act unilaterally and at his own discretion.

For the foreseeable future, the United States must reserve the option of acting precisely in this manner, unilaterally and at its own discretion, not to subvert the rules of international liberalism but to uphold them. Otherwise, the geopolitical system supported by these rules will collapse as would any other trust system that has lost its mooring in its traditional code of honor. In the epoch we have entered, some agency must have the capacity to act quickly, decisively, and with overwhelming strength in order to keep ruthless gangs from charting the course of the next stage of history. Today those ruthless gangs are Muslim—but there is no reason why this will be true twenty years, or two years, hence. But in whatever incarnation such ruthlessness appears, it must not be allowed to decide the direction of mankind's future development.

Second, intellectuals in America, Europe, and elsewhere must abandon the pursuit of abstract utopias and fantasy ideologies and return to the real world. They must undertake a critique of their own inherent distorted point of view, in order to comprehend the visceral and emotional dynamic at the foundation of all human cultures and their history. They must cease to attack those codes of honor that the modern West has inherited from its various traditions, political, cultural, and religious. They must not permit the culture war within the West to degenerate, as it threatens to do, into a civil war.

Third, and perhaps most important, we must all struggle to overcome the collective tendency of civilized men and women to forgetfulness. For that, in truth, is the ultimate question facing us today, Can the West overcome the forgetfulness that is the nemesis of every successful civilization? If it can, then there is hope that mankind will be able to move forward to a higher stage of historical development. If it cannot, then the next stage of history will be one that we once hoped never to see again.

June 5, 2003
Stone Mountain

ACKNOWLEDGMENTS

I HAVE BEEN extraordinarily lucky in the editors whom I have worked with, both on the articles that were incorporated into the present volume, as well as the book itself.

First, I must thank Tod Lindberg, the editor of *Policy Review* of The Hoover Institute, who, in the spring of 2002, generously encouraged a complete unknown to write an article for his journal and whose request brought into being not only "Al-Qaeda's Fantasy Ideology," but what was in effect the first draft of *Civilization and Its Enemies*. There is no way that I can ever repay Tod for taking an interest in my ideas or for the wisdom and sanity he has unfailingly displayed both as my editor and as my friend and colleague.

Second, I want to express my gratitude to Nick Schulz, editor at TechCentralStation.com, not only for being an absolutely wonderful person to work with, but also for championing "Our World-Historical Gamble" on his Web site, despite my own misgivings about the excessive length and density of the piece.

Third, I must thank Bill Rosen, the editor at Free Press who, after reading "Our World-Historical Gamble" in early spring of 2003, called me to ask if I might be interested in writing a book for him, and who subsequently did everything in his power to make the initial stages of this process as pleasant and rewarding as possible. Bill's role in bringing greater clarity and order to my ideas has been immense.

Finally, I must thank Bruce Nichols, who took over as editor of this book after Bill Rosen and whose unflagging enthusiasm for the project has been an inspiration to me. It is Bruce I must thank for providing the final focus of the book and for permitting me to write it in my own words.

In addition to my four editors, I have been helped by the many friends I came to know through the publication of my articles on the Internet, with special thanks going to Robert Hessen of Stanford University, both for his early encouragement and for his valuable assistance in helping me to edit and improve "Our World-Historical Gamble" prior to its original publication.

Thanks also are due to Michael Lynch of John Marshall School of Law, who read through the earlier drafts of the present volume and offered invaluable help in matters relating to both substance and style.

And last, but hardly least, I must thank David Warren, whose article on my Al-Qaeda piece in *The Ottawa Citizen* in September 2002 prompted an e-mail from me that has blossomed into a lively Internet correspondence wonderfully enhanced by the participation of Heather McFarlane of Whitehorse, Yukon Territory. Together, David and Heather patiently permitted me to try out many of my ideas on them first, and have been absolutely invaluable in the many insights that they have offered me from their own treasure trove of wisdom.

Yet I would not be in a position to thank any of the above were it not for the love and loyalty of my extended family—or perhaps, more appropriately, team. These include my dear friends Sid Gough and Stacey Parr, whose generosity and kindness can never be adequately repaid, and my marvelous neighbor, Marci Simpkins. It also includes my unofficially adopted son, Sundown Walker, his wife, Melissa, and their son—my godchild—Gavin Walker. Without Sundown, this book could never have been written.

And the same must be said of Sundown's fellow dedicatee, Andy Fuson, who for sixteen years has shared my life and has served as my interface with reality, and whose love and devotion are the ground of my being.

INDEX

abstract expressionism, 136
abstract reason, 137–38, 139–42, 147–54, 209, 217–18
Achilles, 125, 126
Aeschylus, 209
Afghanistan, 14, 19, 32
agôge, 80, 94
agonistics, 88, 121, 124
Alexander the Great, 123, 189
Algerian War of Independence, 14
Al-Qaeda. *See* Qaeda, Al-
Althusser, Louis, 205
American Revolution, 21
amour de soi-même, 157, 161
amour propre, 157, 158, 161, 187
anti-Semitism, xiii–xiv
Apologia Pro Vita Sua (Newman), 209
Arab world, 15, 25, 27
    democracy potential in, 23, 84
    radical Islamic fantasy ideology and, 12–13, 15, 18–20, 25
    response to 9/11 attack by, 108
    source of wealth in, 26–27
    viability delusions of, 31
Archilochus of Paros, 93
Aristotle, 129
"Arrogant Empire, The" (Zakaria), 212–13
Articles of Confederation, 100
Athens, 82, 94–95, 120
Augustine, Saint, 209
authority
    external vs. inner conscience, 185–87
    paternal vs. team, 123–26
Aztecs, 1–2, 3, 88

Bagehot, Walter, 49, 69, 97, 135
Balkans, 76
barbarism, 69–70. *See also* de-civilization

barracks system, 80–81, 95
behavior controls, 132–33, 192–93
Belgium, 50, 59
Bildung, 162–63
biological barrier, 75, 78, 84, 132, 143, 147, 162. *See also* family system
blackballing, 89–90, 130
Blake, William, 208
bluffing, 166–69, 170
Bodin, Jean, 194
Bonaparte. *See* Napoleon I
Book of the Courtier, The (Castiglione), 40
Bourbon dynasty, 102, 178
boys' gang. *See* gang
bravery, 127
Bright, John, 39
Brutus the Elder, 96
bullying, 169–70
Burckhardt, Jacob, 88
Bush, George W., 105, 198, 214, 215
Butler, Richard, 28

Cabot, Sebastian, 174–75
Caesar, Julius, 21, 42
Calvin, John, 191
Calvinism, 198
Campbell, Joseph, 112
cannibalism, 70, 75, 77, 161
capitalism, 85–86, 192–94, 207, 216
    end of history and, 37, 39, 42
    expansion possibilities of, 130
    family system decline and, 96
    as gangster rule preventive, 193–94
    Marshall's theory of, 96–97
    Marx's theory of, 42, 43, 96
    Protestantism and, 187, 193–94
    trust system and, 191
Castiglione, Baldassare, 40

221

ABOUT THE AUTHOR

LEE HARRIS entered Emory University at age fourteen and graduated summa cum laude. After years spent pursuing diverse interests, he began writing philosophical essays that have captured the imagination of readers all over the world. With three of the most controversial and widely shared articles in the history of *Policy Review,* Harris has emerged as one of the most talked-about writers of recent times. He lives in Stone Mountain, Georgia.